Remembering Nureyev

Florida A&M University, Tallahassee
Florida Atlantic University, Boca Raton
Florida Gulf Coast University, Ft. Myers
Florida International University, Miami
Florida State University, Tallahassee
New College of Florida, Sarasota
University of Central Florida, Orlando
University of Florida, Gainesville
University of North Florida, Jacksonville
University of South Florida, Tampa
University of West Florida, Pensacola

Das Wohltemperierte Klavier (The Well-Tempered Klavier), Nureyev playing his harpsichord. Drawing by Toer van Schayk, 1986.

REMEMBERING

Nureyev

THE TRAIL OF A COMET

Rudi van Dantzig

Translation by Katie de Haan

UNIVERSITY PRESS OF FLORIDA

Gainesville · Tallahassee · Tampa · Boca Raton · Pensacola
Orlando · Miami · Jacksonville · Ft. Myers · Sarasota

English edition copyright 2008 by Rudi van Dantzig
Dutch edition copyright 1993 by Rudi van Dantzig
First Dutch edition published by Walburg Pers bv, 1993

Printed in the United States of America on acid-free paper.

12 11 10 09 08   6 5 4 3 2 1

Library of Congress Cataloging-in-Publication Data
Dantzig, Rudi van.
Remembering Nureyev: the trail of a comet / Rudi van
Dantzig; translation by Katie de Haan.
p. cm. Includes index.
ISBN 978-0-8130-3209-2 (alk. paper)
1. Nureyev, Rudolf, 1938–1993. 2. Ballet dancers—
Russia (Federation)—Biography. 3. Nationale Ballet
(Netherlands) 4. Dantzig, Rudi van. I. Title.
GV1785.N8D36 2008
792.802'80929–dc22
[B]
2007031352

The University Press of Florida is the scholarly publishing
agency for the State University System of Florida, compris-
ing Florida A&M University, Florida Atlantic University,
Florida Gulf Coast University, Florida International
University, Florida State University, New College of
Florida, University of Central Florida, University of
Florida, University of North Florida, University of South
Florida, and University of West Florida.

University Press of Florida
15 Northwest 15th Street
Gainesville, FL 32611–2079
http://www.upf.com

For
Maude Lloyd Gosling
Douce François
and
Marika Bezobrazova
Jeanette Etheredge-Bali,
Rudolf's "women"

"He was a man with great talent
and he did not waste it."

CONTENTS

FOREWORD

This biographical remembrance of the Russian dancer and force of nature Rudolf Nureyev, by the Dutch choreographer Rudi van Dantzig, belongs to a class of ballet memoirs so unusual that you can count their number on the fingers of one hand and still have a finger left over: disinterested and probing, book-length eyewitness portraits in English by a distinguished dancer or choreographer of a contemporary. The "book-length" part is what makes this category so exclusive. Although theatrical dancing has produced copious memoirs where star dancer-authors are able to step back from their own spotlights for a while in order to depict and ponder their mentors and/or colleagues for their own sakes, very few stars either want to or have the time to take on the labor, written and emotional, that would be involved in composing a long essay, much less an entire volume about someone else. Memoir biographies of that kind require one to try to peer outside oneself in order to keep one's attention firmly on another individual. For performers of any tradition, this can be a challenge so daunting, so against the grain of what they need to be stars in the first place, that it is almost unfair to expect it.

The standards for this type of memoir have been set by literature, and they are formidable, ranging in scope from Izaak Walton's tender life of the poet John Donne to Nadezhda Mandelstam's monumental memoir of her husband, poet Osip Mandelstam. In dance, to my knowledge, the group of such extended portraits includes—perhaps consists of—the remembrance of Vaslav Nijinsky by his sister, the choreographer Bronislava Nijinska, in her *Early Memoirs*, choreographer Agnes de Mille's *Martha*, her outstanding biography of her revered friend Martha Graham; and ballerina Moira Shearer's biography, *Balletmaster*, of her cherished choreographer, George Balanchine (although most of Shearer's book was not the product of the author's firsthand experience but rather of her research and interviewing). If the genre of memoir is expanded to include volumes that are limited to concerns of the studio, then ballerina Suki Schorer's study of Balanchine's teaching could be added to this group of rareties.

Even among these few examples, though, van Dantzig's portrait is unique, for Nureyev himself requested that van Dantzig should write about him. Knowing that any book would be published after his own death, Nureyev trusted his colleague and friend to be both honest and fair. This was something of a risk on Nureyev's part, as the men clashed on a number of occasions, and van Dantzig—who had made three new ballets for Nureyev and featured him in a fourth, the 1965 *Monument for a Dead Boy*—was eventually put in the painful position of having to turn down Nureyev's request to perform with the Dutch National Ballet when the quality of the latter's dancing was on the decline.

Still, in desiring the Dutchman to be his literary portraitist, Nureyev demonstrated both taste and excellent judgment. Rudi van Dantzig (b. 1933) is an award-winning choreographer whose ballets have been danced by leading companies in London, Copenhagen, New York, and Beijing, as well as by the Paris Opéra Ballet and the Dutch National Ballet, his home company; and he is also an award-winning novelist. His mastery of tone—suggested eloquently here in the English translation from the Dutch by Katie de Haan, the first translation since the memoir's initial publication, in 1993—leads the author to report events with a conversational intimacy that never deteriorates into gossip and that permits him to re-create actions and undercurrents without recourse to hyperbole, fictional interior monologues, synthesized detail, or invented dialogue. He relates what he knows only from firsthand experience: although this makes for a narrow account of Nureyev's achievements, it also grounds the dancer's outsized personality in a realistic context. Rudi van Dantzig's Nureyev is neither an epic hero nor a cartoon, as he is in some memoirs, but rather a complex human being who is also a genius, and van Dantzig makes no effort to compete with him or to aggrandize himself at Nureyev's expense. The reader is given the impression of a mutual, hard-won respect between Nureyev and van Dantzig: as dancers, they were not equals, yet as colleagues and, ultimately, friends, they were equally fascinating—both individually and engaged with one another.

In terms of its emotional delicacy and its illumination of an artist who could be puzzling at best and maddening at worst, *Remembering Nureyev: The Trail of a Comet* stands up well when considered in the company of, say, James Baldwin's essay-memoir of the novelist Richard Wright or Gore Vidal's of the playwright Tennessee Williams. It is a "dance book" because its author and subject happen to be dancers, but the way it is written aligns it, too, with a much wider group of artists' remembrances. As an insider's guide, it goes very deep.

—Mindy Aloff

ACKNOWLEDGMENTS

For the realization of this American edition of *Remembering Nureyev: The Trail of a Comet*, I would first like to thank Katie de Haan, who began translating what we had taken to calling *The Comet* on her own initiative. When Katie and I met for the first time, after a brief telephone call not long after the book appeared in the Netherlands in 1993, I found to my amazement that she had already completed most of the translation. "Your book about Nureyev is a really unusual and evocative one, and I feel more people should have a chance to appreciate it, not only readers of Dutch," she explained.

When the translation was completed, Katie and I together made several attempts to interest an English language publisher in the manuscript. Our endeavors soon stalled, however, mainly because it was an especially busy period for me in which I had undertaken a great deal of work outside the Netherlands and it was not easy to establish contact with international publishers. I felt sorry for Katie, but her translation lay untouched in a cupboard for years after that, forgotten almost, but not entirely.

Years later, when I was in Moscow in 2001, I met Leslie Getz and her husband, Don McDonagh, who had arrived from New York. Don and I were both on the jury of the International Ballet Competition organized by Yuri Grigorovich. During our meetings there in faraway Moscow, a mere decade after Gorbachev's government had been overthrown by Yeltsin and his followers, when Yeltsin himself was about to resign in favour of Putin, we naturally came to speak of Rudolf Nureyev, having met passionate admirers of his in the theatre. I mentioned to Getz and McDonagh on that occasion that I had spent a fair amount of time with Nureyev and that our company, the Dutch National Ballet, had gone on tour with him in North America and that, following on his death, I had written a book about him that had been published in the Netherlands. At the end of the competition our international jury disbanded, each one returning home; whether we should ever see one another again remained uncertain, despite promises to visit, call, or write, the way these things often go.

A long time went by after that, until Leslie suddenly called me from New York, asking whether she might read Katie's translation: "If I like it, maybe I can try to find a publisher for you," she offered. She was true to her word and helped to shepherd the manuscript through the long and complicated acceptance process. Astoundingly and quite unexpectedly after that, the *Comet* gained momentum.

Besides Katie de Haan and Leslie Getz, I would like to thank my friends Toer van Schayk and Gertjan Evenhuis for their patience and help in reading and organizing manuscripts, correspondence, photos, and all the other careful work that was essential to bring together the various parts of the book again, skills in which I was often sadly lacking.

I would especially like to thank Barbara Palfy for copyediting the manuscript for the American edition, because, faced with enormous personal difficulties, she continued to work on this book; not many people would have had that courage or inner strength.

To Minou Bijl, Coordinator for the Dutch National Ballet in Amsterdam, I am indebted for her helpfulness and perseverance in tracing the photographic material. My gratitude is also due those photographers whose pictures have been included in this book—or their relatives, since some of them, sadly, have died—for their cooperation. Many of the images are from the period between 1970 and 1975 and were not easy to trace again. From the other side of the Atlantic came assistance from Nancy Sifton, who generously loaned photos from her private collection to be scanned for my consideration for the book. The technical support in transmitting these images was provided by Min Zhu. I understand there were many difficulties, but he stayed with it until the job was successfully done.

My thoughts also go to the dancers of the Dutch National Ballet from that time, for all the enthusiasm and devotion with which they endowed their work, and for the way they surely made Nureyev feel he was "one of them."

Lastly, I would like to recall for a moment Maude and Nigel Gosling, Douce François, Wallace Potts, and John Taras, all close friends of Rudolf's and no longer with us, but remembered in gratitude.

Linda Maybarduk and her husband, Bill Alguire, have drawn a trail through time with their children. We became godfathers, Rudolf to their daughter Alexandra Nureyeva Alguire in 1989, and I to their sons Michael and Cameron Alguire in 1983 and 1985: three young people entrusted to two "Uncle Rudis," and a family where Nureyev is ever-present and will remain so.

I should like to thank Meredith Morris-Babb at the University Press of Florida, for giving the book a chance, and Mindy Aloff for writing the foreword.

Remembering Nureyev

1 🙾 *"What You Want?"*

It is 1968, a beautiful spring day in Amsterdam and I am seated on a window-sill in a dressing room at the Carré Theater,[1] watching an exotic-looking young man—powerful build, strong head with very pronounced features—accentuate his eyebrows with a few nonchalant strokes, draw jet-black lines around his eyes, and pencil a deep, brown shadow between his eyelid and eyebrow. He has eyes like a fox hidden among the shrubs, spying on an intruder.

Outside the room, I hear the sounds heralding a performance: instruments being tuned, the ringing of a bell, a voice calling, "Five minutes!" Between the deftly moving dancer and his visitor, not a word is exchanged. One is applying his makeup, while the other watches as the face gradually becomes a mask. Both are eyeing one another from their vantage points.

The eyes, flashing like lightning from me and back to their own reflection, are discerning. There is a blend of suspicion, curiosity, and aggression glinting in them; the fox may disappear in the wink of an eye or launch a sudden attack.

"And, what you think?" His question is more like a command; no contradiction is expected. The sound of his voice is hoarse and, despite the unmistakably Russian intonation, his English seems almost affected. Each word is articulated with care, as though he savors it before letting it go.

I am caught unawares and shrug my shoulders: "I'm not sure."

---

1. The Carré Theater was built in 1887 by the Carré family as a place to show their famous circus. The French architect Gustave Eiffel was responsible for the construction of the roof. The circus had a show of horses, lions, and bears, among other animals and, at the time Fonteyn and Nureyev performed there, the remnants of manure might waft into the dressing-rooms from the stables below the stage. Nowadays Carré has become a very popular musical theater, even allowed to add "Royal" to its name.

"Well, you'd better make up your mind, the world is not going to wait *that* long for you." He casts one last, dissatisfied glance at his reflection, sprays a stifling amount of lacquer on his hair, and all of a sudden, without bestowing on me so much as a second glance, he stalks out of the room.

No, indeed, this world does not intend to wait; any moment now, this world is about to embark upon a successful performance, quite decidedly. He leaves me in no doubt about that whatsoever.

I realize that this dancer teaching me a lesson in such an abrupt manner is five years younger than I am, but it feels quite the other way round.

What should I do? Should I wait? A man puts his head around the door, "Mister Nureyev says that if you want to see the performance, I'm to show you the way." But that will not be necessary; I know the theater like the back of my hand.

As I walk slowly downstairs backstage, I hesitate: what shall I do? Shall I go outside or into the theater and watch the cunning fox perform?

"I'll be back in a minute," I say to the doorman, "just need some fresh air."

Amsterdam is full of early-summer sounds; small clusters of people are scattered here and there, strolling at leisure along the Amstel[2]. The water in the river reflects the warmth of a myriad pools of light, and the trees lining the quayside seem top-heavy with showers of young green leaves.

A day for feeling very happy.

In 1961, following a sensational escape, Nureyev had exchanged his life in the Soviet Union for an existence in the West. His spectacular flight and the many incidents he was involved in or gave rise to later became world news— and remained so for a long time. In no time at all, he had made himself a reputation as *the* leading dancer in the Western hemisphere, seen everywhere and discussed everywhere, the talk of both professional and society press.

It was not until seven years after his flight that audiences in Holland had a chance to become acquainted with the artistic achievements of this illustrious dancer: the Royal Ballet, the English company Nureyev had joined, was giving a short series of performances in Amsterdam.

2. The name Amsterdam originates from the dam constructed in the Amstel River. The Amstel is the river along whose banks the city was originally built in the thirteenth century.

Although I had never seen a performance by Nureyev, I had not bought tickets for this ballet event. Together with Robert Kaesen, and following Sonia Gaskell's departure, I had only recently taken up duty as artistic director of the Dutch National Ballet and, as far as I can remember, we were up to our eyes in organizational and artistic problems. I was in no mood for going out, even for professional reasons. Besides, I was no great admirer of the English company or the repertoire it had brought to Holland, even if the performers were world-famous stars like Margot Fonteyn and Rudolf Nureyev.

To my amazement and initial disbelief, during the company's run at the Carré Theater, I received a message that Nureyev wished to speak to me and the request to report to his dressing room before the matinee on the Sunday afternoon.

Expecting either a mistake or a misplaced joke, I knocked on the door bearing Nureyev's name on that Sunday and soon realized that a meeting had indeed been his intention.

"Hello. Sit down." He pointed to a chair, but I chose the windowsill, a little farther away, and was immediately aware of his defensive attitude. It did not seem to make matters any simpler.

"You did ballet that I heard good things about. I wonder if I can perform it," he said, when the silence between us had lasted long enough.

Two years before our meeting, I had staged one of my ballets, *Monument for a Dead Boy*, for the Harkness Ballet in New York. It was not unsuccessful and I realized he was referring to that ballet.[3]

The first thought to cross my mind was that he wanted me to ask the Harkness Ballet management to allow him to dance *Monument* with them; it never occurred to me for a moment that he would wish to appear with our group.

"But if you've never seen *Monument*, how do you know you want to dance it?" I countered. "Maybe you'll think it's awful."

A surly shrug of the shoulders: "I have perfect system of information, spies

3. *Monument for a Dead Boy* had been staged in New York by the Harkness Ballet. Lar Lubovitch and Dennis Wayne, both choreographers now, appeared in that version. Wayne was "the friend," with Larry Rhodes as "the boy" and Lone Isacson as "the blue girl." Their interpretations were impressive, and *Monument* was a great success, apparently catching Nureyev's attention.

everywhere. But if you're not interested," and he began dabbing away furiously with his makeup sponge.

What on earth did the man want? I felt the warmth of the sun on my back through the open window and I heard children calling out as they ran along the canal behind the theater.

"Maybe you ought to see the ballet first," I ventured, but either he did not think it worth answering, or he was too absorbed in his transformation: colorful sticks of greasepaint, brushes, sponges.

Whatever it was he meant or wanted, the future did not look at all promising.

On returning to the theater after my stroll along the canal, I saw the third act of the ballet *Raymonda*, that Nureyev had rehearsed for the Royal Ballet. A large group of dancers in shiny, cream-colored costumes, waving about wildly on too small a stage and an insistent soloist in the middle, Nureyev, hurling his temperament into space; it was hard to know whether he was furious or enjoying himself or even, if possible, both at the same time.

I saw Margot Fonteyn going through her steps, smiling and controlled in her variations, a geometric and evenly balanced sequence of movements, performed at a steadily increasing tempo and ending with a resounding clap of the hands.

Later, Nureyev would explain to me, "That clapping shows the temperament of the woman in the ballet. The dancer must give the impression she has the heavy, rounded arms of a Slavonic mistress, sensual and masterful. You must feel that the fingers on this matron's hands are laden with glistening, precious gems."

On stage, I saw a ballerina giving a performance as an extremely welcoming, well-mannered, ambassador's wife. While the audience cheered and stamped in their enthusiasm, I made my way back to the dressing room. "And, did you like?" Greasepaint and sweat had mingled and were trickling down his costume. I explained that I had seen the second half of the ballet and then, only from the wings, hardly the ideal way to form a reasonable opinion.

"All right," he measured his words carefully now, "what you want?"

Praise, I would later come to realize, could irritate him intensely, but lack of it would do so even more. His tone now was not only downright hostile but he had even turned the tables on me: if I were not mistaken it was *he* who had wanted something, was it not?

The net result of the afternoon was that I scribbled my address on a napkin lying beside his tea glass with one of his sticks of greasepaint and was almost relieved to leave the theater afterward.

What a spitfire the man was. The whole *Monument* idea was a whim, of course, a sudden notion; that was clear. The following day, the English company would go on its way and Nureyev would have forgotten Amsterdam and the conversation with that strange Dutch choreographer altogether.

And I was supposed to regret that later, I assumed.

A few days later, however, he called me up and asked when we could begin rehearsals. Only then did it become clear to me that he had no intention of dancing *Monument* with the American company, but that he wanted to appear with *our* company. He wanted to work with our dancers!

Suddenly, I saw things in a whole new light and it began to dawn on me what it could mean if someone of Nureyev's standing was willing to link his name to the Dutch National Ballet, if only for a while.

I suggested a few dates maybe a season or more away, assuming that the Dutch National Ballet's performance schedule was already fixed from September 1968 until July 1969. Planning was dealt with by our commercial director, Anton Gerritsen.

"No" he protested, "too far away. Impossible. If you want to do something with me it will have to be soon. I can't wait."

"What do you suggest, then?" I asked, "After all, I have no idea how you're used to working." "I'm free for a few days in October. I could come to Amsterdam then. How long do you think I would need to learn the choreography?"

"Two weeks, three at the most." That was the time we needed to work on a part like that within our own company. Rehearsing with the Harkness Ballet in New York had taken me five weeks and that had been with dancers who were used to contemporary work, something I was unsure of where Nureyev was concerned.

He laughed scornfully. "Two, three days is all I can give you. At the *most*, my dear. Nothing more."

"And the performances, when?"

"I shall have to see, my diary is not fixed yet."

Never before had I heard a dancer speak of "my diary," like a businessman. For me, and for most dancers in Europe in those days, it was usual to work for one company and we were available all the time. Our "diaries" were posted on the notice board in the studio every day. There we would learn when the rehearsals, performances, and tours were planned.

For a moment, when it dawned on him that I was unable to produce a diary with performance dates, he appeared somewhat crestfallen. It was checkmate. Out of the blue, he changed tack—a red herring? "Why don't we make new appointment? I'm working in Milan next week; come and see me there."

In Milan, Nureyev was a different person altogether from the edgy individual I had become acquainted with in Amsterdam. The man waiting for us at La Scala was charming, interested, and even prepared to listen and be reasonable! The elusive impression he had created at the Carré Theater, the remote tyrant, had vanished, and before me stood a pleasant, occasionally even uncertain youth, who could dissolve into wild and inexplicable laughter out of the blue.

I was with the Dutch society journalist Henk van der Meyden, who had shot up like lightning as Nureyev's Dutch impresario. Rudolf showed us around the Scala in model fashion, brought us coffee, and, reclining on a couch to take the weight off his legs, he listened to the proposals van der Meyden put forward. Within the hour, everything was arranged, without the slightest discord.

On my way back to Amsterdam, I had a slip of paper in my pocket with the dates of rehearsals in October and the first performances, which were to take place two months later.

The adventure was about to begin.

2   ⤳   *Monument*

On arrival at Schiphol Airport, Nureyev was greeted by a small group of reporters, a few stray admirers among the inquisitive travelers, bouquets of flowers and the constant clicking of cameras.

He obliged the press radiantly, answering their—sometimes rather impertinent—questions readily and with witty repartee, his mouth moving as though he were devouring a tasty morsel. Articulating his sentences with a lusty eagerness, he recounted how he had boarded the airplane immediately after a tiring tour across America. "And here I am. Ready." And once again, like applause following a performance, there was a dazzling fireworks display from the cameras.

I myself had flown home to Amsterdam that very morning from Munich, where a group of Dutch National Ballet dancers had been recording for a German television company.

It was hard to imagine a greater contrast than between the flashy show at Schiphol and the Munich television studios. The German director had had the rather original idea of filming the choreography, *Fractions*, in a jet black, blinded and darkened studio, where seven dancers carried out their work by the beam of a single spotlight.

Every morning, the dancers would step into the black box, where all idea of direction, time or dimension vanished within minutes. Groping their way around like insects underground, the dancers were thrown off-balance as they moved around and suddenly no longer knew what was back or front; even a fly crawled groggily into a piercing ray of light on the jet-black dance floor, too dazed to fly away.

The man at Schiphol Airport was far from dazed and seemed quite effervescent with energy.

"What time would you like to rehearse tomorrow?" Although it was late in the afternoon, I thought Nureyev still might like to see our studios and meet the part of the company that was not in Germany and maybe exchange thoughts with me on *Monument*.

"What do you mean, rehearse tomorrow?" He looked at me in disbelief. "Nothing tomorrow, now, at once! What time is it?"

While he disappeared into the hotel elevator with his luggage, I called the Municipal Theater, home to the Dutch National Ballet.

"Nureyev wants to start rehearsing now, so the other rehearsals will have to be cancelled." At that time, we had only *one* reasonable, and thus frequently occupied, studio in our theater and, whatever happened, I wanted to work with him alone in this initial rehearsal. It would turn out to be the first of a long series of last-minute changes in our collaboration.

A half hour later, when we arrived at the artists' entrance to the Municipal Theater, we saw that there, too, a cluster of journalists and photographers had gathered, keen to be present at the first rehearsal, but I was feeling uncertain and nervous and could not imagine I would be able to steer this important first session between the two of us to a satisfactory close, and certainly not with a number of unfamiliar onlookers there as well.

"But you want publicity, don't you?" Nureyev asked, a hint of mockery in his voice.

"Not now, at any rate. Later, tomorrow perhaps, or the day after."

The studio was empty, but I had seen the inquisitive faces of our dancers in the hallways and behind half-open dressing room doors.

Nureyev strolled across the deserted dance floor, placed an enormous bag on the bench, and began arranging innumerable pairs of ballet shoes, towels and sweaters, ignoring me altogether. In silence, he tried on one pair of shoes after another, tied a hairband around his head, blew his nose into a towel— clearly from a hotel—and tried out a couple of dance steps. A quarter of an hour went by.

"I want to warm up first." He walked over to the barre and, agonizingly slowly, began a series of exercises while I looked on. In this way an hour passed in an almost deathly hush. He changed shoes, gave a short commentary intended for himself on a difficult exercise, pulled on an extra leotard, and meanwhile, played the game with the probing eyes once again, from his reflection to me and back again, a hypnotic séance.

It was the first time I had seen him at work, so I was not bored—in fact dancers at work never bore me—and yet, maybe owing to the utter lack of communication, I felt like some immobile and mesmerized victim being slowly but surely encapsulated.

"So, ready." He was sweating and looked pleased with himself. "Can we hear the music?"

I switched on the tape with Jan Boerman's (electronic) score, curious as to how he would react.

"Noise," was his only comment, "noise. Interesting."

He walked over to the center of the studio, turned a pirouette, as if to say there was nothing like "traditional," and tightened his hairband.

"Can you mark time to the music?"

No, that was a matter of listening, making the music your own, and finding a communal rhythm with the other dancers. Becoming one with the sounds.

I received an incomprehending glance.

"*Monument* is not a ballet in the ordinary sense of the word," I warned him. "There are no entrechats, pas de bourrée or tours en l'air. There are movements which have to become your own, as though they come from inside you."

"What do you mean, can I do what I want, do I have to improvise?" and he pulled a wry face. But no, he would have to stick to the rules, my rules.

"Okay, that's what I'm here for, let's begin." I got on his nerves, that much was clear.

As I showed him the first steps, I felt my knees knocking and my voice wavering. It all seemed so ridiculous. What was this man supposed to do with my strange movements?

"Once again" was the command and I obediently began again, while he went back to the pile of shoes and began rummaging through it. What sort of an exhibition was this? I stopped.

"Go on, I can see you." But then he would have needed eyes in the back of his head. Once more, then, and this time he joined in, copying my movements; we had gone through the first thirty seconds of the ballet.

"Can we do this to the music?" I switched on the tape and we went through the process once again. Suddenly he clapped his hands. "Enough, now me on my own."

I sat down and watched him give a vague, watered-down version of my movements—or rather, not vague but actually overemphatic: each gesture followed by an exclamation mark, as it were. And it did *not* fit the music either.

"All right?"

What was I supposed to answer: no?

"The music is complicated and you still have to get used to my way of moving." I tried to evade the thorny question, but that did not go down well.

"Good is *good*, not good is *not* good, please."

He repeated the piece and this time really made a caricature of it. "This better?" The question was oozing sarcasm and I began to feel myself breaking out in a cold sweat: where was this leading to, this agonizingly slow learning process with a mulish, stubborn child?

"Would you like us to go on with the next part?" because that seemed to me wiser, even though the atmosphere could be cut with a knife. "Now it all seems strange, but tomorrow you'll probably see it in a different light." Although, to be honest, tomorrow did not bear thinking about.

We struggled on and, teeth clenched, I refrained from giving directions or comments. He slaved away behind me, moaning, puffing, panting; it sounded far from encouraging.

It was a mystery to me. The moves I showed him were complicated but hardly tiring, and yet he gave the impression he was doing the work of a docker.

"Rudi, there's a call for you." Liberated, I tore downstairs to my office; away from the stifling atmosphere for a moment!

"How's it going, what's it like there, when are you going to start rehearsals?" The *Fractions* dancers were gathered round the telephone in Munich, eager to hear about the great adventure.

"He's already started," I sighed, "and I feel lousy."

When I returned to the studio, I caught him going through the choreography on his own, something he stopped instantly, almost startled, the moment he noticed me.

"Shall we try one more time?" The short break had broken the tension, and suddenly the work went far more quickly. As the rest of the dancers were missing from the ballet, it was like working on a kind of jigsaw puzzle, with most of the pieces untraceable, so that he only learned his solo parts. The main thing we were doing now was the reconnaissance of unmapped territory: the sound of the music, the color of the movement idiom. Above all, it was a comparison of characters: how does he work, how do I respond, what does he want, to what extent do I drop my guard? All questions of the utmost importance in rehearsals, which can give rise to strong emotions and outbursts of uncertainty during initial meetings between dancer and choreographer or, on the other hand, to feelings of profound satisfaction.

By the end of the rehearsal I saw he had absorbed quite a bit of *Monument*, and Nureyev himself did not seem discontented either. Puffing and panting, he took off his shoes and sprawled out on the floor, thrashing around with his arms and legs like a beetle on its back. I laughed, he laughed; the ice was broken. For today, at least. The first rehearsal seemed to have been a chastening process, but I was glad it was over.

Outside it had grown dark. He gathered his things together and asked for a masseur, who—hardly surprising at that unlikely hour—was not available and had to be summoned in a hurry.

"And what happens tonight?"

"You'll want to rest, won't you?" I ventured, referring to his possible tiredness, the time difference, and the jet lag; but he would have none of those lame excuses.

"Can't I work with someone this evening, a partner?" Yvonne Vendrig, who danced the *Girl in Blue*, lived in Utrecht, but I called her and explained the situation. "I know it's a nuisance, but can you come back right now?"

He rested for a couple of hours and then he was back in the studio, now, to my amazement, ignoring not only Yvonne, but me, as well. Were we going to start all over again?

"Come on," I said, taking Yvonne by the hand and leading her up to him, as though to a dangerous animal, "Rudolf, this is Yvonne."

He spun round, cast her a stern glance, stuck out his hand and snapped "Hello." It appeared he was not fond of lifting women—something which is almost inevitable in a pas de deux—and certainly not of twisted lifts, unavoidable in *Monument*.

I began to discover the amount of effort it sometimes cost the great dancer to move when the movements were beyond the familiar. How awkward he could then be, how uninventive.

The rehearsal began again, full of collisions, falls and stinging abuse, and once more I wondered: "Why bother with all this, if he finds it such a chore?"

Going by his mood and attitude, it seemed most likely he would pack his bags the following day and say: "This is no good for me; I've made a mistake."

Yvonne was a fair match for him. Like everyone else, she was full of awe for our guest, but she would not allow herself to be maneuvered into a corner.

"No, not like that," she said, taking his hands and placing them around her waist the way she wanted, "Like that." And a little while later: "Ow, you're hurting me, is that necessary?" She glared at him angrily and he seemed intimidated and overwhelmed, but later he slammed her down on the ground unnecessarily hard, with a vindictive look in his eye.

They opposed one another like two Kilkenny cats in what was sometimes a silent battle, snappish, curt. I stood looking on with no idea how to come between them. In my heart I took Yvonne's side, but I knew of no way to curb Rudolf's temper.

"They are fascinated by each other," I tried to explain the implications of the pas de deux to him. "They are both feeling their way toward each other, both afraid of going too far. The boy keeps withdrawing sooner than the girl; it is she who takes the initiative, over and over again."

"She's a bitch," Nureyev muttered, clearly audible.

Yvonne was still very young, eighteen at the most; I had discovered her in the corps de ballet and given her a number of important roles, which she had interpreted brilliantly in her burning, obsessive expression.

I felt sorry for her: her first disillusioning experience with a "real" star. It reminded me of a young, adventurous kitten, being reprimanded out of the blue by her furious, hissing mother, with a few, deft strokes of the paw.

At the end of her brave fight, she sat sobbing in a corner of the studio, while Nureyev sullenly got ready to go. I sat down beside her and put my arm around her. So, that should be perfectly clear to him.

A curt "bye," and he had left the studio.

When I knocked on his dressing room door some half hour later—just to be certain, for he was sure to have gone—I found him still sitting there all alone, like a child sulking.

"Let's go and eat." I later came to realize that this was his magic formula which was supposed to resolve almost every situation. And did.

By now, it was eleven o'clock and hard to find a restaurant where we could still dine; suddenly I felt a little ashamed of Amsterdam, he would think us very provincial . . .

After a few abortive attempts there was a restaurant, *The Oyster Bar*, whose owner recognized Nureyev. "For *him* we'll open up the kitchen again." And so the thorny situation was resolved.

Even though he wanted to dance *Monument* and had begun rehearsing it, he had asked me nothing about its content yet, concerning himself only with the movements; I had given a few sporadic clues. Not that this is so unusual in the world of dance; a choreographer is often like a guide leading a blindfolded person by the hand: "Here is a bend." "There is a man with a child." "There's a bird flying toward the sun. Can you hear it?" "Now there's a group of people coming, avoid them." And thus, slowly, gradually, and with a minimum of words, the drama line unfolds. The dynamics of the movement, the waves and explosions, the silences, and withdrawals do the rest, conveying the essence: a body language which, if spoken well, escapes no one. "Tell, me, what is the ballet about? He loves boys, no?" Rudolf inquired after the character of his role.

"No, that's just it, he's a boy who's still unsure whether he's attracted to boys or girls. He's imprisoned in a series of nightmarish impressions and experiences."

"A stupid boy, then," was the down-to-earth comment. But I think he was enjoying his salmon.

"Some people know earlier than others what they want, but I wouldn't call it stupid," I said protectively, in defence of the hesitant boy in *Monument*, but Rudolf did not respond to that remark.

Later, on the Spiegelstraat[1] window-shopping for antiques: how old I thought those wineglasses were, and whether that table was genuine. I was at a loss for an answer.

---

1. The Spiegelstraat (literally "Mirror Street") is a small street full of antique shops in the heart of Amsterdam.

"What can we do now?" We were strolling along one of the canals and he had linked his arm with mine and seemed not at all about to give up. I told him where I thought he could find the type of nightlife he seemed to be looking for and accompanied him a little way in that direction.

"I'm sorry, this is something you'll have to do on your own." I was utterly exhausted, and said I had an appointment early the next day and wanted to be fit. How long ago had he set off on his journey from America to Amsterdam, seventeen, eighteen hours?

The notion that not every human being has an equal store of energy to draw upon was small consolation to me.

Two days later, the *Fractions* dancers were home from Munich, a little wan from their "reminiscences from the subterranean," but at least our company was complete again.

Toer van Schayk—the original interpreter of *Monument,* who had created the leading role in the ballet *and* designed the sets and costumes—was in the Munich group as well. With his impassioned interpretation, he had been a source of profound inspiration to me in the creation process, and I was sure he could give Nureyev artistic and technical advice for his role.

The rehearsal schedules had been adapted by now, so that entire days were devoted to *Monument*, or rather to Nureyev, who was following a crash course. During our second rehearsal day, he had suddenly announced he was unable to stay in Amsterdam for as long as we had originally agreed upon, but that he still wanted to know the entire ballet before he left. That meant our whole company had little option but to repeat infinite variations on *Monument* morning, noon, evening, and—if Rudolf had anything to do with it—night, as well.

The dancers who were not involved in *Monument*, but were so very curious to catch a glimpse of our famous guest, sat on the studio sidelines during rehearsals and to them, in the beginning at least, Nureyev was really amiable. He made jokes with them and tried to win the dancers' audience over when differences of opinion arose between him and me by showing off in a sort of commedia dell'arte way—pulling faces, making grotesque gestures—or using them as personnel: "Can you get me tea?" "See if masseur is in." "Ask office to call London for me." Never "Please." He gave orders.

Toward his partners in the ballet he was as changeable as a chameleon: one moment he was effusive in his expressions of affection, the very next he would be downright rude and tormenting.

And Toer's presence was not appreciated at all. When certain things went wrong with Nureyev time and time again, I was foolish enough to ask Toer, who was modesty and helpfulness in person, to demonstrate them. Sometimes, the chance to see a movement performed and be able to analyze it can help a dancer immensely.

Nureyev, however, walked over to his bag abruptly, threw in shoes and towels and said: "Why don't you let *him* do it then?"

We were amazed. To interpret help offered in good will in such a manner was an unpleasant form of provocation. After the door had slammed shut, everyone in the studio went rigid, wondering what would happen next.

I shrugged my shoulders in resignation; the past two days had taught me a great deal.

"I'm not going after him," I said, and I did not want a well-meaning dancer to go to his dressing room either. No pleading.

"We're going to continue, everyone." I switched on the tape recorder again.

Two minutes later, the door opened and he stepped into the studio again, gave me a long, blank stare, and resumed his position. Had he lost a contest?

But in my heart I felt for him. He stood there looking so disillusioned, as though he could not cope with his own emotions or how the outside world responded to them. Did he see the dancers' friendliness toward him, even after the incident, as condescending or groveling? And did he feel my behavior was hostile, or disrespectful? Did he think I was taking sides?

Over the years, when I had gotten to know him better, I would notice that whenever he entered a new environment or an unknown company he would harbor suspicion and mistrust, as though everyone were conspiring against him: the inhabitants of the safe, protected nest against the unknown intruder.

And of course, it *was* hard for him—world-famous, adored by a massive audience, feted everywhere and accustomed to receiving enormous fees—to gauge whether the friendliness he saw around him was sincere, or whether people were playing up to him, currying favor; a fear of flattery and insincerity that can soon become an obsession.

"Get out," he said, "go away," and suddenly all the interested dancers had to leave the studio. "I can't work like this."

Toer stayed, seated beside me but silent now. We agreed to go through all that Nureyev had learned in those two-and-a-half days and at the end everyone, including Toer, was amazed: he had learned so much in so short a time.

Suddenly I saw Nureyev's self-confidence grow, he relaxed perceptibly and even went as far as asking Toer for help, watching patiently and in amusement how a move could be made without the danger of damaging a knee.

More and more ice was broken and, as the afternoon drew to a close, a number of photographers were even given permission to register a few rehearsal scenes.

Before the photo-call began, Nureyev changed practice clothes, tried on shoes endlessly, and made sure his hair was impeccable, all preparations I found surprising and disappointing. Surely the idea was to capture the working atmosphere, not to make an official portrait?

The run-through began, cameras clicking, but after no more than a few minutes Rudolf clapped his hands: "Stop!"

I became irritated. Who was in charge here, he or I? Who decided whether a rehearsal was interrupted? But I still stopped the tape recorder. He grabbed hold of a photographer who was trying to take pictures in a corner of the studio by the shoulders and directed him toward the front of the studio.

"I will not have ugly photos taken of me," he snarled, as though *that* had been the photographer's intention. "Photographs may only be taken from *here.*"

There was a commotion among the photographers, sniggering, mumbling. We began again from the beginning to the sound of furious clicking, nerves clearly strained to the utmost. And, sure enough, Rudolf tripped and fell. Immediately he called a halt, sat down, and ordered tea, toweled himself off, changed his shoes, while dancers and press waited. Ten minutes passed and one of the photographers—sensibly!—gathered up his things and left.

When, agonizingly slowly, Nureyev arose and walked over to his place again, that moment was registered behind his back, click. He wheeled round, flung the glass in his hand across the studio, and yelled: "Finished. Go, go away!"

"You do want publicity, don't you?" he had asked me two days earlier.

"You go too, everyone," I said, for this was quite pointless for the dancers as well. "Enough for today."

That evening, in a fine mood, he took Toer and me to a restaurant.

Eating out with him in those days could be rather embarrassing. He would happily send back a bottle of wine, "Not good enough," and stare in disgust at the remarkably thick steak which was often placed on the table with pride by the chef himself. Rudolf would cut the meat and taste it with his tongue: "Too small. And cold inside. I want it hot, not half from fridge."

He seemed to assume on principle that there was nothing worthwhile in Holland, an attitude which infuriated me. A year later, when I dined with him in Paris, at the Ritz Hotel on the Place Vendôme, and he was served a wafer-thin steak, I said mockingly, "Well, send *that* back, then." But he ate it meekly, without so much as a whimper.

"What a fantastic profession we have," he would sometimes say when he was enjoying himself. "We do the work we love and get paid for it as well!" This is a thought pondered by many a dancer, only Rudolf happened to be very lavishly rewarded for his work. Around the time of *Monument*, he told me he was earning some $5,000 dollars for a performance, "and I dance at least two hundred and fifty performances a year. Expenses I hardly have, because hotels, traveling, and food, everything is paid for by the companies I work with. If I stop working *now* I can live gloriously for the rest of my life."

How different he would sound in later years.

"But everyone is enthusiastic," he protested when I told him I considered a second rehearsal period absolutely essential.

By the end of the fourth day, we had gone through the whole of *Monument* and he was, indeed, roughly familiar with the choreography. However, performing the moves more or less correctly is not the same as an interpretation that has become a fusion between form and expression. Dutch audiences were familiar with Toer's interpretation and a comparison was bound to be to Nureyev's disadvantage. (Later I discovered that, no matter what his performances were like, audience and press would still be jubilant.) These arguments aside, however, *I* was unhappy with the way the ballet was looking at that point, and surely *that* should have been the decisive factor for him.

He grumbled, leafed back and forth in his diary, and called the Royal Ballet.

"I'm appearing in Paris for two weeks. If you can come there we can work together."

It took me considerable persuasion to convince him that it was precisely the work with the other dancers that was crucial, the emotional bond between him and his partners. All the rest would be largely a waste of time. I knew that if I gave in to him now, I was finished, putty in his hands.

"Take it or leave it. After all, what is it you want, to learn something from our collaboration, to experience something new, or simply to find yet another way of dazzling your audiences for a while?"

He eventually agreed to an extra series of rehearsals and off he went again, laden with cases, parcels, and bags (he had clearly visited the antique shops after all!) on his way to Schiphol and his next destination.

"Bye." Such a curt farewell, as though we were strangers once again.

Meanwhile, he called me up several times and, to my surprise, asked whether he could stay with Toer and me on his next visit.

He had visited our home only once. We lived in a small, old property that had begun life as a grocer's shop, in the Jordaan district of Amsterdam.[2] The shop floor now served as a studio for Toer's painting and sculpture. It was a somewhat primitive abode, with a narrow, winding staircase and a ladder up to the loft where Toer and I slept, and only a tiny spare room. Was that what he wanted, used as he was, I now realized, to large houses and lavish hotels?

But arrive he did, larger than life, in the Eerste Looiersdwarsstraat, causing quite a stir in his attire, which was extremely eccentric, even in the era of the hippies, Stones, and Beatles.

All dressed up in a leather coat nearly down to his ankles, an enormous fur hat, flamboyant shawl, and colorful harlequin boots, he had the air of a captain on some fairy-tale galleon: our house was immediately bursting at its seams.

2. The Jordaan area of Amsterdam is a seventeenth-century neighborhood said to be reminiscent of Greenwich Village.

But what now? Could we saddle him with our messy and rather bohemian way of life?

The first problem proved to be alcohol, a delicate matter, as neither Toer nor I was an expert on drinks; a bottle of wine on birthdays at the most, and then often only of the cranberry sort, I fear.

"I only drink vodka," he announced, but it had to be "Stolichnaya," and no other. And that was in 1968 . . . I cycled halfway round town, but that particular Soviet brand was nowhere to be found, until, in sheer desperation, Toer suggested trying our old corner off-licence. And sure enough, a mere ten yards from our very door: Stolichnaya!

"Here in the good old Jordaan," as the song goes![3]

The following morning I left the house while Rudolf was still asleep. I usually arrived at the theater early, in order to deal with various business matters with my co-director Robert Kaesen before work got underway in the studio. Classes for the dancers began at ten o'clock and Rudolf had impressed upon me how essential they were for him, but by quarter past ten—the overflowing class was waiting patiently—there was still no sign of Rudolf.

I rang home, where Toer said in despair: "I can't get him out of bed, but he swears he'll be there in fifteen minutes."

The class began almost an hour late but, miracle of miracles, none of the dancers or even the teacher complained; after all, this was Nureyev.

The *Monument* rehearsals had been allotted far less time than during his previous visit, for we were unable to go on devoting all our time and space to the one ballet. Strangely enough, however, the rehearsals went far more smoothly; either he had done all his home (studio) work thoroughly in the meantime, or had thought it all through and absorbed it surprisingly well.

When he had kept the company waiting scandalously long the next day as well (and now I did hear grumbling), and as I suspected him of trying to string us along, I came up with a ruse. I set the alarm clock in our house three-quarters of an hour ahead.

On the third day, when he discovered that this time he was not even the last person to arrive in the studio he glanced at the studio clock as if stung by an adder and hissed at me furiously, "You fiddled with my alarm."

3. "Bij ons in de Jordaan" (Here in the good old Jordaan) is an old song, an ode to this neighborhood in Amsterdam, dating from when the Jordaan was a poor but cheerful area.

His preparations for the barre work were somewhere midway between performing a play and the celebration of high mass. Poker-faced, and looking at no one, he went through a series of rituals, pointing a toe, adjusting a leg-warmer, checking an arm position, tying a hairband, arching his back extremely slowly, and uttering a deep and tortured sigh.

It was surely effective; all eyes were on him.

At the barre he maintained his own tempo, which was exceedingly slow, and, as he was a famous guest, after all, the teacher felt there was no option but to follow his tempo. And, when that was still too fast for him, Rudolf went on imperturbably in his own rhythm, ignoring everyone around him.

During the exercises in the middle of the studio, he would sometimes stop everyone and say, "Me, alone," and then carry out a combination of leaps quite different from those demonstrated by the teacher. Rudolf often entered into a discussion when he disagreed with a particular sequence in class, half-accusing the teacher that he, or she, was no good at the job.

He was brilliant at upsetting people.

Inside me an elevator,
   full of people, full of faces,
   slowly moving up
   and downwards,
   an elevator heavy
   with memories and lives.

Toer and I tried hard to translate the fragments of verse by the Dutch poet Hans Lodeizen,[4] which served as a guideline in the *Monument* program, but rendering those simple but oh so fragile, lines into English of the same calibre for Rudolf was by no means easy.

Monument is a ballet covering a period in the life of a boy coming of age and those around him who played a role in his life: his parents, a girlfriend from his earliest youth, his adolescent schoolfriends, and the boy and girl with whom he tries to experience love. His encounters merely bring him to the sorry conclusion that there is an unbridgeable chasm beween emotion and sexuality. The boy seems unable to find a way out of his dilemma.

The ballet consists of a series of brief, dreamlike and nightmarish scenes,

---

4. Hans Lodeizen was an influential Dutch poet who died young (1924–1950).

a chain of obsessive experiences leading ultimately to the boy's choice of death.

"And I play with the sorrowful rope of time . . ."

The entire Nureyev project had begun only a few months earlier and our own theater was already booked over Christmas by the Dutch Opera. Consequently, our company's first performances with him took place in the RAI Arena, which was a cold building, intended as a conference center, and a far less suitable location for dance.

Besides *Monument*, Nureyev danced the *Nutcracker* pas de deux with Royal Ballet ballerina Merle Park as a guest on that occasion because, he explained, the audience had a right to see that he was also a first class classical dancer, as well.

"I have to think about my reputation," a sentence I would hear often after that.

The RAI rehearsals were a disaster; Rudolf's mood was a combination of swearing, hurling things around, threats, storming off, and then again, out of the blue, all good will and hard work. He had become accustomed to the atmosphere and size of the stage at the Municipal Theater and, in contrast, he hated the RAI: the floor was too hard, the hall too large and too chilly, the acoustics impossible.

The members of the National Ballet hung around together in silence, allowed the storms to pass over them and waited to see what would happen.

Fortunately for Toer and me, he had moved into the Hilton for that period, because the idea of sitting across the table from one another amicably in the evenings seemed impossible under the circumstances and, besides, I was relieved to be free of him for a while.

When the curtain rose on *Monument* in the RAI on 25th December, he had made the audience wait in their seats for twenty minutes, procrastinating endlessly and giving everyone in the wings a nervous breakdown.

But this delay, as well, was swallowed by the audience without noticeable grumbling. If one of *our* dancers had tried something like that . . .

Of how Nureyev worked, how he interpreted the role of the boy in *Monument* in those first performances, I remember little, hardly anything in fact.

From later performances, I know that my main objection was—and remained—that he created the impression of a hero in *Monument*, militant, sensual, and extrovert, quite the opposite of the reluctant antihero I had had in mind. But he was quite astounding, a fiery presence confronting his destiny like a caged panther. Nureyev hurled himself into every situation, whether frightening or repulsive or even calm, with a keenness and zest for life that made it hard to believe the man could ever be prey to doubt.

He had a superb group of dancers around him: Christine Anthony and Ivan Kramar were the parents, Lieven Verkruisen the boy as a child, Ellen Brusse the little girl, with Benjamin Feliksdal and Yvonne Vendrig as his contemporaries, each providing a wonderful foil to the hurricane Nureyev. In my view, the hurricanes of applause following the performances were due to them as much as to Nureyev who, it must be said, was quite emphatic in allowing them to share in the well-earned success.

There will have been a party after the premiere, but this, too, eludes me now. I remember that when he left the theater, a small cluster of admirers were gathered waiting for him (and his autograph) and I saw the rather astounded look in Rudolf's eyes when he saw so few people: "Is that all?" In other countries, as I discovered later on, people would throng at the stage door, clamoring to see the star at close quarters, and it might be a quarter of an hour before he could free himself from his fans.

At the Hilton Hotel later that night—and wanting to prolong for as long as possible the festive mood that overtook him following a performance—he spoke to Toer and me of his impressions, what he thought of our company's calibre, the contrasts between modern and classical dancing and how important it was that these differing directions be drawn together.

The fourth person there that evening was Zizi Jeanmaire,[5] who was performing with her company in the Carré Theater at that time.

"There is nothing like seriously approached dance, whether it's modern or classical," she sighed, "I can't tell you how much I miss that."

Jeanmaire was a dancer trained in the classical tradition; she had achieved great acclaim in contemporary choreographies by her husband, Roland Petit, who later had her climb the stairs of the far more lucrative music-hall.

5. Renée (Zizi) Jeanmaire, dancer with the Paris Opéra Ballet, was married to Roland Petit in whose Ballet Roland Petit she was the huge attraction.

"I do it for Roland, because otherwise . . ."

And she consoled Toer: "I know from experience how hard it is to see someone else take over a role you have created and consider your own. Like having your child taken away from you, *ça fait du mal.*"[6]

"Oh, Toer," I said later, "for me, you're by far the more convincing one. No matter how much success he has, Rudolf can't make me forget your *Monument*. Quite the reverse."

We repeated the series in The Hague, Rotterdam, and Antwerp. The studio rehearsals were almost over for Rudolf, so that he was free to spend the long afternoons as he wished. He lured Toer and me along to exhibitions, antique dealers, or film theaters with him; he could neither sit still nor be on his own for long.

I was faced with the dilemma that I really needed and wanted to be with the dancers and in the theater, where dozens of urgent matters were always cropping up, but, then again, I did not wish to leave Rudolf to fend for himself alone.

After his success with the audience and with the company—something he seemed to find most important—he relaxed noticeably and began to enjoy his surroundings; his mood became far less volatile and his company was virtually uncomplicated. And yet, still he had not learned not to keep the audience waiting endlessly; that occurred time and again at each performance.

The final performance in the series took place in Antwerp. Merle Park had returned to London and Noëlla Pontois, a ballerina from the Paris Opéra, took her place in the *Nutcracker* pas de deux.

On stage at the Antwerp theater, I came upon a quiet young woman who asked me the way to Rudolf's dressing room.

"I have danced that pas de deux with him before, but it was quite a long time ago and I would like to rehearse with him this afternoon."

It was no more than a natural request, but I feared the worst; Rudolf had taken refuge in his dressing room and was unapproachable: "I can't work now."

"Rudolf, you can't do that; she's very unsure of herself."

6. "That sure hurts."

"She knows the steps, she danced it already with me." As though that were enough to dance such an extremely difficult and exacting piece.

He eventually came on stage, partnered her in a pirouette, did one intricate lift with her, said "enough" and vanished again. Pontois remained polite and went on rehearsing alone.

And that night, with the theater packed to the brim, the audience was not spared Rudolf's bad mood either. Once again, he kept the theater waiting, but here in Belgium, they did not take it so lightly; there was regular demonstrative applause and even yells in the direction of the closed curtain. All this time, Pontois stood on stage alone, trying to keep her muscles warm and herself calm. When the curtain finally rose, the hostility in the theater was almost tangible; one could cut the atmosphere with a knife.

A few minor things went wrong in the pas de deux, no catastrophes, but clearly visible and the audience—not star-struck now—made no secret of their sympathy and appreciation for Pontois after the initial duet. The response to Rudolf was cool and curt, barely even time for one bow.

The variations and finale that followed degenerated into a competition for the audience's favor, a contest Pontois won with flying colors.

After the performance, Rudolf's room was too small to contain him. He fumed and raged so terrifyingly that everyone kept their distance. What was in store for the *Monument* dancers I wondered?

In the end, I plucked up courage and went and sat down with him. I waited in silence, for there was nothing to say that would not rake the fires, but I hoped my presence would gradually calm his rage. I laid out his costume: "Rudolf, we *have* to begin now," for the almost provocative, slow clapping had been audible again for some time now. Gripping him by the arm, a prisoner almost, I took him to the stage, where the dancers who were to work with him in *Monument* hung around uncertainly, wearing forced smiles.

It was a poor performance, a lost contest. He failed to achieve contact with the dancers, who were no more able to penetrate the unyielding barrier he had thrown up around him than he could himself. Toward the end of the ballet, I saw how he shook off dancers who came too close for his liking, even dealing out a few heavy blows.

From Antwerp, he was due to travel on to Brussels, where he was to work with Maurice Béjart's Ballet of the Twentieth Century. One of Béjart's dancers, Robert Denvers, a friend and admirer of Rudolf's, was waiting for him in the dressing room, where Rudolf once again turned everything upside down, knocking over chairs, yelling.

"Don't just sit there like that, pack those fucking things," and Denvers began gathering up soaking wet leotards, shoes, towels, greasepaint, the whole circus, thrusting it all into bags and cases while Rudolf removed his makeup.

"We *have* to catch the last train," Robert whispered to me, "but we'll never make it, the performance has run at least an hour late."

The bags were not packed to Rudolf's liking, so he turned everything out onto the floor again and snapped at Robert, "Go and do something constructive, for once. Hold that train!"

Poor Robert.

When Nureyev, Toer, and I finally emerged from the taxi at the station, puffing and panting, and ran onto the platform—quite in vain, I was certain—the train was still standing there waiting obediently, some twenty-five minutes overdue; in mortal fear, Denvers had wrought a small miracle!

The driver was standing helpfully at a compartment door with the ticket-collector, and all along the train silent, curious passengers were hanging out of the windows. Those were the days!

The luggage was hurled through a window and into a corridor and the train drew out of the station; Rudolf was on his way to prove himself in yet another company.

Toer and I made our way back slowly down the deserted staircase and out through the empty hall; did this finally mean peace, or was it the beginning of a bad hangover? Finding our way back through Antwerp in the dark, I tried to cope with the turmoil of anger and sympathy, disgust and compassion, respect and incomprehension arising within me, in turn or all at once.

To no avail.

3   *Frog Jumps*

But our collaboration was extended, once again, on Nureyev's initiative.

In spring 1969, a few months after his first visit, he was in Holland once again. He had informed me that he wished to dance a full-length classical ballet with our company and inquired after the artistic standard of *Swan Lake* as staged by the Dutch National Ballet.

No easy question for an artistic director: if I were to recommend it, then later he could challenge me on the quality we were offering; if my judgment were negative then he might—justifiably—say, "Do something about it" or "Then don't dance it."

The idea that the kind of works that served as a measure for ballet companies had developed by means of repeated trial and error seemed to be an unfamiliar problem to him. This was because he had been used to working with established companies in Russia and in England whose evening-length academic works like *Swan Lake* or *The Sleeping Beauty* had been in their repertoire for decades or more.

My opinion of "our" *Swan Lake* was somewhere between positive and negative; often it was patently obvious that the classical showpieces were beyond our reach but, on occasion, the whole company seemed to become inspired and would dance an impassioned and technically fairly sound performance. However, in those days, it could not be denied that this only occurred on rare occasions.

"Why not come and see for yourself?" I suggested to him.

He came to Rotterdam, but missed the first act. In the second act, when the Swan Queen—one of our chubbier dancers on this occasion—makes it clear to the prince that he should come no closer (expressed in ballet-mime by a constant crossing of the hands back and forth in front of the pelvis, while the head is insistently shaking "no") I heard him chortling away beside me: "Delicatessen is closed," a fatal comment at a moment intended to be the epitome of romantic chastity.

The expression would retain its suggestive power between us for twenty-five years; if ever something did not meet with his enthusiasm, then I would hear him chortling "delicatessen is closed."

There was small hope of a serious response from him, I realized; in the fourth act, where rows of white swans are startled by an agitated sorcerer, he nudged me and, half-amused, pointed upward where, to my horror, I saw a pair of legs belonging to a spotlight technician, dangling from a stage opening and enlivening the atmospheric forest scene.

No, in many ways, the Dutch National Ballet was not yet ripe for *Swan Lake*. So it was to be *Giselle* for Nureyev, a romantic ballet from an era when the merciless demands on the dancers' technique were less excessive, and where the movements served more to convey the dramatic line.

Additionally, we had a young ballerina within our ranks, Olga de Haas, a brilliant title-role interpreter, light as a feather, vulnerable, pure of line, and utterly convincing as well.

This time, the rehearsal period could be fairly short, since Rudolf's version of the choreography could easily be fitted into ours. He would only need a number of rehearsals with the principals and with Olga de Haas in particular.

The first clash, however, occurred at a stage rehearsal, as soon as he set eyes on Olga's costume for the first act.

"That's no good, she looks exactly the same as the other girls." *Giselle* is the story of a simple village girl, seduced by a young nobleman disguised as a villager. However, the young prince is soon seen to be deceiving her; there is a noble fiancée waiting in the wings and so Giselle, feeling betrayed, falls prey to madness and dies.

One of the most impressive dancers of the twentieth century was Galina Ulanova. With her interpretation of what was once a sugary, superficial dance piece, Ulanova had given the role of Giselle (in Lavrovsky's restaging for the Bolshoi Ballet) so much content and psychological depth, that the ballet experienced a renaissance.

In Ulanova's conception, the title rôle was remarkable, not for the way she was dressed, but for the budding beauty and naive enchantment of the interpreter. It was Ulanova's version upon which our *Giselle* was based and I refused to adjust Olga's costume to Rudolf's demands.

It all became clear to me, however, on the arrival of Rudolf's British partner, Lynn Seymour, who was to dance several performances with him, Seymour's Giselle emerged from her humble peasant dwelling with a bouffant hairdo studded with artificial marguerites and, in contrast to our calf-length costume, her shiny skirt barely skimmed her knees: a mini-skirt avant la lettre. A mockery, to my mind.

"But she's mother's pet," Rudolf remonstrated. "Giselle has been spoiled and pampered by her mother. She doesn't have to work in the fields like the other girls from the village."

As far as I was concerned, from the very first steps she took from her little peasant dwelling, this Giselle remained an artificial apparition, already verging on madness, for whom I could conjure up little sympathy.

Olga was an exquisite Giselle and, during rehearsals, our company was spontaneous in its admiration and quite absorbed in her interpretation.

Above and beyond this, the story seemed to acquire a new dimension: here was a barely known Dutch dancer literally and figuratively being up-lifted by this exuberant, international hero, who seemed to have strayed into these parts by some mere chance.

And even the prince's betrayal seemed set to come true when, in one of the last rehearsals, Rudolf put Olga down so roughly and indifferently that she sprained her ankle.

There was a great commotion in our "camp" (for that was how keyed up and tense the situation had become). Would Rudolf dance all the performances with his English partner now? And had that been his intention all along? many people asked themselves in silence.

But Olga gritted her teeth, her ankle was bound up tightly, and she danced.

I felt that Nureyev was at his very best in *Giselle*; the role of Albrecht fitted him like a glove. He united authority and arrogance convincingly, in the scenes with the hunter Hilarion, Giselle's village admirer, or in the company of his servant, who was in on the plot with him. He displayed a roguish yet paternal humor toward the younger villagers—and a burning, heartrending desire for Giselle.

His grief in the second act, during the search for Giselle's grave, hidden deep in a nocturnal wood, was utterly compelling, his interpretation a monument of guilt and penance; the variation he danced in that act was no show of virtuosity, but merely served to convey his despair.

The ovations he received every time were altogether justified.

In *Giselle*, especially, the training he had received at the Leningrad Kirov Ballet was clearly visible. That precise execution of certain technical principles which he would not—often could not—relinquish on any account, made him into a solitary figure on stage, a brilliant, glittering diamond among shimmering, rounded pearls.

He admired developments in dance in the West tremendously but, no matter how he scoffed at the parchment-dry stuffiness of the Soviet ballet, he still always returned to its achievements. He would preach almost fanatically to us the ballet commandments from his old school: Thou shalt, thou shalt not.

During performances, he would carry out his steps as though he were giving a lesson in precision, demonstrating how classical ballet should be performed, the clear-cut positioning of the feet, perfect arm movements following through the sequence of positions, well-planned pirouettes.

Olga de Haas, whose technique was a little less dazzling than her partner's, was ideal opposite him in this ballet, because of that very contrast. Pure of line and vulnerable in every fiber, she was utterly persuasive as the consoling shadow hovering over her adulterous lover. Her simplicity almost seemed to radiate light.

The Dutch National Ballet ended the season that had borne Rudolf's mark so clearly with a number of performances in the open-air theater at Nervi, a seaside resort on the outskirts of Genoa.

While we awaited our guest, the dancers, who had arrived two days earlier, rehearsed their own repertoire and enjoyed the sunny Italian countryside in their spare time.

Italy was at its most beautiful, parks lush with flowering shrubs and fragrant pine trees, the sound of the sea all around, and our hotel a beautiful fin de siècle villa with creaking wooden halls and endless red-carpeted corridors.

During a stroll along the rocky coastline, all of a sudden I encountered Rudolf, apparently just arrived from Rome. He was in the company of a strapping young man.

"This is Wallace, Wallace Potts; he's going to make a film about my work."

The boy, tall, friendly, shy, obligingly gave a meaningful, lopsided grin.

Sitting at a terrace table overlooking the sea, Rudolf explained that all his work would be recorded on film by Wallace, a kind of diary in moving-pictures: "My rehearsals, my productions, the performances, the traveling. And the next big project is with you." He grinned when he saw my bewildered expression: "I am negotiating with the Royal Ballet about a new ballet and you're going to make it. A great opportunity."

Nothing asked, nothing discussed, just: "You're going to make it."

And an "opportunity" for whom? For Wallace, for me, or for Rudolf himself?

"I have no idea whether I can, or want to do that," I remonstrated weakly, but in Rudolf's eyes, the matter was resolved.

During the ensuing days, I got to know Wallace somewhat better, a young American would-be filmmaker, who was apparently as overwhelmed by the many Nureyev projects as I was.

"He wants me to travel with him everywhere he goes, but I have to go on studying and he just doesn't seem to understand that," and he showed me a piece of paper.

"Rudolf's itinerary: Paris, Athens, Chicago, New York, London, Manila, and that's just the next two months. But after Nervi I'm going home to America. I *have* to go back."

It was in Nervi that I had my first serious clash with Rudolf. I had promised myself that the waiting for our great star would become a thing of the past and that classes would simply begin on time.

Rudolf turned up half an hour late that morning, trailing a small cluster of admirers in his wake (yet another aspect that began to play on my nerves, as though classes and rehearsals were some kind of reception).

"I see, sausage-train rides on time," he sneered when he found the lesson was well under way.

"What do you mean: sausage?" I yelled back, imagining he was referring to the size of our dancers.

Only years later, when we were raking up the past and laughing at old memories, did he explain to me that he had not said "sausage" but "socialist-train," a charge I would hardly have seen as an insult.

The performances in Italy, however, began punctually. Rudolf was finally beginning to show signs of being social.

The audiences in Nervi seemed to embrace him indiscriminately, hero-worship seeming to suit the Italians more than the Dutch; that much was patently obvious and audible. Rudolf lapped up the adoration and, in my view, often rather overdid his dancing.

"The audience simply has great expectations of me, and I must live up to that. They saw me here two years ago and have retained certain memories; I can't disappoint them now. I'm the best and *that's* what they want to see."

"But art isn't the same as sport; ballet is not just about achievement."

"High C is an achievement too, and when you can no longer reach it, or not with ease, then you're finished. That's all there is to it," he ended the discussion.

During the breaks, Wallace brought me up to date on Rudolf's admirers: "That's Zeffirelli and Sylvana Mangano, that's Visconti and that man on his own there is Luciano Berio; he only tags along because his wife is a ballet critic."

I also saw the group of mainly English women I would later come across all over Europe wherever we appeared with Rudolf, at the theater, in the intermissions, outside the hotel. Waiting, watching, smiling.

"We adore him," one of them told me. "We want to see everything he does, wherever he is."

Rich they apparently were not. They mostly had office jobs in London and had to scrimp and save to allow themselves all that traveling. Rudolf generally treated them ruthlessly, pushing them away from him roughly: "Fuck off, leave me alone." But they stared after him tenderly and followed at a distance. They were in their forties; I was unsure whether I felt compassion for them or revulsion.

After the final performance Wallace did indeed leave, having stuck to his guns, which was no mean feat in the face of Rudolf's determination! Toer and I traveled to France with Rudolf at the wheel; winding, congested coastal roads, in the burning heat. But he was enjoying himself. Our vacation, and his as well, had begun; ours was to last four weeks, Rudolf's a mere five days.

With a mixture of pride and indifference, he had told us of his summer home, high in the mountains above Monaco; it would be the first of a steadily increasing list of real estate, houses that maybe served as beacons in the stormy seas of his existence.

The mansions he owned reminded me of the story of the profusion of glittering jewels on the ballerina's fingers in "Raymonda."

A tiny, hushed village, where we arrived at the end of an interminable journey along a high, winding road: La Turbie.

Perched on the hillside, some way outside the hamlet, the house was concealed among the cypress trees and afforded a dizzying view over Monte Carlo from the garden. From behind, the French Alps reigned silent. Here we were treated to another facet of Rudolf's character: utter hospitality. He drove us around up and down the coast, revealing sight after sight in the vicinity; we bathed in the sea and clambered up hills—everywhere he was recognized and was often asked for his autograph—and he seemed to lap it all up as much as we did.

"Look," he said, stretching out on a towel by the sea, "does that one not ring a bell?" pointing toward a woman who had nestled down near us, unnoticed.

A familiar face, but where was she from?

"She is one of those Nervi-women," he sighed. It was one of the women from the fan club; a mystery how his admirers somehow even managed to find such a holiday spot, announced nowhere.

"You can't stop them." But it did not enhance our sojourn by the sea.

Restaurants were avoided because, he said, "Madame Claire is the best cook possible."

Claire, Rudolf's housekeeper, turned out to be an elderly French lady exuding an air of rural aristocracy. Rudolf bestowed on her a remarkable amount of respect: she was one of the very few people toward whom I never ever saw him show even a shadow of irritation.

Madame Claire, on the other hand, subtly made it quite clear when something was not to her liking. He showered her with compliments on her cooking and ate like a horse, dragging us along to the kitchen to see the delicious morsels in store for the following day and suggested his favorite dishes to her.

In the mornings, breakfast was served on the terrace on the Monte Carlo side, and in the evenings we would dine in the huge kitchen or the garden with its Alpine view.

In a corner of the garden a coach house had been converted into a ballet studio. "Here we can work on the new ballet for Covent Garden." I stiffened, considering him quite capable of wanting to start on it out of the blue and unprepared. Fortunately, it was the last time he mentioned the "new project."

After only two days—"enough holiday!"—Rudolf took off for Monte Carlo in the afternoon, to take classes with Marika Bezobrazova, one of the many White Russians whose better-situated parents had settled on the Côte d'Azur following the revolution.

Bezobrazova's studio was bursting at the seams day after day; it was summer and the students, mostly would-be dancers, had come from far and wide to follow the summer courses at her school. To my amazement, surrounded by often laboriously toiling pupils, Rudolf followed the exercises in total concentration, as if Maria Callas were practicing her scales together with the ladies of the village choir.

A suffocatingly hot late afternoon in the garden; we made our way through the undergrowth of shrubs and collapsed onto a wall, too inert to speak; Rudolf gave the impression he had never yet penetrated so far into his own domain. Way below us lay the harbor of Monte Carlo, with its toy yachts and the water shimmering silver around it. Toy cars like beetles crawling along the winding roads.

"The old pond,
   frog jumps;
      kerdoing. . . .!"

Amid peals of laughter Rudolf recited a haiku. Precisely what was so hilarious eluded me, to be honest, but to Rudolf it seemed to be the peak of absurdity. "Frog jumps" he repeated several times. "Kerdoing!"

Halcyon days, but, after a mere week, Rudolf's vacation was at an end. It was as though he could hardly wait to start work again. "Stay on by all means if you want to, there's a car and Claire will cook for you." But we had plans as well, holiday plans.

"I'll call you in a few weeks' time, and then I'll know more about our project." And, this time, I no longer saw that promise as the whim of a pampered star.

4 ⟶ *The Ropes of Time*

For the Covent Garden premiere he had spoken of in Nervi, Rudolf had in mind a piece that would have something new in store for Royal Ballet audiences. "It's time we dusted them down," as he put it so graphically.

"Use electronic score, no orchestra. It's good for the dancers too. They'll learn what listening *means*."

He had become a staunch admirer of the composition Boerman had written for *Monument* and was intrigued to know how such sounds came into being: were there instruments involved, or was it all purely electronic equipment? He insisted I allow him to keep the score—which bore a certain resemblance to an abstract, graphic design but was also reminiscent of the fever chart of a chronic illness—so that he could have it framed later on. I never set eyes on it again.

Boerman had an existing piece—*The Sea*—which he had agreed to arrange as a composition lasting some half hour. He promised to have the music ready by the end of November, leaving me a month to prepare myself before rehearsals in London were due to begin in January.

At the beginning of the new season, Rudolf had appeared with our company once more, this time with Margot Fonteyn opposite him in *Giselle*; an event of prime importance for balletomane Holland.

In 1962, after his flight from the Soviet Union, Nureyev had formed a bond with the Royal Ballet and, more especially, with Fonteyn, the company's first soloist, who had been on the verge of ending her dancing career when Rudolf's comet blinded the Western world of dance. On seeing Nureyev perform, she revoked her decision to bid the world of dance farewell and, it was generally recognized, set out on a new phase in her career.

She was then forty-two, Rudolf twenty-seven.

"It will look like mutton dancing with lamb," was her own observation.

For all my reservations about Fonteyn's interpretation of the first act of *Giselle* (she had neither the swiftness nor fluidity of movement to allow the audience to forget her age and, besides, her interpretation was more reminiscent of a well-meaning debutante), in the second act, the glow of their two-in-oneness, hailed as phenomenal, suddenly shone through. Rudolf seemed to efface himself as Fonteyn's partner, he melted into her movements and was so entirely absorbed in every nuance of her interpretation, so wholly at her disposal, that the very tension of this took the spectator's breath away.

In the meantime, the new ballet was not progressing at all well. The date by which Boerman had promised me the music had long passed and still, when I rang him, I received the apologetic answer, "I'm sorry; another week, I think." I had been hearing that answer for almost a month now, and I was beginning to panic.

Without the music, I could scarcely get down to work on the ballet. A choreographer needs to know the structure of the composer's score, the movements which go to make up the music, the dynamic sequencing, the coloring. I had the oppressive feeling of heading toward the dreaded British Judgment Day in utter idleness and, because my plans were stagnating, Toer, who was to design the costumes and sets, could not get under way either. If I decided to look for other, existing, music at the last moment, it would mean that Boerman had worked so hard for four months in vain, and Rudolf's desire for electronic music to be heard in the Royal Opera House would go up in smoke as well. I felt trapped.

Two days before my departure for London, I was able to collect the music tape in Boerman's studio in The Hague and heard it for the first time, but, by then I was already under such stress that I was barely aware of the music.

I was not new to working in London, having already produced two choreographies, *Jungle* and *Night Island* with English companies, but this expedition was different: in those days, the Royal Ballet was seen as *the* leading ballet company in the world but I had never felt quite so unprepared as on this of all occasions.

Before rehearsals began, I had already traveled to London to talk with the artistic director of the Royal Ballet, the choreographer Frederick Ashton—Sir Fred, as he was affectionately known by his title—to inquire whether my ideas for the ballet would fall on fertile British soil.

"My secretary will meet you at the airport," Rudolf had said, but I made my own way by underground to the studios in Barons Court. "I was looking out for someone far older," Joan Thring apologized later, but I suspect she had been on the lookout for someone far more formally dressed.

Without an introduction it was by no means easy to gain access to the studios: according to Ashton's secretary, he would arrive only around midday and, as for an appointment with Nureyev . . .

"Every day we have to send at least ten people on their way who say they wish to speak to Miss Fonteyn or Mr. Nureyev," and my name clearly meant nothing to her. Somewhat reprovingly, she added that I should wait in the corridor until the dancers' classes were over.

Seated on a bench, I whiled away the time observing the constant stream of children passing me by dressed for class, chattering like monkeys, since pupils and professionals shared the building.

"What are *you* doing here?" Merle Park, late for practice, caught sight of me sitting on my penalty bench. "Why didn't you just go straight through?"

Simply walk into an unfamiliar studio on my own, while the class was already under way?

It was an enormous studio, with dancers at the barre all round and Rudolf, who was all wrapped up like Santa Claus, grinned broadly when he saw me, but made no further move; Merle introduced me to the teacher and gave me a chair. I had no sooner sat down than Rudolf grabbed hold of my arm: "Ashton's waiting for you."

As it turned out, Sir Fred was there after all, guarded by the self-same lady, Iris Law, who ushered us into Ashton's room with a sugary smile, looking as though butter would not melt in her mouth. It was an unbelievably depressing cubbyhole where, every few minutes, underground trains thundered past the windows, high up in the wall: was this the domain of a world-renowned choreographer? Gracious as a geisha, Ashton shuffled out from behind his desk, treating Rudolf with the utmost charm and exclaimed in a half-coquettish, paternal way.

"So you're Rudolf's new discovery." Fumbling nervously at a cigarette, he said: "Well, we'll see what happens."

"If I don't hunt down the choreographers myself, nothing happens," Rudolf retorted. "Nothing is created for me here and I'm not going to sit and wait."

Ashton giggled daintily and then gave Rudolf a commentary on a charity performance he had attended, with an abundance of names, but in such lisping English that half of it eluded me.

Then he turned to me again—"My dear, you can do whatever you want"— but I was not to expect him to come and check on the progress of the piece. "I'll see it on stage."

"Maybe you'll be taking a risk, then," I countered, but not even the electronic music met with either his resistance or astonishment. "Feel free, *you* decide."

When would the set designs arrive? How many dancers did I intend to use? Who, besides Rudolf, were the soloists? Those were the other questions, which were answered within five minutes, and then the conversation was resumed, and I learned that Rudolf had returned from Manila the previous evening, following a number of guest appearances there.

Ashton emitted tiny puffs of smoke, Iris Law brought in three mugs of tea, and Rudolf kept fishing more and more towels and leotards out of his bag because the small room was icy cold. It began to dawn on me that being with Rudolf also meant endless waiting around.

After the Ashton rendezvous, Rudolf looked round for an empty studio, where he ran through a number of variations, followed closely by dozens of pairs of children's eyes through a window in the corridor. "I have very few performances here, so I have to keep up my condition."

In a car piled high with boxes, cases, and plastic bags— "these are the costumes I need this month"—we left for his London house, miles from the center, on the edge of Richmond Park.

Somewhat in awe of the size of the house, I allowed myself to be shown around by Rudolf, glowing with enthusiasm, through spacious rooms, an imposing hall, a library and a music room. As in La Turbie, all the rooms were filled with wondrous antiques, immense solid oak tables and ditto settees, wrought-iron gates and imposing candelabra, four-poster beds, dazzling chests, paintings, and carpets, all strewn around in an improvised fashion as though the real work had still to begin, and thus creating an illusion of great freedom.

Here, too, Madame Claire seemed to be running the house, if only for the time being.

"No one else will work here, so I must have her come over from France."
And then, during lunch, I finally came face to face with Joan Thring, a robust,
beautiful woman with a resounding laugh, who hauled heaps of mail out of
her bag. Spooning his soup, and casting no more than a glance at the papers
it seemed, he leafed through them and quickly pushed the whole pile to one
side. "You decide," he said to her. "I can't read all that."

Joan later told me that he was acutely aware which letters and contracts
were important, and she took care not to do anything on her own initiative:
"He'll give me hell."

Rudolf vanished upstairs for an afternoon nap, Joan withdrew to the library, and I explored the house with its enormous garden and placed my mea-
ger shaving things in one of the bathrooms.

To my amazement, it turned out that Rudolf was to depart as early as the
very next day, to dance three performances for the shah of what was then
known as Persia, but—before he took off again—he wanted me to meet two
friends who could offer help and advice, should I require it. "They are like
parents to me, my parents in the West."

Maude Lloyd and Nigel Gosling—he was an art critic for *The Observer*,
she a soloist in the pioneering English company, Ballet Rambert, in the 1930s
and together they wrote reflections on dance under the name of Alexander
Bland—had taken Rudolf under their wing almost immediately following his
escape from Russia.

"They have a self-contained apartment for me in their house that's always
available," he told me, "if it's too late to drive out to Richmond from the center of town."

Following Rudolf's departure, I lived alone for three days in his vast and
really rather empty house. As if to emphasize the emptiness, the telephone in
the hall would ring at the most unlikely hours nearly every night, a sound that
echoed through the vast house, and it would almost always be soft, women's
voices:

"Is Rudolf there? Could you tell me where he is at the moment?" or simply
the rustle of someone silent at the end of the line. Rudolf's most fanatical
admirers (and, as I had discovered in Nervi, he had quite a number) followed
him everywhere: to his home, the theater, and especially by telephone.

I soon found out that the part of Richmond where the house was situated was very difficult to reach without a car; buses were rare, the underground station was miles away and even the London taxi-drivers said "Richmond Park? No, that's too far."

"That's why," said Madame Claire, "he can't find anyone to run his house; it's a voyage round the world each day."

Strange situation at 6 Fife Road: I ate on my own at a twelve-foot-long table in an enormous room, and somewhere farther along in the same house, Madame Claire was camping out. As she showed no sign of encouragement, I did not seek out her company, but to have shared a meal would have seemed to me only pleasant and logical.

Did Rudolf always pass his domestic life in such isolation?

For the London period of work, which was to last two months, and after discussing the matter with Nigel and Maude, I decided to live in with them in Victoria Road, in Rudolf's apartment, which they put at my disposal. Rudolf's Richmond Park abode, which he had offered me as a place to stay, was too far away and isolated and, besides all that, it seemed to me that in Rudolf's company I would have little peace; in order to work I needed a place of my own, although the rooms available in Fife Road were sorely tempting for Toer's design and my choreographic work. And work I should *have* to: to become familiar with the structure, I played Boerman's music all hours of the day, until I could dream the hallucinatory sounds.

Maude and Nigel were incredible friends, providing us with advice, assistance, and practical help; they'd stocked up our kitchen with all imaginable wares, understanding we would have no time at all for household concerns the first few days but often, in the evenings, there were places laid for us at their table as well.

Early every morning I began by discussing the sets with Toer, then I would work out bits of the choreography on my own, travel to the studios to become better acquainted with the dancers during class, rehearse, and then hurry back home to continue listening and working: the month that Boerman was overdue with his music had to be caught up in less than no time.

The choice of the dancers I determined myself, of course, but Rudolf always kept an eagle eye on the names that appeared on my list. Sometimes he would remark, "Look at that girl, very promising," or "Are you sure you want him?"

Initially, he was amazed I had not planned on Margot Fonteyn as his partner: "Then success with the English is guaranteed." But he had made it so clear to me that this was to be a ballet for him that, in my view, all other figures must be secondary and I felt unable to allow myself that freedom with someone like Fonteyn. And besides, she did not particularly inspire me, no matter how I admired her otherwise. There was no way I could envisage her dance idiom in combination with Boerman's shrill, ominous sounds—or with my probably rather chaotic choreography.

He seemed content with the two women who were to dance with him, Antoinette Sibley and Monica Mason. From the first instant I had seen Mason work—down to earth, natural, never giving up—she had inspired me with confidence ("a real trouper," as they say), and Sibley, capricious, quick and witty, seemed a fine foil for Rudolf's sultry temperament.

I immediately noticed that Rudolf displayed a particular interest in Sibley: "Did someone recommend her to you?" he asked. "Why her and not one of the other ballerinas, Merle Park or Deanna Bergsma?"

Later I realized that Sibley represented a special challenge to Rudolf because she was the regular partner of Anthony Dowell, a young, virtuoso star of the company. So Sibley was new territory to be conquered by Rudolf!

For most choreographers, starting out on a new work is a question of exceedingly tense nerves which can flare up even in the familiar area of one's own company and studio.

But a first day in front of a group of dancers who are utter strangers is doubly devastating: what can you achieve with them, how much will they understand of your ideas, how much of their energy and enthusiasm will they be prepared to give you?

One of the dancers in the group was Wayne Eagling, then still a very young dancer just starting out with the Royal Ballet, who would succeed me as artistic director of the Dutch National Ballet, twenty-one years later.

Rudolf showed himself to be clearly the best pupil in class. That first week he was all ears to everything I said and amenability itself. It was patently clear to everyone in the studio that he considered this ballet as much his enterprise as mine, an attitude that was a great support to me and at the same time, made me doubly unsure of myself. What if I did not live up to his expectations?

I had named the ballet after a poem by the Dutch poet Hans Lodeizen

The Ropes of Time, and to go with it I had sought a theme that would not be unfamiliar to Rudolf.

In a fathomless void, a person is born, an insignificant insect, wavering about, uncertainly finding its way. He becomes part of a society, struggles, and by an enormous feat of energy manages to rise above that society, until younger forces measure themselves against him and overshadow him. Then, gradually, he abandons his struggle for supremacy.

For the boy born into a working-class family in a provincial town in Russia, who later became world famous, that seemed to me to be a recognizable theme.

Sibley was the driving force behind the rising current, and Mason the ebbing current behind the receding man, movements of ebb and flow which never come to a standstill. It was a banal and much-used theme that would rely heavily on the form in which it was presented, of that much I was aware. Whether I would succeed was quite another matter.

At the apartment in Victoria Road, Rudolf's antique furniture, piled high with music tapes, records, and art books, was moved to one side. Toer constructed his set designs in one room, while I occupied the larger one as a studio. Outside, a dreary London winter reigned and upstairs the Goslings were as helpful and interested as they could be.

How hard it was at the start. The dancers had great trouble with the music, which they felt gave them nothing to grab on to. Although I assured them I knew from experience that it was a question of time, for quite a while they gave the impression they felt at home only with harmonious melodies with an even tempo. Rudolf often came along to the group rehearsals, out of interest, but I also suspected him of keeping track of how much time and space in my choreography I devoted to the ensembles or left over for him.

"Don't worry, Rudolf; you'll be in action from beginning till end."

"But surely not the way it was in *Monument*, where I only stand and watch." It was almost insulting, that "only." I wished I could show him how hard and important precisely those moments were for me; maintaining a motionless pose demanded far more dramatic talent than turning x number of pirouettes.

"No, you'll be dancing nonstop from the beginning of the ballet right up to the end," and, for the moment, that was enough to set his mind at rest.

Sometimes, if he was dissatisfied with the group rehearsals, it would be he who would suddenly clap his hands: "Once more." And occasionally he even went so far as to demonstrate movements to the dancers or tried to correct them: "He wants it that way." Upon which I was forced to say "No, Rudolf, that's not the idea either, I want it like *this*."

The real difficulties began during the rehearsals with Sibley. From the very first soloist rehearsals of their pas de deux, I felt that Nureyev was tense and distant and reacting moodily toward both of us, making for an electric atmosphere.

Each time he was required to lift her—something almost inevitable in a pas de deux—he puffed and panted as though he were moving Stonehenge. He deliberately allowed movements to go wrong, put Sibley down like a sack of potatoes, and walked off to the side demonstratively: "Do it yourselves," an expression that infuriated me.

Sometimes the situation looked so hopeless that I broke out in a cold sweat, nothing seemed to be accomplished, valuable time flew by, and relations among the three of us became extremely strained. I felt that Sibley came into the studio reluctantly, and I did not feel much better myself.

She tried whatever she could but was able to achieve little on her own, and unfortunately I was not such a good partner that I could show Rudolf *what* it was I had in mind.

"If you hold me like that now, it's bound to work," Sibley suggested, and suddenly, from Rudolf's answer, I understood what the problem was.

"I am not Dowell," he snarled, referring to her regular partner. "Maybe you should dance with him if you think I am that bad." Was he unsure of himself, or jealous? But why should he be?

After some of the rehearsals I could hardly exchange a word with him, it was all so childish, so petty.

To make matters even worse, Toer left because he had finished the *Ropes* designs and there was work to be done in Amsterdam. How I should have loved to have gone back with him! No one to pour my heart out to anymore, or to give me advice or a word of encouragement before I left for Barons Court in the morning with a heavy heart.

One morning Iris Law passed me a note: "Dear Rudi," I read, "I don't feel well at all and my doctor suggests I take a rest. I've left for the South of France, forgive me. I hope your ballet will be a success. Antoinette."

Message understood.

But Rudolf vanished from time to time as well, to give guest performances in Holland, among other places, with the Dutch National Ballet.

As my entire choreography revolved around Rudolf and there was an unfillable gap in rehearsals whenever he disappeared for yet another three days, I went to Ashton.

I told him I could not and would not continue without an understudy cast, that work was not proceeding as it should, and that I was afraid we would not be ready in time for the premiere date.

"But you know Rudolf is adamant about not having a second cast. You were there yourself when he stipulated it."

I was indeed aware of that, but I had never been told that he would be away so often. Eventually, Sir Fred put Anthony Dowell on the list as stand-in for Nureyev: "I think he'll be the best."

Naturally Rudolf considered the decision as a vote of no confidence on my part and for a whole day he behaved accordingly, working indifferently and marking out all the steps, shrugging his shoulders every now and then. The entire company, including Dowell, stood looking on tensely.

"Five-minute break." I was really at my wits' end and felt that if this went on for another day I would pack up my things and leave.

"I want to see the whole piece once again. Anthony, you take Rudolf's place this time."

But it was Rudolf, larger than life, who strode into the middle of the studio.

"Is your name Anthony?" I had never felt so distant from him as at that moment and I felt dreadful having to put him in his place like that, in front of the whole company, but on the other hand I knew it had to happen sometime.

At the end of the afternoon I informed Ashton that Rudolf had departed with the announcement that I would not be seeing him at rehearsals anymore.

Ashton chuckled. I think he was rather enjoying the commotion.

"He'll be back and otherwise you can just go on with Dowell."

That evening Maude rang me, and I thought I heard a hint of uncertainty in her voice.

"Rudi, would you like to have dinner with us tonight?"

Why not? I thought. No work this evening. After that miserable confrontation in the studio, I was in the mood for a carefree evening.

But I might have guessed, of course: Rudolf turned up to dinner as well. I had no idea how Maude had heard about our war of nerves, but it was clear that in her own discreet way she was trying to offer a helping hand.

Maude had finely drawn features, with eyes of an indefinable hue that always seemed slightly startled or taken unawares. She moved lightly and somewhat hesitantly, as though she went in fear of disturbing others, and despite her girlish voice and apologetic manner, she had a mournful air about her. She was someone whose charm it was hard to resist.

Rudolf seemed shaken, I *was* shaken, and the mood during dinner remained strained.

I went back to my floor early—"Tired, headache"—and a half hour later Rudolf knocked on the door.

"Can we talk?"

"We *have* to talk, I think."

I tried to make clear to him the tension I was under with all the conflicts that had arisen during the past three weeks. How many more could I expect in the following five? I had come to work pleasantly and as well as I could, not to engage in continual pointless fights.

We decided to go for a walk. The Goslings' house was near Hyde Park in a neighborhood full of large gardens and pleasant streets.

"I'm under pressure there, too." He tried to make me see his side of the problem. "They still think of me as a stranger, a barbaric intruder in the Royal Ballet. They see me as a threat to their male principals, and the critics trash me whenever they can."

From that evening on, his attitude changed and he worked without a hitch. His new partner, Diana Vere, who replaced Sibley, did not have the position of first ballerina in the company and Rudolf clearly enjoyed playing the experienced soloist helping the young girl over her uncertainty; Diana could make blunders, fall, or accidentally punch him on the cheek and he would still remain goodhumored and helpful.

It was a major breakthrough for Vere, working with Nureyev so unexpectedly, and it might have been a failure but, with his help she progressed by leaps and bounds.

There had never been any problems with Monica Mason; Rudolf clearly respected her down-to-earth, energetic approach and the speed with which she dealt with difficulties. In that far more constructive atmosphere, work progressed enormously, the choreography began to take shape, and things fell into place musically, as well.

The moment in the choreography where two younger dancers try to outdo the protagonist in a technical trial of strength—leaping higher, moving more buoyantly, shooting up and down like lightning—was hard for Rudolf to accept.

"The audience will just think that those two dance better than I do. It will look as though I can't keep up with them."

"Well, you can't"—I saw him stiffen—"but then you've been dancing for twenty-five minutes and those two boys have just stepped in as fresh as daisies. Of course, the audience will see that and understand what the scene represents. It's just as in ordinary life: at a certain moment new faces appear, even in a ballet company, younger, stronger, more energetic."

"Sorry, but I shall do everything in my power to work better than they do." But I knew that, whatever he did, those two young and gifted boys would always seem to outstrip him.

The idea of being the loser offended Rudolf's sense of pride, but the fight he would engage in with his youthful rivals would only make "the survival of the fittest" even more exciting.

When the premiere came into view, Rudolf became more uncertain. "Are you happy with what I'm doing. Is it right?" But he could tell that in my view there was still a great deal wrong with it. So he organized private rehearsals on Sundays, sometimes just the two of us, sometimes with the two ballerinas as well. He labored on endlessly, starting over and over again, but I still retained the impression that the movements did not come from within him but had been glued onto the outside, as though he were speaking a second language: even if he spoke all the words and if a sentence were grammatically correct, a different background could still be heard.

"Try not to make a drama of it," I warned, when he overdid things with the strangest of grimaces. "The drama shows in the movement, in the situation, in the structure of the ballet. Don't lay it on so thick that you're exhausted, because you *will be* by that time. And showing that will be very impressive; you let the audience feel the truth along with you."

He had found a new housekeeper for Fife Road, Alice, a small, black woman with an absurd sense of humor: she and Rudolf were like beings from different planets.

Sometimes, when he was in one of his grumpy moods, she would suddenly come in with a tray, all dressed up in the strangest garments from his wardrobe, a brightly embroidered dressing gown, oriental beads around her neck, and a towel draped like a turban around her head: clearly a caricature of Rudolf himself. Rudolf would remain staring icily into his plate and ignore her act, while she would screech and point and wink at me. Time and again she tried it, probably hoping to put him in a better mood, but her performances remained unsuccessful and she would slink off back to the kitchen, without a smile ever appearing on her "boss's" face.

On a few occasions, he organized large dinner parties, for which he had Claire come over from La Turbie; he would not dream of trusting Alice with those.

On one of these evenings, with Fonteyn and her husband at the table, the Goslings, Joan Thring, his impresario Gorlinsky with his wife (whom Rudolf called 'la croqueuse des diamants'[1]: "Every time I've been on tour, *she* acquires another diamond") and a number of society people, Alice reported that there were two young men at the door: "Nice-looking. They say they have an appointment with Mister Rudolf."

Rudolf, in a wonderful mood, cursed and then leapt up and disappeared, followed by Joan, who returned soon after and remarked drily, "he'll be back again in ten minutes." We heard Rudolf and his visitors go upstairs.

While the gathering ate on somewhat disconcertedly, Joan could apparently contain herself no longer.

"That's just the way he is," and she laughed her resounding laugh. "He

1. *La Croqueuse de Diamants* ("The Diamond Cruncher"), 1950, is a ballet by Roland Petit, about a gangster's moll who claimed diamonds were like vitamins to her; she could not get enough of them.

tosses them like pancakes," illustrating the remark with her hands, slapping one hand onto the other and then flipping them back and forth."

The guests smiled politely. And comprehendingly?

When the front door had slammed shut again, Rudolf resumed his place at the table, radiant and with eyes twinkling: "That really tastes excellent."

Claire handed him his warmed-up dish with unconcealed disapproval in her eyes.

"Toer, get up, the house is falling down!" I wrenched open the door, ran out of the house and through the garden, and stopped short in the middle of the street, barely dressed. Toer was standing slightly dazed and drowsy in the doorway. It was midnight and freezing.

A clearer sign that the première was looming ahead there could not be.

In the final weeks Toer had rejoined me for last-minute preparations for the production and to take care of the lighting for the ballet.

Ropes was largely completed, as it had to be, because a new piece was rehearsed at Covent Garden a week before the premiere, unlike in Amsterdam where, in those days, a new piece had its first and only stage rehearsal on the morning of the first performance.

New, time-consuming problems arose: for the opening scene Toer had designed a large half-globe, on which Rudolf was to carry out the initial sequence of movements.

That delicate balance created problems in itself, but the winching up of the globe and its disappearance up into the dome of the theater far more so. For the safety of the dancers and especially of Rudolf, the vanishing trick was repeated again and again, while the other dancers in the ballet hung about in the wings in practice clothes.

I saw the prospect of a productive session fading by the minute and wanted to defer the troubles to a later moment in time: "We'll work that one out later, Toer." But Rudolf remained stoic, demanding that the same scene be repeated time after time until he was satisfied.

"But there are other dancers, Rudolf, I want to see them as well."

"They'll get *their* time. First my things have to be in order." No "socialist train" here.

Ashton, sitting behind me in the darkness of the theater, tapped me on the shoulder and said "If you want to go on, then do so, Rudolf will have time enough," but he had forgotten that the microphone in my hand was on, so that the dancers on stage heard every word.

"Are you conspiring against me again?" Rudolf had come to the edge of the stage, peering into the dark with his hand above his eyes. "Fred, can you please go away and leave Rudi alone?"

There we were, company director and guest choreographer, both eliminated; Rudolf had the ropes firmly in hand. But he fought for the ballet, threw all his energy into it, made demands and caused arguments if he felt he had to, even with the ballet's creator, if need be.

Naturally, above all, it was a fight for himself: he wanted to be a success, to come up trumps, longing to show there was no new avenue in dancing he could not go down and that even if that avenue proved to be the wrong one, he himself would make it right.

At the end of the first entire run-through with lighting, sets, and costumes, he appeared intensely satisfied, in contrast to Toer or me; there was a lengthy list of items requiring a solution.

Outside the theater, at the artists' entrance in the narrow street off Covent Garden, after one of the final rehearsals, we were followed by a portly, older woman, whom I had noticed earlier.

She trailed us in a manner akin to an old-fashioned detective story, occasionally hiding behind the piles of baskets and boxes (there was still a fruit and vegetable market around the theater in those days) and hissing at us or calling out.

"Who on earth is that? What does she want?"

Rudolf grinned: "That's one of Anthony Dowell's fans. She's one of the ones who wants to get rid of me."

Many fanatical fans knew when the dancers they idolized had rehearsals and would sometimes wait hours for their favorites. Since I had made a ballet for Rudolf, this Dowell fan apparently thought I belonged in the enemy camp and, sometimes, when I left the theater alone, I would suddenly hear her voice: "What are you doing here? Go back where you came from."

When we got into Rudolf's car, she stationed herself in front of it and made thumbing gestures as though she were showing a dog the door: "Out!" But she took to her heels hastily when Rudolf started the car and sounded the horn loudly.

One of his favorite outings was to the antique market in the Portobello

Road and, to celebrate the end of the dress rehearsal, we ate there, roving around afterward among the stalls and booths and in and out of the antique shops. Self-assuredly, he had left his car in a no-parking spot but, when we returned, we found the vehicle had gone. A policeman informed us that the car had been towed away.

"Was it your car?" And, after being recognized everywhere and stared at in the street, he was now asked, "What's your name?"

Very curtly: "Nureyev, Rudolf Nureyev."

The policemen, quite innocently: "How do you spell that?"

Rudolf, sneeringly: "N-U-R-E . . ."

Only a tiny sting, but his pride was hurt and a shadow cast over the sunny day.

"English, stupid cows," he complained, as we drove back to Richmond by taxi and stepped out into his magnificent, sloping garden where the bluebells and daffodils were already in flower. But he was oblivious to them. Joan Thring was called up and delegated to retrieve the car. He sat in one of his enormous carved armchairs in silence, a lonely, sulking child.

Was the première a success? It certainly sounded like that and, for Rudolf, it *was* a success, but then everything he did at Covent Garden received frenzied applause: the audience was always grateful to see him. A shower of daffodils rained down upon him and the man who had just displayed an exhausting and isolating decline in *Ropes of Time* took the tribute like a gladiator.

The critic John Percival wrote, "For The Royal Opera House audience, "*Ropes*" was decidely avant-garde, even introducing *musique concrète* into that building for the first time. Once again, Nureyev danced an odyssey through life, but, this time aided by Van Schayk's moving sculptures, the choreography unfolded itself in unusual and remarkable images. There was an affinity in the metaphors danced that must be familiar to every top sportsman or artist, the struggle to retain mastery, despite the challenge of youthful rivals and the inevitable passage of time."

Toer and I celebrated the London première with our parents and a small band of dancers who had come over from Amsterdam. After an excited and happy time together, we left for a supper to which we had been invited and arrived far too late. When we entered the lavishly expensive house, there was a slightly appalled mood at our long delay—dessert had already been served—and as soon as our food had been brought the conversation was resumed.

The host and his wife, Lee Radziwill, were swapping experiences with Ashton, Rudolf, and the other guests about the various countries in which they invested their capital: not one word—more?—was devoted to the performance.

After listening to the chatter for a while I suddenly became incensed by that exchange of stock-market news and the fact that Rudolf acquiesced in such bigoted society chitchat.

During a brief lull, I inquired mockingly of Toer what *he* did with his money, whether he maybe hid it under a mattress?

"How could you do that?" Rudolf asked on the way home, "you shocked everybody."

"Easy," I said, "just like you: by getting angry."

In the days following the premiere he arranged an evening for our parents in Fife Road, was cordiality itself, and did all in his power to ensure they felt at ease, showing them around the house and telling them how happy he was with the new ballet.

"Make yourselves at home." He passed dishes around, poured the wine, and glowed like a boy who has just received a good report; it was clear how much he missed his own family life.

5 ∽ *Sweet Grass*

Some two months after *Ropes*, Nureyev was back in Amsterdam yet again. Owing largely to Rudolf's involvement, the Dutch National Ballet had been invited to give its first series of performances in London, a crucial happening for any company.

Appearing with our company at his home-base, Rudolf wanted to show English audiences not only *Monument*, but also a classical duet, and his interpretation of Balanchine's *Apollo*.

Although he wished to dance *Apollo*, Rudolf's appreciation of Balanchine—one of the most prominent and influential choreographers of the century—was still variable in those days. He was unable to understand our reverence for that great man's work.

"Why do you get so excited about him? He made a few good ballets, but the rest is so dry and bare. Gymnastics."

In a similar way, he considered Toer's passion and mine for the Diaghilev era absurd: "What's the matter in Europe, everybody carries on about Nijinsky, Massine, Lifar, Stravinsky. Why? It's just another period in dance."

Diaghilev, a great ballet innovator, presented seasons of Russian art, music, and ballet in Paris in 1907 and 1908, and in 1909 was invited to form his ballet company, Les Ballets Russes, there. When Nijinsky resigned from the Maryinsky Theater in 1911, he and Diaghilev remained in Europe and never returned to St Petersburg. After the Russian Revolution, Diaghilev's revolutionary movement in the world of music, dance, and fine art was, if not smothered, played down to a minimum in its country of origin.

Rudolf's attitude and preference still betrayed his origins. The Soviet Union ballet repertoire consisted largely of narrative works and dancers were required to be expressive, conveying lyrical, heroic-dramatic emotions to the audience, sustained by pompous scores and sumptuous, excessive scenery and costumes.

Balanchine at his best was quite the reverse. His ballets were bare in the athletic sense: superfluous fat was trained away, the skeletons of his choreographies clothed only by muscles. No scenery, few costumes: the dancer's body and the mathematics of the composition alone defined Balanchine's choreography.

Apollo (1928), to Stravinsky's score of the same name, is an early work from Balanchine's Diaghilev period, and the heritage of the older traditions is still sometimes apparent in the new avenues Balanchine was exploring in the ballet. Its combination of drama and the abstract made this ballet an ideal piece for Nureyev.

Apollo allows the audience to witness the birth of the young god. Initially, the youth is led and guided by three Muses—poetry, dance and mime—and he gains control from them as he develops (the reins are almost literally in his hands), gradually ascending to divine heights.

Tottering uncertainly at birth, like a foal taking its first uncertain steps away from his mother, and gradually gaining in certainty, precision, and power, Nureyev's interpretation was brilliant. The ballet became an ode to dancing.

He plucked the three Muses right out of the ranks of our company—for a while, I had feared he would demand at least *one* Royal Ballet muse beside him—and the work of Olga de Haas, Sonja Marchiolli and Hélène Pex was in perfect harmony with his.

The Sadler's Wells Theatre stage was small and rather primitive; I was amazed at the circumstances in such a renowned theater and at the fact that Rudolf agreed to appear there: three large movements and he was right across the stage!

"You have to adapt," he preached to me, "that is number one. Always work everywhere, no matter how. Number two is that you must make yourself indispensable, make sure you're always everywhere. Without even noticing, the audience must become addicted to you, first they can't get rid of you, but later they can't do without you."

"Full house," a triumphant placard announced every evening in the foyer at Sadler's Wells, but I was tormented by the thought of how it would have been without Nureyev. No matter how splendid their achievements, would not our Dutch Muses have been performing for a "quarter full house"?

The year was brought to a close by yet another tour with Rudolf. He seemed to have become a permanent member of our company. We traveled through Germany and Switzerland, ending in Nervi once again. I was somber on that trip: Robert Kaesen, with whom I ran the Dutch National Ballet, had informed me that he wished to leave the company, and the prospect of taking on that gargantuan task alone overawed me; not even all our recent success could change that.

And besides, success is like thin ice; if you stamp on it hard enough, you'll go through it. I realized that our Nureyev success was exactly that kind of slippery, transparent substance: "Frog jumps: kerdoing. . . ."

But I had problems of my own, as well, and Rudolf felt that intuitively.

"Don't hide yourself," he said, concerned, when I wandered off on my own during the tour, "you can't afford to lie low. You're the boss." I was reading *Ada* at the time, the Nabokov novel that had just come out, and I devoured the book; it was the best possible company for me at a difficult time. Curiously enough, parts of "*Ada*" are set in the very area where we were appearing, Lausanne, Montreux, Vevey.

"Nabokov lives around here," Rudolf tried to persuade me to go out exploring with him, "and Stravinsky wrote *The Soldier's Tale* here in Lausanne."

It was a blissful day in Switzerland as we roamed from one spot to another by taxi, bus and on foot, gazing out across the hushed and occasionally even ominous expanse of lake; swans gliding on the water, sloping orchards, silent houses, sheer walls of rock. We ate our picnic in the lush grass, basking in the sun, Rudolf falling asleep and awakening in sudden confusion.

"That's the first time I've ever fallen asleep like that, outside, under a tree. Am I *that* tired?"

"What do you think, shall we stay here forever?" He laughed, chewing on a blade of grass and said: "Sweet grass, this tastes like home."

After our final performace in Lausanne, while we were dining in a restaurant, Rudolf nudged me under the table.

"Look at that man behind you, do you know who that is?"

I glanced round quickly: "No idea."

"Pasolini."

I had talked of the Pasolini films I admired so much to Rudolf, who was quite a film buff: *Accatone, Oedipus Rex* and especially *The Gospel According to St. Matthew.*

"Go up to him, speak to him."

"But do you want to meet him then?" I asked.

I went up to the table—it was indeed Pasolini—and asked if he would like to meet Nureyev; I saw our program book lying beside his glass, so the suggestion could not have been that strange and yet I felt as though I were making him an indecent proposal.

It only really became indecent when Rudolf said: "Rudi admires your work; he has just seen *Il Conformista.*

That was true, but *Il Conformista* was one of Bertolucci's films. Pasolini grinned, winked at me and sipped his wine, ignoring the remark.

The contrasts between their backgrounds and interests—Pasolini's sympathy for the working classes and Rudolf the society figure—were unobtrusive. Or maybe they were not so divergent after all?

Rudolf dominated the conversation, which was conducted mainly in Italian. (Without a single lesson, he had mastered Italian as well as French and English.)

Mutual acquaintances, films, and the boys, especially, were the topics, the qualities and features of youngsters in America, in Italy, in France; like gourmets they savored the masterchef's dish.

I was aching to know how Pasolini achieved such fantastic work with amateurs in his films, how he worked with them. Might I come and take a look one day?

Pasolini scrawled his Rome address on a napkin and slid it across to me: "Who knows . . .?"

And "Who knows?" I saw Rudolf thinking, "Maybe there might be a film in it for me one day?" What neither he nor I could know was that, five years from then, Pasolini would no longer be alive, murdered in Rome, and that Rudolf would not work with us again for another five years. It would be 1977 before he entered the Dutch National Ballet studios again.

6 ～ *Mishenka*

The Dutch National Ballet began the 1970–71 season with a new, two-man leadership; Robert Kaesen left and the American Benjamin Harkarvy took his place.

Harkarvy had already worked with the Netherlands Dance Theater in Holland for some years and was not unfamiliar with the state of dance in this country, the subsidy system, welfare arrangements, the artistic potential, the quality and mentality of our dancers. But Rudolf said "Bad news," when I explained the situation. "Why him?"

"We need to start with a clean slate," was Harkarvy's opinion, as he felt there was room for great improvement in the quality of our company. He proposed giving fewer performances, more intensive training—provided by him—and a limited number of dancers—the "advanced" ones—would be allowed to perform. He made us feel we were sitting a grade school exam to enter high school.

Harkarvy waived aside Nureyev's opinion of the company and the successes achieved with him, and there could be no question of further collaboration with our guest.

He had designed a three-year plan, by the end of which the company would have achieved a different and far higher level. "It requires much application, many sacrifices, but it is the only way; we must clear up a great deal of superfluous ballast."

The excruciating plan was put into operation—and Nureyev was dropped, at least, as far as the Dutch National Ballet was concerned; we were headed for a new and better future!

After an extremely difficult six months, for Harkarvy as well, during which much was turned upside down, the innovator informed me he had decided to return to America: the three-year plan had fallen apart. There was indeed a great deal that needed clearing up.

On the positive side, Alexandra Radius and Han Ebbelaar had joined the company and, the following season, Hans van Manen decided to join us as choreographer. These would prove to be swifter and better injections to strengthen the fabric of the group.

In the winter of 1971, I traveled to the Soviet Union with Ivan Kramar, a Yugoslavian and one of the ballet masters of our company, to try to arrange a tour of that country.

Stowed away in my luggage, too thick to hide inconspicuously, there was a wad of dollars with which Nureyev had entrusted me. Smuggling was no mean risk in a highly suspicious Russia and the small pouch moved around with me during the journey, from the bottom of my hand luggage, to my inside pocket, and back again to a side pocket in my bag. Mission impossible?

After visiting Moscow, talks with state agents, ministries, and influential ballet people, we took the night train to Leningrad, hoping to see performances and classes at the famous Kirov Ballet and to try to interest a teacher from that school in working for the Dutch National Ballet for a while. We had been assigned accommodation in the Anglisky Hotel (Hotel d'Angleterre), a large and somber building, with long, high corridors and smoky dining rooms, crawling with people in full winter regalia who all seemed to be going about secret missions, gliding in and out of doors, up and down stairs.

Room 5 in the Anglisky was where the poet Sergei Essenin, lover and later husband of the American avant-garde dancer Isadora Duncan, hanged himself in 1925, but the door to our room had another number. Beyond that door was a stately room, furnished in a style that can scarcely have been different from when Esenin moved in.

Our room afforded a view of the imposing contours of St. Isaac's Cathedral and, below us, the secret missions seemed to continue furtively on the snowy boulevard. Besides searching for a teacher in Leningrad, I had also agreed to try to visit Nureyev's mother and deliver the parcel burning a hole in my inside pocket.

"Please, when you are in Leningrad, call Monique," Rudolf had impressed upon me. "She arrives from New York, and it's her first time in Russia."

That same afternoon, Ivan and I set off for the Europeiski Hotel, yet another piece of dance history, for that was where Diaghilev first met the dancer Vaslav Nijinsky, who would later become world-famous. Now Monique van Vooren was staying there.

In the lobby of the Europeiski we soon discerned a conspicuous lady, even by western standards, being ogled at by almost every passer-by: a huge fur hat with a tail dangling from it, perched atop a stunning blond hairdo, her coat of pale green dyed panther-skin hanging open nonchalantly over the scantiest patent-leather hotpants we had ever set eyes upon, the suspenders stretched promisingly over an aggressive bust.

The lady gave a shriek and strode across to us: "Rudi?"

That evening, the three of us saw a performance in the Kirov Theater, the place where ballets like *Swan Lake* and *Sleeping Beauty* had their premieres at the close of the nineteenth century, and where the career of many a dance celebrity, including Nureyev, had begun.

Among the extremely soberly dressed audience, Rudolf's American friend, who, for this occasion, had even donned green contact lenses, was especially eye-catching; wherever we took her, she caused a stir.

"I'd keep that coat on, if I were you; the theaters here seem barely heated at all," Ivan lied, for fear of the effect the hot pants might cause. The attendants, however, two resolute matrons, grabbed Monique's coat and made it clear that coats belonged in the cloakroom. A small skirmish ensued, in which Ivan and I were bent upon keeping the green fur coat on and the two ladies did all in their power to remove it.

Breathless, but content, and with Monique swathed in fur from top to toe, we took our seats in the excellently heated theater. To our regret, the Kirov ballet turned out to be on tour, and that evening was the final examination performance by the ballet academy: brilliant young dancers in often amazingly virtuoso and stylish work and there was one boy, who danced a variation from *Les Sylphides*, whom the audience and we found quite enthralling. He seemed to float, was vividly expressive, and maintained a lyrical quality, even in powerful leaps.

Rudolf was clearly not the only, or the last, great dancer the Kirov Ballet institute had brought forth.

Two days later, after numerous inquiries, telephone calls, and fruitless waiting, we finally made contact with Rudolf's sister Rosa, with whom Rudolf's mother, who had traveled from Ufa specially for the occasion, was staying.

"Dress simply," I had tried to impress upon Monique. "It must be strange enough for these people to receive visitors from abroad as it is."

Nureyev's sister lived with her little daughter, Gouzel, in a drab tenement block in a city suburb. It was three o'clock and already dusk had fallen. The taxi driver dropped us in a wide street, indicating which way we should go. Wading through the snow, we passed under a low gateway, crossed a deserted courtyard, climbed endless stone stairs, and found Rosa there—clear resemblance—waiting for us on a landing.

A rather bare room, where Rudolf's mother sat huddled over a table, a small, somewhat bowed woman, with an almost peasant-like demeanor, her fingers wandering clumsily and nervously across the table. Communication was limited to a minimum because Ivan, who spoke Russian, had returned to Amsterdam the evening before and I possessed only a scant number of words and sentences.

Rudolf's parcels were handed over—he had given Monique gifts to take along too—and I spread out a number of photos of him: colorful pictures of an unreal, elegant, fairy-tale prince. They looked at them in silence, as though he were a missing soldier. What were they thinking? What impression did they gain of him? It was hard to imagine a greater contrast than between his present circumstances and those of his family; Rosa and Gouzel had another tiny room to sleep in and the mother slept on the divan by the stove.

As it was too dark in the room, we went outside again to record the meeting on film for Rudolf; Mama on sturdy Rosa's arm, crunching through the snow, with Gouzel's small voice ringing out and echoing back from the somber houses. Here and there at the small windowpanes around us, we saw faces eyeing the curious scene, two obvious tourists from the West, armed with a camera, revolving around the trio seated on the bench.

Gouzel made a snowball, Mama drew her shawl around her more tightly and wiped her eyes and nose dry on a corner, while Rosa made a brave attempt to laugh into the camera. At any rate I had managed to record a memory for Rudolf.

Somewhat abashed, we got into a taxi afterward and returned to our large hotels.

"When I was accepted into the Kirov Ballet in Leningrad, I gave it everything I had. All I did was work, work like a horse," Rudolf had told me. "My colleagues didn't take to me, but I was dancing the leading roles immediately, and with the best ballerinas in the company."

Rudolf was nineteen years old then, very much a provincial boy and seen as the odd man out, dangerous because of his ambition.

"I was alone, no one had anything to do with me, but I didn't care; all I was interested in anyway was becoming as good as possible."

Alexander Pushkin, Rudolf's favorite teacher to whom he said he owed the most, was not only an influential educator, but a father figure for the young dancer, as well. Pushkin took the gifted and solitary boy into his home, where he and his wife, Xenia Jurgenson, were able to make his life a little easier and more agreeable. As teachers at the Kirov School, they had a more comfortable home and the food rations they received were better, too.

"When I went over to the West, my only feelings of guilt were toward Pushkin, the sorrow I caused him and the consequences my flight might have for him."

Pushkin died in 1970: "Go and see his wife, tell her about me, ask her how she is."

Xenia Jurgenson lived in an apartment belonging to the academy on Rossi Street, and a few ballet pupils showed us the way there the following evening.

I had been imagining a somewhat awkward visit to a quiet, mournful widow, but Madame Pushkin, a ballet pedagogue herself, turned out to be an effervescent lady, full of life and surplus energy. She hardly spoke of her dead husband or Rudolf—there was the obligatory, and very Russian, sigh— and then she seated us on a divan and almost immediately fished out from under the divan a box, out of which she conjured piles of photographs of Pushkin's last great pupil, telling us that he had taken Rudolf's place in their household.

"Rudolf used to sleep here,"—she tapped our divan—"and now Mishenka. Misha is doing television recordings this evening; he'll be here later."

Between the plentiful snacks and the sips of vodka, she talked of her beloved pupil. She praised him, occasionally kissing his photograph, and in broken English and French sang songs of praise that began to sound more and more like love songs. It gradually became claustrophobic and monotonous; time passed, conversation topics became scarcer and Madame Pushkin was clearly stretching time. Monique, however, was determined, and left after a time: "I met a very nice man at the hotel."

My attempts at departure failed miserably, hindered as they were by my hostess with all her might: "You *have* to meet him! Misha will be very angry if I let you go."

He arrived home around midnight, a small, blond athlete whom I suddenly recognized: it was he who had danced *Les Sylphides* so beautifully in the examination performance. In the theater world of Leningrad his name already had a magic ring of expectation to it, but several years later his dancing art would be seen and make its impact in the West as well: Mikhail Baryshnikov sought political asylum in Canada in 1974.

7   *The Duchess of Malfi*

Spring found me in London once again, since the film-director Jan Vrijman was making a documentary about the Dutch National Ballet and wanted to include some recordings with Rudolf Nureyev and, to my amazement, he cooperated with patience and goodwill: no scenes, no snarling.

I stayed for a week; the Kirov Ballet was appearing in London and I explained to Rudolf that I should really like to meet a good friend of mine again, Anatoly Nisnevich, who had given guest performances of *Giselle* with Natalia Makarova and the Dutch National Ballet in 1965.

"Tolya," Rudolf grinned. "Of course, he was a classmate of mine."

We attended the performance together and the rumor that their former classmate was in the theater must have traveled swiftly to the Kirov troupe in the wings. Rudolf nudged me and said, "That is a secretary with the company; and that one is a teacher; the man walking past now is one of the directors." One by one they came to size up the situation "inconspicuously."

And yet Rudolf was still in mortal fear of the Soviets, refusing to visit the Kirov dancers backstage, although there were several people he was aching to see again.

"But what can they do to you now?"

"They might take me back . . ."

While Rudolf waited outside in his car, I visited Nisnevich and, in an unguarded moment, whispered whether he would like to meet Rudolf.

"But not here." Rudolf was not the only one frightened. "Tell Rudolf to wait for us in another street."

We moved a few blocks away from the theater, got into his car hastily and decided that dining at his home, unspied upon, would be by far the safest place for Anatoly.

If Nisnevich was overwhelmed by the opulence of his colleague's princely residence, then he managed to conceal it, moving around at ease, as though such an abode were the most usual thing in the world: the servant opening the door, the dishes served, the secretary who had Rudolf select photographs between courses.

Rudolf reveled in it all. A fire was ablaze in the hearth, there were candles burning at the top of the staircase, the library was viewed. A mere ten years earlier, like Tolya, he, too, had dwelt in poverty-stricken surroundings in Leningrad.

Walking back along the Thames to his hotel—Rudolf again waiting at a safe distance—Tolya assured me he was not envious, that he would not care to change places with his old classmate. Soviet doctrine?

He preferred to say goodbye at the corner of the hotel, "because at the entrance they could see me with you."

Before Rudolf went abroad for a few weeks with Fonteyn, they gave another London performance of *Marguerite and Armand*, a ballet created by Frederick Ashton specially for the famous pair in 1963.

The morning before the performance, there was a dress rehearsal planned, as the piece had not been performed for a number of months. That morning, I drove into town with Rudolf and, as was usual for him, we had left far too late and were navigating grimly through the hectic London traffic, risking life and limb. His mood, not good to start with, plummeted further with every minute, but I now knew the reason: there was another journey looming.

Fonteyn welcomed me at Rudolf's dressing room with her familiar greeting: "Ah the Duchess of Dantzig, how are you?" I was not keen on that particular "nickname" and failed to see the humor in it. She and Rudolf were wont to give people nicknames; she rechristened Nureyev "Never-off" and Han and Lex (Ebbelaar and Radius) became "Ham and Eggs." I was often "Mishkin" in those days, Dostoyevsky's "Idiot," a name I appreciated far more than Fonteyn's "Duchess." Only much later on did I discover the connection: there was an operetta called "The Duchess of Malfi"; I could finally grin at her pun.

The Covent Garden rehearsal was attended by a small audience—mainly women, probably a circle of friends of the Royal Ballet. In work light, the stage appeared bare and dreary, and the dancers were visibly tired; it was quarter past nine in the morning.

"Where's Rudolf?" Ashton's voice sounded through the theater.

"He was held up, the traffic," Fonteyn apologized for her partner. "He's warming up right now." Her "Never-off" was frequently "off" for rehearsals.

But they could not afford a delay; the orchestra was waiting and time was limited. Rudolf appeared like a leaden weight from the wings, threw a scathing glance in the direction of the audience, and then strutted across to his place in an excessively stiff manner. "Alright, let's get it over with." The mood was set for the romantic drama.

Halfway through the rehearsal, Fonteyn fell headlong on the ground at Rudolf's feet, with a nasty smack. A low moan went through the audience and Ashton stood up. It was unclear whose fault the fall was, but Rudolf stood back and waited, hands on his hips and a face that said "You see?" until Fonteyn had clambered up again. He even declined to offer her a helping hand.

"Come on," I said under my breath, "give him a box on the ears," but Fonteyn dusted off her tutu and called out a giggling apology to the conductor. "Can we please take it from . . ."

I left the theater—it was a warm, spring day—and walked toward Hyde Park; a dog bathing in the Serpentine, riders on horseback cantering by and calling out to one another in affected English, small knots of tourists strolling around at leisure, and for the moment, I had had enough of theater life and of Rudolf.

"You were upset?" he demanded that evening with angry mockery in his voice, for he never failed to register the reactions to his doings with acute precision.

"Yes," I said, "I was."

"Well," he said, with a sullen shrug of the shoulders, "too bad."

Marguérite and Armand, based on *La Dame aux Camellias*, was a ballet I considered rather ungainly and lachrymose. It was clearly created as a vehicle for two superstars, revolving entirely round the title role interpreters, with the remainder of the ballet draped around them like moving scenery. Critics described Marguérite as "a great love drama, performed by the dance pair of the century, displaying the theatrical qualities of the two stars as never before."

Rudolf had told me that the New York audiences had cheered them for half an hour and in London as well the applause went on and on. Time and again they took curtain calls, and the two public pets seemed to thank each person present in a personal tête-à-tête.

Storms of cheering, the air raining flowers and bouquets, this was a love drama between the audience and its idols, a new performance in the simplest of choreographies.

Outside the theater, hordes of fans thronged at the door to see them both. On some occasions, Rudolf would patiently sign the many programs that were thrust at him, but now he forced his way through the throng of admirers, cursing, and strode up to his car. Fonteyn, on the other hand, remained inconceivably courteous; uncomplaining, and with admirable discipline, she signed her autograph, spoke to everyone, and listened patiently to the outpourings of her fans. Not a sign of irritation, every inch a lady.

The Goslings had organized a farewell as well, in the form of a midnight supper and then, at Rudolf's request, films were shown. "The Roxys" he called these private performances, in which he reveled. In fits of laughter he watched Chaplin, whom he adored, and asked for the best parts to be shown again. "Ah, what genius."

Fonteyn, I saw, was fighting manfully against tiredness and sleep; the next morning they had to be at the airport by twelve o'clock sharp.

Rudolf and I spent the night at his Victoria Road flat in order not to have to make the journey to Richmond again. It was irresponsibly late and he must have been exhausted, but he was like a child: if he was enjoying himself, he could not bear the pleasure to be brought to an end.

And yet, the following day, on the way to the airport, he still insisted on paying a visit to a strange sort of exhibition. The artist-pair Gilbert and George had organized a kind of sit-in for acquaintances, one of whom was Nigel Gosling, the Observer art critic.

In his car, loaded with Rudolf's inseparable cases, boxes, bags, and sacks, Nigel drove us to a house where the two artists had arranged themselves in a sparsely-furnished room, as immaculately dressed shop-window dummies, one leaning at the window, the other beside him, seated in an armchair. Frozen smiles, not batting an eyelid, no noticeable breathing, a macabre house of death.

What should I do? I was afraid Rudolf might poke them, but he merely stalked right up to the pair, his nose almost touching their skin: "They're real!"

It was half past eleven, the journey to Heathrow might take more than a half hour; Nigel drove bravely like one possessed. Fortunately, it was Sunday and traffic was light.

"Don't worry, we'll make it." Reclining calmly in his seat, Rudolf left the feelings of panic to us until Joan Thring took over in the departure lounge.

"Margot has boarded already. Please, hurry."

Before he vanished in among the customs officers, he spun round and yelled in my direction, "And, whatever you do, no drugs in my house!" an extremely compromising yell, certainly for Nigel, in England in those days.

On the way home, Nigel related to me how, during a dubious party in America that he had attended with Fonteyn, Rudolf had been arrested on suspicion of using drugs and they had spent the night in a cell. From then on, Rudolf was certain the whole of Scotland Yard were now just waiting to pounce on him in another such scandal so that they could deport him.

Rudolf was anything but a drug user: he was uninterested and he had better things to do with his energy, but I had told him I had experimented with LSD, something that was part and parcel of everyday life in those days. On top of that he was aware I knew a number of people from the London pop scene. One evening, to his amazement, I had been dropped off at his door in a jeep by the whole of the group "The Who." "I don't want you bringing them to my home any more," he said. "It's fatal for me."

He lived in constant fear: of the KGB, who might haul him back to the Soviet Union; of Scotland Yard, who might be hunting him as a Russian spy; and of the Royal Ballet who, he was sure, would sooner be rid of him yesterday than today. Paranoia.

Joan Thring's laugh rang out throughout his house: "If only he knew! Alice's son sometimes comes and helps his mother with the shopping and then he sits here in the kitchen chain smoking joints."

That afternoon she confided in me: "I won't be here for much longer," she whispered, as if Rudolf could hear us. "He wants to get rid of me." I had noticed that the atmosphere between them had cooled; he seemed to have little confidence in the way she took care of his business.

"She's cheating on me, the only thing she's interested in is to profit from my rich friends. While I work hard, she gets herself invited on cruise holidays by Onassis and Niarchos."

It sounded almost jealous.

"But he wouldn't dare do it: I know too much. If he fires me his whole life will appear in the newspapers," Joan said grimly and bent over his daily pile of contracts, agreements, bills, itineraries, invitations, and fan mail: zip, zip, one envelope after the other.

Feeling threatened on all sides—is that the price one has to pay for fame?

Over the following three years little occurred between Rudolf and the Dutch National Ballet. Occasionally, he came over to Holland to see the company, and to learn whether there was any new work he fancied—for his own ends!

He saw new choreographies by Hans van Manen and Toer van Schayk and insisted on seeing the opera *The Dream*, by Ton de Leeuw, in which Toer, besides designing the sets and costumes, had also had a major share in the choreography and the production.

Together with Han Ebbelaar, we traveled to Utrecht, Rudolf as untiring as ever. He appeared excited about *The Dream*: "You should take this to a small theater in London, it would be a huge success, it's so different!" But *The Dream* was a Dutch Opera production, not ours.

Back in Amsterdam he met Alexandra Radius as well, but was shown the door in their house that evening when he became rather disparaging about Harkarvy.

"That man has not a clue about classical ballet; he copies other people, that's all."

Han, who had worked with Harkarvy for years with the Netherlands Dance Theater, was incensed. "If that's your opinion, you better leave my house." No sooner said than done.

Although little concrete took place, we kept in touch. Rudolf would call me, now from Australia and then from Sweden or California, enquiring, "What's up? When are we going to work together again?"

However, either the dates he was free were unsuitable for us, or he had "better fish to fry," as he called it when something else offered better artistic or financial prospects. But our company had better fish to fry as well; the company was busily involved in creative processes and consolidating its own, Dutch, identity. A new generation of dancers arose that began to determine the image of the group more and more, in a diversity of new repertoire by Van Manen, van Schayk, and me.

So, in every way, it was better that the company was left to its own devices to develop in absolute peace and in its own manner.

Rudolf did not allow himself that vital respite, but danced evening upon evening, traveling around the globe, learning new works everywhere like the wind or staging versions of full-length classics which he knew from Leningrad, with large companies. Nonstop; he allowed himself barely any vacation, a week here, two days there. Sometimes I read of his little scandals in the press: he had struck a dancer here, offended a conductor there, thrown a photographer off the stage elsewhere.

He had told me of the immense sums of money he earned each evening— gargantuan in my eyes—"but I will never charge your company that," he reassured me.

"You're murdering yourself," I sometimes told him, and I did not mean merely physically, but in a spiritual and artistic sense, too. The lengths to which he drove himself seemed unsustainable, a senseless pursuit.

Wallace Potts rang me from London: "Can I come and stay with you?" He had fled from Rudolf and his hectic existence.

"I can't keep up with that life. He always asks me to fly over again from America to keep him company when he's on tour. I pack his cases, arrange taxis, race off to airports, watch endless rehearsals and performances, and then, when I finally think I can begin shooting my film, he takes off again. Sometimes I don't even know where we are, and then I ask myself, 'What are you doing? Who are you?' And Rudolf expects me to love him, too."

He did not unpack his luggage, merely wanted to stay in bed, with a blanket over his head. Not to see anyone, just to be alone; I heard him weeping.

"I meet all sorts of people, but I don't exist as far as they're concerned. All they're interested in is Rudolf. I'm a shadow."

Rudolf called every day, impatient, angry, or worried.

"Tell him I'm not here, that I've gone." But Rudolf was not to be fooled: "Wallace is there, I know it. Hand him over to me, " and, suspiciously, "What are the two of you up to?"

I had told Wallace he must go back to America, but one morning he got into a taxi and waved goodbye with a weak smile: "See you."

He did not go home, but returned to Rudolf's nomadic existence, of which he had really had his fill.

8 ⤙ *Pressure Cooker*

When Nureyev returned to Holland in 1975, I was startled to see see how he had changed in those few years. His face was lined and aging fast, and in class I saw he sometimes moved with difficulty, as though each movement were painful.

"I have to keep to my own tempo," he declared, when he noticed my astonishment on seeing him. "My body just doesn't get along with all those fast movements that your company likes, so early in the morning. That's for the young ones."

He was thirty-seven and one does, indeed, begin to feel old around that time in the dance profession.

I introduced him to the company and our new repertoire with pride. Besides Alexandra Radius, Sonja Marchiolli, and Han Ebbelaar, Maria Aradi, Monique Sand, Francis Sinceretti, Henny Jurriëns, and Zoltan Peter had come to reinforce our ranks as well, and a group of young soloists had arrived on the scene, including Joanne Zimmerman, Valerie Valentine, Jeanette Vondersaar, Karin Schnabel, Clint Farha, David Loring, and Wade Walthall.

He saw new work in rehearsal and on video: *Daphnis and Chloe, Adagio Hammerklavier, Twilight* and *Sacre du Printemps* by the choreographer Hans van Manen; *Before, During and After the Party, Pyrrhic Dances, Eight Madrigals* by van Schayk and our joint piece, *Collective Symphony.*

He was impressed—"So many new ideas"—but insisted that, if he were to work with us again, a new piece should be made for him. "I need something dramatic, I am very interested in Byron at the moment, the Romantics. Eternity, death, love."

He called his manager, Gorlinsky, in London: "Sandor, tell me, when am I free for Amsterdam?"

Beyond that, however, little had changed, his work schedule was as limited as ever: he barely had time for rehearsals and everything had to be done quickly.

"You have to get used to pressure cooker," he added with a malicious little laugh.

He seemed to undergo rehearsals as a necessary evil, a process he liked to get behind him as soon as he could. The adventure really only began for him when a piece went on stage: sets, lighting, the sound of the orchestra, and above all, the audience.

"When I'm rehearsing I just lose performances and I can't afford that."

Surely, giving fewer performances and devoting more time to the work he was dancing would have been a healthy and vital change.

I hesitated, was it worth it, another via dolorosa? He had in mind a tour across America and Canada for our company; "It's time they see you over there."

That prospect settled the matter for me.

He was to dance one act from *La Bayadère*, a ballet from his Leningrad period that had been rehearsed with us by a former colleague of his, Marina Shamsheva, and a pas de deux from *Le Corsaire*, which had long been his showpiece with Fonteyn. "Radius will be excellent for these works."

But the new work was quite another problem. I could hardly create a new piece in two weeks—all the time he gave us—while he would also insist on time for *La Bayadère* and "Corsaire." My two capacities, artistic director and choreographer, would be in conflict; as choreographer I should want to claim all the time for the new piece, but as artistic director I should have to allow the other pieces, especially *La Bayadère*, which was a very demanding ensemble piece, to take precedence.

"The only solution is for me to start work with another dancer in your place." I knew the importance he attached to a ballet being created to his specific capacities, and how jealously and suspiciously he could react to other dancers, but there was no other solution.

I suggested Henny Jurriëns, a young soloist whom Rudolf clearly appreciated, correcting him regularly during class and often taking him aside for advice.

"When you come, Henny can teach you everything. He'll always be at your disposal."

Nureyev found it an excellent idea.

I was burning to show him the film of his mother and Rosa—whom he had not seen for nearly fifteen years—but he did not appear to be very enthusiastic about it.

"Don't you long to see them again?"

"Well, not exactly; not like this, I mean."

The reel was already in the projector; I drew the curtains and turned on the machine. Images of Moscow flashed across the wall, Ivan in front of the Kremlin, wooden houses in the Arbat, the Bolshoi Theater. Then, just at the point where the Leningrad part was about to begin, the film became jammed in the machine, the picture flickered and faded away.

Rudolf got up in agitation: "Stop, don't try to fix it. This is a sign, I knew it, I shouldn't see it, it's bad for them," and he drew back the curtains.

Together with Rudolf, I listened to suitable music. He suddenly seemed interested in Nijinsky and asked whether I could make a new arrangement of his *Till Eulenspiegel*, a ballet to music by Richard Strauss that Nijinsky had created for Diaghilev's company in 1916. A piece that could really scarcely be called Romantic, or in a Byronic mood.

Joseph's Legend was considered, another Strauss composition performed from 1914 by Diaghilev's dancers, but the thought of an arrangement did not appeal to me and we ended up with Strauss's *Death and Transfiguration*, a symphonic poem with vehement mood swings that seemed to suit Rudolf's emotions.

In *Blown in a Gentle Wind*, a man propelled by two winged figures looks back on his life one final time. Memories drift past, people he had known in his lifetime, his expectations, his deeds. When the storm subsides and the feverish dream seems to ebb away, he allows himself to be led on by the beating wings of the angels of death.

My choice of music was an unfortunate one; I was swept along in the lachrymose melodrama of Strauss's cries from the heart, allowing myself to be engulfed, drowning in the music instead of creating a sense of balance.

I could steer rehearsals with our own dancers—Jurriëns as the man, Farha and Walthall as the "angels of death"—in such a way that they approached the theme soberly and with great restraint, emphasizing the alas not so imaginative movements, but Rudolf threw an enormous amount of histrionics and vehement expression into it, causing the already unreliable vessel to keel over precariously.

I had created two duets with young people for him (or rather, for *them*), Karin Schnabel and Peter Boyes, but I had no idea how they would react to the confrontation with the temperamental star, or of how he would react to the "young ones." I felt that the contrast between the died-in-the-wool Nureyev and the inexperience and vulnerability of Schnabel and Boyes might be a catalyst for something exciting.

But Rudolf's lack of time affected everyone, not merely himself. On arrival he seemed totally absorbed by other things, he was tired, appeared confused and neglected even, and, for the first time since I had known him, gave the impression his diary was becoming too much for him. Above all, though, he seemed to have grown lonely. I sometimes caught him unawares in the corner of a studio, out of breath, perspiration pouring off him, panting like a hunted animal with a stricken look of suspicion in his eye, as though he were waiting for me to criticize him. At moments like those he behaved as though we were strangers.

"Will you ever learn?" I wondered.

After a few rehearsals—through which Jurriëns guided him with the patience of a saint—he informed me out of the blue that he did not want to work with Clint and Wade: "They are not concentrated enough and are unsure of the music."

It even went as far as scenes in the rehearsals, when he accused his two partners of bad behavior, punched them, and communicated solely by means of snarls. An untenable situation.

Farha and Walthall were two highly gifted young dancers, with splendid line and superb form, too perfect in the eyes of Rudolf, who wanted to be the only one to shine in the trios. I had long discussions with him, saying that this behavior diminished his own performance, but his only retort was, "What the audience wants to see is me, not them."

The costume Toer had designed for him was a torn shirt intended to give a worn-out impression, an aging skin from which color and luster have faded.

"You're trying to make me look as ugly as possible, I'm not wearing this rubbish," but I was adamant. I refused to change it and said to Toer, "Whatever he says, don't give in."

In the choreography, as well, he changed things he claimed he could not do—"I'm not Henny"—or did not want to. "I need steps, I need to move. If you make me stop there, at that point, right in the middle of the ballet, then I can't get started again after that."

It was not merely the lack of time, but the working atmosphere that was alarming as well. I was hardly enthusiastic about my own work in the first place, but Rudolf made me come to dislike it and I began to dread rehearsals.

I did alter a number of things for him, because my task as choreographer was to find a solution with the dancer that was agreeable to both, but he would still try to change some passages according to his own insights, something I did not allow: "Sorry, but this stays as it is."

It was discouraging later on, during the performances, to see how, when I could do no more about it, he would suddenly dance his own version after all.

In that respect, dance is one-of-a-kind in the interpretive arts; things are possible which are unthinkable in any other art form: in an opera or a concert, the audience knows that the singers and orchestra follow the score in detail as the composer wrote it, and in a play, the actors keep to the original text.

In dance, however, the audience can never quite be certain whether a given passage is what the choreographer intended or a compromise according to the insights of a dancer or even that of a répétiteur with his own ideas.

In the *Blown in a Gentle Wind* period, I began to understand something of the reason for Rudolf's agitation; he spoke bitterly of the bad reviews he had received in various parts of the world, and of Mikhail Baryshnikov, who had been bringing the house down in America for the past year.

It was astounding that the amiable, fair-haired athlete should be seen as a threat by Rudolf; was there no room in the world for two such talented people?

Naturally, comparisons were drawn between the two dancers, both of them from Leningrad and both having fled during a Kirov Ballet tour, but those comparisons were almost always in favor of the new star. And rightly so: Baryshnikov was a dancer with a phenomenal technique and an amazing and highly intelligent stage personality who gave me, too, the feeling I had never seen a dancer quite like him before. He clearly hailed from a younger generation and fitted with far more ease than Rudolf into contemporary choreographies, giving brilliant interpretations.

Nureyev found it hard to deal with all the attention and praise his younger colleague received.

"I must expand my horizons," he said, "do other things."

"Yes, why not? I can imagine you've had enough of all those appearances." I thought he meant he wanted to devote more time to producing ballets, something he did rather well.

He gave me a withering look. How on earth could I imagine such a thing? Of course he would still keep on dancing! But he was negotiating a film role and was hesitant, wondering whether it was wise to step into such an unknown medium; it would mean taking elocution lessons and being coached in acting. In short, it would consume a great deal of his time.

"But I'm tempted!"

Altogether, he calculated, it would cost him six months, meaning that, during that time, he would have to be available for the film from early morning until late at night.

"Make sure you know what you're doing, it'll mean you won't be able to take classes or give performances."

"I'll do my classes on the set. I'll take my own teacher along." And performances? "I'll have it put into my contract that I can leave every now and then."

But he did not really seem convinced.

If *Blown in a Gentle Wind* was not the most fortunate of experiences, Nureyev truly came into his own in the two classical pieces he danced with Alexandra Radius; this was clearly his domain.

Together they formed a remarkable pair, Radius and he, as though they had worked together for years, both with equal control over the stage, seemingly perfectly synchronized, each other's match.

Sometimes he put her to the test, did not support her, or deliberately held her far off balance, but Radius did not give an inch, remained firmly in balance, and, if need be, did the technical stuntwork without his help. Seeing them dance together could be like watching a thrilling game of tennis, swift, skillful and scintillating.

What amazed him and filled him with respect was that he seemed unable to get a grip on his partner. Radius never allowed herself to be carried away or even affected by Rudolf's tantrums, making it quite clear to him that she had come to the studio to work and for no other reason.

He considered the high technical demands that *La Bayadère* made on performers as a measure for himself: "As long as I come through that impeccably I know I still count as a classical dancer." In later years he sometimes asked me to put *La Bayadere* in the repertoire, "to get into condition again."

Of course, not every performance he gave was of the same caliber, but whenever he danced at his peak, he swept everyone along in his determined bravado; he ran enormous risks and pushed himself to extremes.

"Now he's going to fall," you would think, "he'll never make it" but all the time you were aware of his willpower and determination to bring the variations he danced to a perfectly wrought conclusion.

On those occasions, it was as though he needed to cling to the triumph he felt on such an evening for as long as he could. Performances would be followed by prolonged dinners, preferably with a large group of friends, a ritual he kept up until nearly the end of his life. It was almost always the guests who were the first to show signs of fatigue, the host was indomitable and seemed to know no exhaustion.

For some time, he had been considering buying a house in Amsterdam and had asked Toer and me to keep an eye open for a characteristic house on one of the canals: "The canals remind me of Leningrad." He loved the atmosphere in Amsterdam, but especially what went on there in ballet. On evenings when he did not have a performance, and to acquaint him with other aspects of Dutch culture besides dance and painting, I would try to read him letters by the Dutch author Gerard van het Reve, from his books *Nearer to Thee* and *Towards the End*, translating them as best I could.

Once, in a fit of enthusiasm, when Sonia Gaskell was director of the Dutch National Ballet, I had given her the same two volumes, because she too was unfamiliar with Dutch literature. But she responded negatively, saying she found what she read narrow-minded and self-absorbed: "You people here are so absorbed in your own small problems." I recall how disappointed I was and especially upset by her condescending reaction.

With Rudolf it would be different: I was sure Reve's blend of tragedy, humor, self-mockery, and bitter earnest would appeal to him, that he would recognize a great deal of himself in it. But translation, I would discover, was a craft in its own right; I failed miserably at turning Reve's wayward and often archaic use of the Dutch language into similar English.

At the end of the season, I invited a large group of dancers to my home to celebrate our collaboration with Rudolf; in spite of all the problems and conflicts he often caused, everyone was fond of him and his whims were easily forgiven. And after work, when the tension had eased, he seemed a different person altogether, more relaxed and full of stories and jokes.

It was a beautiful evening. The windows and doors were thrown open and the dancers sat in the garden until the early hours. When the last guest had gone, Rudolph and I cleared away the worst of the mess in the house and, outside, dawn was breaking. Rudolf sat down in the doorway, listening to the first birds starting to sing in the treetops. I put on a record, Mozart's *Don Giovanni*, and I suddenly saw tears rolling down his cheeks. "This comes straight from heaven," he said, "the most beautiful thing ever created."

The following morning he packed his ancient, dog-eared cases and bulky, overflowing bags. I had managed to get hold of *The Acrobat and Other Stories*, a book by Reve that had been published in English, and I stowed it away in among his luggage, hoping to keep his thoughts of Holland alive that way.

The messiness and poverty-stricken appearance of what he dragged around with him never failed to amaze me. He seemed unable to part with old belongings; I saw the same old leotards, shawls, and sweaters turn up in his luggage year in year out, ancient towels, bags of old and worn-out ballet shoes, a jumble of odds and ends of greasepaint, and dozens of music cassettes which he stuffed into nooks and crannies in his bags. Music was his life, even more than dancing.

For months on end, he would wander around that way, from hotel to hotel, from dressing room to dressing room and on to friends, seldom ever seeing his own homes.

9 ∾ *About a Radiant House*

Our tour of Canada and America went ahead, but without Nureyev, who had committed himself to appear in a film after all.

For the self-confidence of the company, it was good to give a guest performance on such an important continent without feeling we were following in the wake of a great attraction; if we were praised, we would be sure it was for our own achievements—and if we were criticized, as well. Before the group's departure he called me: "I wish I could come, too." He wanted to know which repertoire we were going to perform and gave me some advice. "In New York, call this person and that one, and you absolutely *must* invite Mister X personally, the *New York Times* is an important paper." How little he knew me, to think I would do *that*.

The film he was to make in England was *Valentino*, the life of that other Rudolph who had made so many hearts beat faster on the silver screen.

"It's a great challenge," he said, "and I love it."

I was unfamiliar with the deeds and accomplishments of Rudolph Valentino and had never heard Rudolf mention him or his films, while he was such a great lover of old films. From the odd photo, I recalled a man with an unremarkable face, somewhat round and quaint, and in such contrast to Nureyev's profile with its angular nose, alert nostrils, shrewd eyes and sensual, eager mouth. What they did have in common was the fascination they held for women, Nureyev had a throng of women who adored him, and I had the impression they wrote to him, called him up, and trailed after him more and more.

"Me and my women," he would often sigh, with an undertone of mockery, "but where are the men?"

That same winter I returned to La Turbie, for a short vacation without Rudolf.

"Use my house, it's empty anyway. I'll call Serge to prepare everything for you," for with the collections of art treasures they contained, he could naturally never leave his mansions unattended.

Madame Claire had grown too old and left the house and her place had been taken by an elderly Russian émigré, Serge Ivanov.

The fact that Wade Walthall was to be the other guest in his house was accepted by Rudolf without a murmur; no matter how hostile and critical he had been toward his far younger colleague in rehearsals, outside the studio there were different rules.

During our stay at La Turbie, he called now and then, inquiring after the state the house was in ("I've not been there for two years, I think") indicating which books I should search for in his bedroom and take back for him, and offering advice for trips on which we might embark.

"Remember, the car is there for you, use it!" he impressed upon me, but Serge could hardly manage without the car in that isolated spot, so we had rented one.

"Don't tell Mister Nureyev, he will not like that," said Serge a little anxiously. Rudolf was seldom understanding or sympathetic toward the people who worked for him and their often difficult circumstances.

"I never know what's going to happen, when he's coming, how many there'll be," Serge told us. "He often calls me up in the evening to say he's coming home with eight guests, and then I have to prepare a meal for all those people. And if it's not flawless, then I'm in trouble."

We roamed the misty hills, the three of us worked in the gardens around the house and ate together.

"I have to make sure that the house is always in order, because Mister Nureyev may suddenly turn up at the door, unannounced. That happened to me once, the heating was off, there was nothing extra in the house. "The house must always be ready, you can always expect me," he said. "That taught me a lesson." Serge gave me a meaningful look: "When you work for famous people . . ."

We avoided the larger rooms in the house; the grand candelabras, the massive wooden settees, carpet chests, and room screens made us feel we were in a wing of the Metropolitan Museum, splendid for viewing, but not for spending evenings in, especially in winter, with all the windows closed and shuttered, so early in the evening.

"Maybe I'll come for a few days," Rudolf had said, but it did not come to that. Fortunately for Serge, who enjoyed doing things together and really appreciated the coziness of sharing meals. And fortunately for Wade, as well, because Rudolf's arrival would have lent our holiday a very different character.

Ten days later, the garden gates closed behind us and we returned to Amsterdam, leaving Serge behind in that beautiful, large, and empty house.

Rudolf asked me to go and see the premiere of *Valentino* in London; "I think it's wonderful, a very good piece of work." I was unsure whether he was referring to his own work or that of the director Ken Russell.

The evening before, Frederick Ashton visited him in Richmond, sharing stories with us from the past, his early years with the Ballet Rambert and his first choreographies for that company.

"Show us how Pavlova danced," Rudolf asked, because Ashton had seen the legendary dancer perform in his youth and had tried to obtain a position in her company.

Taking a quick drag on his cigarette, Ashton strutted over to the center of the room and began imitating the mannerisms of the aging Pavlova, the hasty steps, her flapping hand movements and coquettishly raised shoulders.

"She was a genius at capturing one's attention. Even doing nothing at all, she was in perpetual motion, fingers, head, eyes. She undulated."

I spied Alice standing in the hallway, gaping at Sir Fred in amazement, as he twirled around ecstatically, pirouetted, and dropped onto one knee.

"Her facial expression varied continually and her mouth moved as though she were whispering secrets." By way of illustration, he opened and closed his mouth, smiled, pouted his lips, a whole arsenal of nervous habits.

Rudolf seemed to lap it up and instantly gave an Anna Pavlova parody. The disconcerting part was that, not long afterward, I saw him making the same gestures on stage, and began to notice the same twitches around the mouth. Was he aware of that, was he copying the "liveliness" of his illustrious predecessor? Was this another form of innovation on his part?

It was strange seeing Rudolf on the silver screen—strange, too, because no matter what costume he wore, whatever unlikely situation he was in, he remained himself, so much so that I was unable to imagine Valentino's life or anyone else's for a moment; it was barely more than watching a slide show. Was that owing to the director or the principal actor? Or was it my taste influencing me, or the fact I knew Rudolf too well? I could imagine that Russell had wrestled with the task of molding Nureyev into another personality, and that Rudolf himself had certainly made every effort to become one, too. His body adopted all the forms and attitudes required for the various scenes, passion, anger, surrender, pain, but in his eyes I was still aware of a distance, he never quite let himself go, remaining cautious and in control, even on the silver screen.

I felt it remained an awkward and rather strained approach. Rudolf did not seem to melt into the narrative, remaining an onlooker and outsider, so it was hard for us, the excluded audience, to become spellbound.

After the premiere, at a party given in the hotel, he planted me at the table opposite Princess Margaret, who was not entirely unknown to me, as she had attended a rehearsal in the *Ropes* period and, years before, I had also met her once in Holland.

"Keep the conversation going," he joked, knowing how bad I was at that, and withdrew.

Later, when festivities were in full swing, I was able to observe how Her Royal Highness's attention was directed entirely at the greatly admired table companion on her right, while the guest on her left made desperate attempts to strike up a conversation, but was completely ignored. Whatever he said, no matter how he approached her or what he spoke of, he simply did not exist for her.

My mouth fell open in awe at so much majesty.

10   *A Faun around the House*

In 1978 two more new works were added to our Nureyev repertoire. Toer van Schayk created *Faun*, his own version of what was originally the Nijinsky creation *L'Après-midi d'un Faune* from 1912, and my *About a Dark House*, a ballet to the composition of the same name by the Austrian composer Roman Haubenstock-Ramati.

We had two weeks of appearances ahead of us in New York, in that same theater where we had made our American debut—without Rudolf—two years earlier.

The Minskoff Theater management and the American agency for the Dutch National Ballet were clearly interested in us, and this time, they assured us that, thanks to our guest soloist, we could count on a better, no, the best house. "But do bring along new works with you," we were advised, "ballets that have never been seen before anywhere."

New work was no problem for our company, which boasted three choreographers, but preparing those new choreographies within Nureyev's eternally tight schedule was a challenge. The pressure cooker would have to be brought to the boil again.

Nureyev's visits to our studios were gradually ceasing to be news, either for the dancers or the press. Rudolf was greeted like an old friend within the company, something which clearly gave him satisfaction and affected his temperament. His whims, such as arriving late for practice and making full houses wait for him, were a thing of the past; we had withstood that baptism by fire.

Of course, there were always journalists wanting to interview him, whom he would then treat at random. Sometimes he would condescend to agree to a talk and then later say he was too busy or too tired for an interview. Another time he would answer the questions with such cynicism and hostility that it was easy to predict how the article would turn out (which then incensed him); and then again, he would often be friendliness and patience personified, until the moment came when he would abruptly call out "Basta," scoop up his things, and be off.

"What have we done wrong now?" the newspaper people were clearly thinking, but often there was no apparent reason for his sudden change in mood.

He frequently grumbled at "the press" and scolded them, announced he would never allow any more interviews, but then he would be shocked when, indeed, no one turned up or called.

One evening, Rudolf mentioned he had met a boy in the anonymous world of a club and had had a drink with him. The film *Valentino* was showing in Amsterdam around that time.

"Did you see that film?" Rudolf had asked him, pointing to the billboard above the cinema.

"Yes," the boy answered, but gave no further indication that he recognized Nureyev as the star.

"And, did you like it?"

"Mmm, so-so," the boy had said, "but I thought Nureyev was really bad." "It was very amusing that the boy had no idea who I was. He left to go to the bathroom and then someone at the bar had obviously asked him how he had picked up Nureyev. When he came back to my table he was furious and left," Rudolf roared with laughter. "Can you imagine, not embarrassed, no: furious! That's Amsterdam for you."

Toer had a marvelous idea for *Faun*: three conveyor-belt workers on a factory floor, two women and a man. When the ballet begins, the workers are hard at work, not to Debussy's wondrously soothing music but to hollow Muzak sounds, the man polishing the pipes on the machinery, the two women performing their mechanical actions on the conveyor belt.

At the sound of the coffee-break signal, the man contentedly removes his lunch from a tool chest he has brought along—the bunch of grapes the sole allusion to the faun—while the women stand there dizzy with exhaustion, until one of them switches off the Muzak in irritation.

And then, to the sensual yet reassuring sounds of Debussy that ensue, a pleasurable, no-strings flirtation develops among the trio, the mischievous laborer like some young, affectionate animal to whom the two women respond in their different ways. A moment comes when the faunlike youth seems about to choose between the two, but the signal goes for the end of the break. The two women dutifully return to the conveyor-belt, but the man is sullen and succumbs reluctantly to the daily drudgery of the slate-belt once again.

A piece full of humor, which came into existence with the necessary embarrassing moments. In van Schayk's own words:

"At the first rehearsal, when I showed Jeanette Vondersaar and Rudolf the initial movements of the duet they were to dance together—gliding steps with knees bent deep, the upper half of the body curved forward with rounded back at right-angles—Rudolf asked somewhat mockingly, *Est-ce que nous sommes des ours?*"[1]

Although he generally spoke English, he sometimes enjoyed repeating phrases in another language. From that moment on, he renamed Jeanette "Oursky," the duet was christened the "Oursky-pas de deux," and I was "Toersky." It had become a marker in *Faun*: "Shall we start from our Oursky-pas de deux?"

I had already worked out large portions of the ballet on my own so, much to Rudolf's satisfaction, rehearsals went rapidly. He threw himself almost lasciviously into my forward-bent body movements and arm curves, which were so unfamiliar to him.

With someone like Nureyev in the studio, I had dared leave only a minimum to the inspiration of the moment and had noted the sequences I had thought up beforehand in a sketchbook. In one of the rehearsals, I was showing him some steps bent over forward and, with my arms circling behind me, I looked around at my notebook, which was lying on the ground beside me. Rudolf obediently copied that pose, thinking it must be part of the choreography.

Jeanette, realizing the misunderstanding, roared with laughter, and Rudolf reacted suspiciously, thinking he was being laughed at. After that, all three of us laughed, but the unforeseen rear-curving-move looked so lovely when Rudolf did it that I kept it in the choreography.

Generally, Nureyev was not too happy with my previously thought-out choreographies, preferring me to work directly on his body, and not with an imaginary, idealized dancer.

1. "Are we supposed to be bears?"

The fairly calm atmosphere of the early *Faun* rehearsals did not last for long, unfortunately and, as the first night drew closer, I noticed Rudolf was growing tired and so more brusque. He often made things difficult for both his partners, Alexandra Radius and Maria Aradi (Jeanette had been forced to drop out because of an injury). If they had to perform a movement at the same time as he did, they were not allowed to raise a leg higher than he did, a scruple he rarely had with Fonteyn.

Nor was he always content with the moves I gave him, once it became clear to him that in *Faun* I had little interest in spectacular turns and leaps.

"Couldn't you give me," he said with a tinge of feigned exhaustion in his voice, "a few leaps here? This," he made a parody of the move I had just shown him, "is not exactly the most interesting movement in the world."

There came an afternoon when, after I had once again stood my ground and not succumbed to his wishes, he silently gathered up his bag and clothes and left the studio. With a resigned feeling of "well, that's the way it'll have to be," I had the rehearsal continue with Han Ebbelaar, Rudolf's understudy.

But ten minutes later, Rudolf returned to the studio with a glass of tea, as though he had only taken a break, sat down on a chair with a somewhat defeated expression on his face and looked on in silence. After a time, still sitting, but indicating the steps demonstratively with hand gestures, he began rehearsing with us again.

I walked over to him; the air had to be cleared. And right in the middle of this awkward and, on his part monosyllabic, conversation, something suddenly dawned on me that had never before crossed my mind: he, too, the great Rudolf, could become nervous before an approaching first night!

If my memory does not deceive me, from that moment on, when he stood up and began to work normally once again, the problems were solved and the final days before the first night passed in a far more harmonious working atmosphere.

Nureyev's own contribution to the role of the faun was considerable; he added a great deal, especially to the facial expression and mime. I still see before me the inimitable sensuality with which the factory worker threw back his head and slowly lowered a bunch of grapes into his mouth."

I had scarcely been around during the rehearsal process of *Faun*, so immersed had I been in a creation process of my own. For all its atmosphere and aura,

Haubenstock-Ramati's was not the simplest kind of music, barely countable and quite capricious in its sound.

After the innumerable parties and receptions I had attended with Rudolf over the years, I would sometimes ask him why he still went along to events like that; did they amuse him, did he go for professional reasons, for the sake of public relations, was it important for him to be rubbing shoulders with millionaires, shipping magnates, film stars and their entourage?

Of course I did not expect an explicit answer, understanding that it was a combination of various things, which were sometimes parallel and then again at cross-purposes with each other. Often he would curse such gatherings—beforehand—but I noticed he thoroughly enjoyed himself and always soon endeavored to become the center of attention.

He was also capable of insulting people badly and, at the end of the evening, under the influence of alcohol, might make a fool of the prominent hostess or pocket a number of dreadfully expensive bottles of wine saying, "This wine agrees with me. Do you mind?"

The reactions nearly always remained polite, and lenient as well, albeit accompanied by a somewhat icy smile, "Oh, such an unpredictable artiste."

How the guests would have responded had *I* taken such a liberty!

"Pretense is what makes their world go round," was his comment, "No one is really himself on such occasions; masks, a second skin. I have a lot of money, but for them I am a simple boy who happens to be in fashion, they tolerate me. When my star has faded, I'll no longer exist for them."

But then he sometimes behaved so impossibly it was hardly surprising. His behavior was, I believe, revenge in advance.

"But do you *want* to belong to those circles?"

"Well, it's a certain power. And it's expected of me," he gave me a crooked grin, "They for sure give a certain standard to my performances."

Did he mean it mockingly?

Sometimes he tried to persuade me to make use of his connections, if not for myself then at least for my *own* company. But the very idea had me cringing in misery; to my mind it was bordering on a sort of high-brow prostitution.

In *About a Dark House*, the curtain rose on a formal gathering in a society salon. Rudolf was among the guests, an outsider remaining aloof and detached from this world, unable to establish any real contact with those around him.

Right in the middle of the ceremonies and formalities, the protagonist undergoes a transformation: his dinner-jacket vanishes from his body and a savage, half-naked figure remains. The furniture, too, goes through a metamorphosis: rising and suspended in midair, it seems to take on the aspect of bizarre celestial bodies.

Then the other guests don another form—their true one maybe? The pattern of movements becomes uninhibited and impulsive; what seemed neatly ordered beforehand becomes anarchic chaos.

In the end, the main character becomes involved in a violent fight and is spat out by the chaotic society into the salon, where the impeccable gathering seems to go on undisturbed.

Nureyev lies there on the ground like some exotic and repulsive insect, and after their initial amazement, the gatherings seem to go on as he crawls across the immense floor to the entrance of the room where he vanishes, all the while not losing sight of the company for a moment. Wounded and humiliated, a discarded animal.

I think *Dark House* was the most satisfying work I created for and with him, even if the rehearsal period did not pass without friction. He seemed unable to work any other way and, overworked as he was, he was under immense pressure.

He learned three ballets in the same short space of time, the existing piece *Four Schumann Pieces* by Hans van Manen and our two pieces, an enormous amount of work, even for a well-equipped and well-rested dancer. But it was he who had insisted on performing three ballets, knowing full well how little time there was.

He often turned up tired and confused from one rehearsal, tried out steps from *Faun* during *Schumann Pieces* and rehearsed *Dark House* in the movement idiom of van Schayk. When it all became too much for him, he would start accusing me that our company was badly organized and that it was impossible for him to work like that.

"What about the others?" I asked him. "Our dancers, Hans, Toer, they work like hell to get the ballets ready too. It's not only you who's tired."

He had added the impossible element himself, as of course he very well knew, only there was no way he could admit that to himself, let alone to us.

Toward the end of *Dark House* there was a scene where the "formal gathering" is standing in one corner of the stage and the "informal" one in another, linked by a long rope held by both groups. Rudolf hangs there in the middle of the rope, suspended "at the edge of being."

My intention was that, with both hands still holding the rope now stretched into a V shape, he should lower himself far out of balance into a sharp diagonal line. His head should then be a mere two feet from the ground.

"Impossible," said Rudolf, "I'm not going to risk my life."

I was convinced it had to be possible and offered to demonstrate it myself. Rudolf positioned himself opposite me on the floor with an expression on his face that said, "Okay, come on then, let's see you do it."

The two groups held on to the rope as counterbalance, while I allowed my body to hang over forward. Aiming to balance almost parallel with the floor, I tried to take it to the extreme.

All of a sudden, my feet shot out from under me and (I was holding onto the rope with both hands so there was nothing to break my fall) I landed flat on my face with a dreadful smack.

There was a jet-black explosion inside my head and for a moment the whole studio disappeared into a deep void, but my first thought was, "Get up, don't let Rudolf see how bad it is." I tried to laugh but he stared at me unmoved, not a muscle in his face betrayed the slightest emotion.

The dancers were shaken; it was clear to everyone how hard the fall had been. Immediately afterward I had to go lie down, my body felt as though it had been run over by a truck.

It turned out that I had a slight concussion and was out of the running for a week. I could not have chosen a worse moment for it: *Dark House* was unfinished.

During my entire convalescence I heard nothing from Rudolf, not a telephone call, no note, no message: he left Amsterdam without my even seeing him again.

Later, when he came over for a few days to allow me to finish the ballet, I told him how disappointed in him I had been, that he had ignored me like that.

"I am very superstitious," he explained. "You know, Mishkin, I keep as far as I can from illness, accident, and death. Otherwise you bring these things upon yourself. You should never dwell on such occurrences." He stated this drily, as an ironclad rule. No shame or remorse, no attempt to put it in a good light; this attitude was his tuxedo, the camouflage behind which he hid.

I enjoyed seeing the three stars, Radius, Aradi and Nureyev, slaving away as factory workers in *Faun*, however stylized it was. After all the "correct" images the ballet world consisted of then—and sometimes still does—it was a relief.

Four Schumann Pieces (created by van Manen for Rudolf's rival at the Royal Ballet, Anthony Dowell) was danced impressively by Rudolf; when he was in the right mood he melted into the ensembles, even harmonizing with his partners Radius, Marchiolli, and Jurriëns. But if there were the slightest thing wrong with the circumstances—and that might be anything from a sore foot to an irritating telephone call—then things were clearly off key and he operated in isolation, a remote island. Although loneliness seemed to be a basic theme of *Schumann Pieces*, solitary behavior of this kind is not beneficial to the work, or to any other piece experiencing the ripples of Rudolf's displeasure, for that matter.

In *Dark House*, Mea Venema was the cool, almost inviolable hostess, only touched and maybe moved by Nureyev. In the impulsive society he came eye to eye with Sonja Marchiolli, Joanne Zimmerman, Karin Schnabel, Henny Jurriëns, Wade Walthall, and Ad Berbers.

I had originally had Clint Farha in mind for the role of the one who would overrule Nureyev's unbridled, untamable passion in a struggle for power. However, Nureyev refused to work with Farha; he had accepted Walthall but Clint, who could be undisciplined and temperamental as well, was too uncertain a factor for him. On the one hand, I think Rudolf recognized his own unruliness and caprice; on the other hand, he felt that the rivalry that was bound to arise between him and Farha might lead to dangerous situations.

"If you put him together with me in that ballet I'll kill him," and, knowing the gentlemen through and through as I did, the idea that they might come to blows seemed quite conceivable. And, besides, I was sure that Clint would win a fight with flying colors.

With an aching heart I spoke to Clint, for I would have loved to have seen him in the role, but he, on the contrary, seemed relieved because, since *Blown in a Gentle Wind*, he had felt the animosity between the two of them and clearly had no desire to prolong the hostile clashes.

Ad Berbers was a young dancer from the corps de ballet, a fine, athletic type with the nonchalant humor of a real Amsterdammer and that very combination of muscleman and vanity that excited Nureyev and endeared him, too.

Berbers was thrilled to bits with his role and worked himself to the bone for me, and for Rudolf. The fight they were to have together was really tricky, not something that could be rigged, no stylized version of a boxing match, but a raw hurling about, slamming, and overpowering of one another.

Rudolf was anxious during rehearsals, approaching them like a panicky infant in a swimming pool. He was far older than his opponent and vulnerable to Ad's raw power. In every way he could, Rudolf tried to impress upon him that his body was the instrument he wanted to go on using for a long time.

"Don't hurt me, be careful, you dance with Stradivarius, don't forget."

But Berbers' camaraderie ensured it never came to serious disagreements and sometimes I would even notice a certain satisfaction in our awkward man when he was being tossed back and forth in Berber's arms.

The new programs had their Amsterdam premieres in March 1978, and three months later we opened on Broadway at the Minskoff Theater, now a familiar place to us. I recall that time in New York as a spell of pure unsullied joy, without the merest shadow of displeasure.

The group worked brilliantly and Nureyev, too, behaved like an enchanting, tame foal. The Minskoff Theater had strict rules about starting times: performances were to commence promptly, everyone was to be on stage five minutes before curtain up; there would be no waiting for anyone, soloist or corps de ballet.

That sounded promising; in Dutch theaters five minutes more or less seemed to be of no consequence. The opening performance was about to begin, with dancers, conductor and orchestra at the ready. Balanchine was in the audience, Martha Graham, Lincoln Kirstein. One more minute, thirty seconds . . . Now?

The theater manager appeared in the wings and made an announcement to the dancers: "The performance cannot begin, because the *New York Times* critic hasn't arrived yet."

We began, in short, ten minutes late.

I remembered Rudolf's advice: "You must invite the *Times* critic personally." How sick and revolting for a theatrical society to be so dependent on one hack; prostitution to the press.

And were we then supposed to run and read the chitchat in the *New York Times* the following day?

I saw little of Rudolf during that time. He was staying in a different hotel on the other side of Central Park and had his own hectic life. And I had mine.

Central Park was in flower, I reveled in the sunny avenues, the Hudson, the amazing assortment of passers-by, farmers straight from Crete mingling with spritely secretaries, motherly black waitresses, film stars out jogging, the odor of horse manure near Tiffany's, sun worshippers under the deep pink blossoms on the hawthorn trees, the fragrance of balmy summer evenings. America still seemed an innocent dream, the threat of poverty only occasionally present.

Rudolf worked at a peak each New York evening, but then so did everyone. I enjoyed our dancers quite as much as I did him.

There were celebrities in the theater at each performance: Lisa Minnelli, Alexandra Danilova, John Travolta, Mstislav Rostropovich, Jacqueline Kennedy, who came and congratulated Rudolf profusely afterward: "Oh, Rudolf, you were great, absolutely the best; what a divine performance."

And yet, amid all the elation I would still occasionally awaken from it all somewhat disillusioned, amazed at the euphoria a one-off success could unchain in an adult society.

11 ～ *American Dream*

That summer found us in America once again, this time for a tour across the continent: St. Louis, Chicago, and San Francisco. The American Dream went on.

Following the New York season and a Holland Festival, our dancers had a three-week summer holiday behind them, but Rudolf had simply continued nonstop with his appearances and I wondered anxiously about the state in which we would find him.

It was midsummer and stifling hot in St. Louis, so that it was fortunate our first theater was an open-air one in Forest Park called Municipal Opera. And what a theater, with seating for thirteen thousand spectators!

As soon as we arrived, our technicians had their work cut out to suit the stage to our needs, an enormous operation which had to take place before each performance: to prepare our own lighting equipment, install spotlights, unpack and distribute the contents of scenery and costume chests, set up the orchestra, and position sound equipment.

The lighting could not be done before dark, so the technical crew would have to work almost the entire night, which meant one fortunate factor: it was cool then.

While I stood at the back of the theater watching the transformation of the stage into a bluish island in a hazy darkness, Rudolf was flying in our direction by private airplane, after his final performance in Washington, and we would be complete once again.

Jan Hofstra, our technical manager, was busy on stage, the air was balmy with fragrant shrubs and insects zooming, and on the horizon there was the dusky urban glow of St. Louis; it all seemed to fit and instilled me with confidence: a sublime theatrical night.

The following morning, I went to Rudolf's room to welcome him and talk the day through with him: what time classes started, the order of rehearsals, and the number of ballets he wished to dance.

His rooms—he had an apartment in our hotel—had already been transformed into the familiar Gypsy encampment, cases lying here and there, bouquets of flowers, tape recorders, mountains of personal and theater clothing, baskets of fruit, piles of mail, everything strewn around the room in disarray. And in the midst of all that there stood a massage table.

I was startled: Rudolf looked crumpled and intensely fatigued, inching his way around the room like an invalid, with small, shuffling steps, on painfully swollen feet.

"I don't know if I'm going to make it, I feel sick." Moaning, he stretched out on the massage table where Luigi Pignotti, the masseur who traveled everywhere with him, carefully felt his calves.

"Ahh," he groaned, "don't touch me there. Start with the shoulders."

I advised him to go back to bed; he could miss practice and, if necessary, we could do the rehearsals without him too. After all, he had danced everything not so long ago in New York.

Way below Rudolf's apartment, I could hear the dancers splashing about and cheering. The company was housed in a splendid hotel beyond the city, an old-fashioned, towering, stylish castle, with a large swimming pool in the courtyard, for cooling down in and having pleasure.

While I awaited my breakfast at the water's edge, a boy approached my table.

"Are you Rudi? Rudolf asks if you'll come."

Franck Duval was a mere slip of a boy, still a schoolboy even, and, like Wallace before him, an admirer of Rudolf's, who had immediately towed him along in his wake. Among other things, Franck had studied Russian, been to the Soviet Union and, as far as I could tell, spoke fluent Russian.

"But I've just come from Rudolf," I answered.

"There seem to be some problems." He spoke English with a charming French accent.

Back in Rudolf's appartment, it turned out that Lilian Libman had arrived as well. She was his theatrical agent responsible for our tour, whom I had already met earlier in New York. Lilian's face spelled trouble.

"Rudolf doesn't know if he is able to perform." I went rigid.

The victim himself lay mute in bed and was slurping his tea noisily.

"This apartment is awful," he complained. "I can't get any air." In my opinion it was an apartment fit for a king, with every imaginable convenience, reception room, bedrooms, kitchen.

"I'll try to get another one," Miss Libman growled.

"Not another one, the best," Rudolf called after her.

A quarter of an hour later, swathed in towels and dressing-gowns, Rudolf stumbled to the lift on my arm, and Franck and Luigi began to pack up the whole luggage-caravan again.

On the top floor, the thirty-second, a veritable palace awaited Rudolf, five vast rooms, three bathrooms, an enormous kitchen, and a breathtaking view: spacious green parks, the St. Louis skyline, and a glistening, meandering ribbon in the landscape, the Mississippi.

"That will do," Rudolf sighed.

He did not appear at practice; it made us all uncertain and the mood plummeted. Was this the onset of a debacle? Seated on a bench concealed behind a rhododendron bush I saw Anton Gerritsen, wearing a sombre expression, in conversation with Libman, papers changed hands—contracts probably, who has to pay for what—and now and then I would hear Lilian raising her deep voice.

But Rudolf *was* present at the dress rehearsal, appearing out of the blue. Libman even managed a smile and everyone's degree of cheerfulness rose noticeably; Rudolf was welcomed like a prodigal son.

To protect them from the blinding sun, the dancers had all been issued a sort of Charlie Brown baseball cap, and a protective sheet spanned the orchestra where the musicians were in danger of being toasted; in short, all preventive measures had been taken for our well-being. Nonetheless, everyone seemed broken, the time difference and the long journey had clearly affected us; to cap it all, the surface of the stage was so hot that the linoleum layer had almost melted, giving some of the dancers blisters on the soles of their feet.

Fortunately, curtain up was far later than usual, so that everyone could withdraw to the hotel for a few hours to recover.

The only one who insisted on working on was our injured guest.

Nureyev had demanded to dance van Manen's *Four Schumann Pieces* at every performance, a bitter pill for Han Ebbelaar to swallow, as he would otherwise have shared the role with him. Rudolf thus danced three pieces each evening: besides *Schumann Pieces*, a pas de deux and either *Dark House* or *Faun*, a reckless burden, especially now that he was so fatigued and injured.

"Then don't dance the Schumann, I argued with him, "if you feel so bad. Han can do it. You have to keep going for another three weeks."

"Three weeks?" he grinned. "For me there is no stop. After this tour I go on for another three months."

No matter how hard I hoped for Ebbelaar, Rudolf did not give up one single ballet: "I need *Schumann Pieces* to get warm for my pas de deux." But he knew that was nonsense: I had often seen him begin an evening with a pas de deux.

I was at a loss to understand why he made things so tough for himself; St. Louis was not New York. I could imagine his wanting as many different works as possible to be seen in that city, but here . . . He was risking not only his own condition, but also the whole tour.

Lilian Libman supported me; we argued, pleaded, and implored, but he would not budge an inch, he bandaged his foot and in the evenings seemed in fine form.

And yet, when he pushed off with all his might for an enormous leap in *Le Corsaire* and landed on his vulnerable foot I knew that quite a number of people—Libman, Luigi, our dancers—cringed in anxiety.

The audience was oblivious and cheered; St. Louis was clearly grateful that such a famous dancer was visiting their city. Each evening they were there, all thirteen thousand of them! In one week, we had performed for as many people in St. Louis as in five months in Holland.

Rudolf led a domesticated life, spending most of his time in one part of the suite, while the rest remained empty, unused. We went to an exhibition in the city—there was an immense queue but, antisocial luxury, he was allowed straight through—and occasionally he would keep our dancers company in the swimming pool. But mostly he preferred to rest, reading and listening to music.

Franck was a calm but lively young man and, despite the impression he gave of a high school boy, he was quite able to fend for himself and unafraid of telling Rudolf what he thought and felt. His French rationale often clashed with Rudolf's impulsive and irrational behavior. He had become friends with the dancers and spent more time with them than with Rudolf, who sometimes inquired about him like a worried father—and a jealous lover.

After a performance, when Franck had dived into the swimming pool with some of the dancers, Rudolf amazed me by asking conspiratorially, "What do *you* make of Franck?"

I was afraid he suspected Franck, and not entirely without foundation I noticed, of marital infidelity: "What do you mean?"

"Don't you think it's strange he speaks Russian so well?"

"Not strange, but very clever. I wish I could."

"I don't trust him. He could be dropped on me by KGB. He could easily be spy."

Cheerful, coltish Franck a Russian spy? He came running in with soaking wet hair, threw his towel on the bed, and ate like a wolf. But Rudolf took the matter seriously and reverted to it time and again during the tour.

Wade and I had rented a car, in which Wade gave me driving lessons on the long and empty roads outside St. Louis. On a day off, we wanted to explore the Mississippi together, but Rudolf insisted we take him along. "But we're leaving early."

Naturally, we left far too late: Rudolf had massages, telephone calls, a meeting with Libman, and then Gerritsen. We were cursing: our Mississippi plan was going up in smoke.

After only a half hour, we ended up in a restaurant: Rudolf wanted tea. Afterward he slept in the shade of a tree and when he awoke he wanted something to eat. When he finally seemed ready to go and view the eagerly-awaited river—I had visions of Huck Finn and Tom Sawyer—he mumbled, "Too late, let's go back."

We had gone no farther than the leafy suburbs of St. Louis.

Lilian Libman and Anton Gerritsen had their hands full coping with Rudolf: he was moody, made demands and caused any number of complications, often behaving like a willful child.

But Lilian seemed a good match for him and not easily alarmed.

She was once assistant to the great impresario Sol Hurok and, for a long time, she had been private manager to Igor Stravinsky and regaled us with exciting stories about him.

She was equipped with a deep, rasping voice, like a cracked church bell, and her laugh—and fortunately she did laugh, albeit with a cynical undertone—could be heard from afar, floors below in the hotel or in the shrubbery around the theater, when she had arranged yet another emergency meeting.

When Rudolf heard her laugh, it sometimes seemed as if his hair stood on end; he would grab hold of his things and prepare himself for another argument. I began to suspect that he believed that causing problems went with his status.

The level of his performances was erratic. One evening, he would dance as might be expected of him but the following evening, if anything went wrong or was not to his liking, he might give up.

And yet, the stay in St. Louis was good for him to regain his strength. After the first two days, like everyone else, he was free during the day to relax and at the end of the week he was visibly recovered and his foot appeared to be healed.

Chicago was a greater challenge to Rudolf than St. Louis, for he had danced there before and had a reputation to maintain.

As beautiful as the city was—splendid skyscrapers with their art deco façades, imposing sculptures on the streets—the theater was at the other end of the scale, a bare congress hall, bereft of all atmosphere and doubly hard to accept after the lush paradise we had left behind us.

In a diary I kept around that time I wrote: "Our theater is a colossal hall, horrifyingly vast and lacking in atmosphere. It holds four thousand two hundred people but . . . we're not sold out. That's a blow for Rudolf: the audience is the barometer of his career."

"The only time I did not sell out was in Hamburg," he says. The press criticize him, too: "Radius and Aradi outdance Nureyev," someone writes. The following day I expect Rudolf to be like a thundercloud, but no, over the years he has become gentler, wiser.

And in the evening he dances better than ever, if only to prove something to the critics in Chicago. It really does me good to see him like that. Working with the legendary Nureyev is still an experience for us and a great education.

Even though, on occasion, there are performances when I would rather not watch him, in the end his devotion, discipline, and zest for work are a great example and no less a miracle. He is forty now, and work he certainly does, evening after evening.

Ten weeks ago I saw him after a performance in Vienna, looking as though he would not last till the following week, fatigued and drained as he was. In a faint voice he said, "I'm about to embark on a twelve-week period of nonstop performances."

My heart sank into my boots. Our tour was to follow those twelve weeks; what were we in for? Now, in Chicago, he says, "In ten weeks I gave ninety performances; the Royal Ballet gives eighty a year." There is triumph shining in his eyes.

He dances three ballets each evening, sometimes four; when there is a matinee that means six ballets a day. He is never too grudging—or too grand—to help dancers with their art and is always on hand with counsel or criticism: "What the fucking hell are you doing, looking like sour grapes? Do you *have* to dance or do you *want* to dance? This is end of ballet, *finale*, you understand: allegro! Smile, be happy," he hissed into the wings on one of the company's down days.

One of the newspapers commented on Rudolf's performance: "Time to stop." Words that drove him to distraction, and he cursed and swore and hurled his things about. It was hard to stay in the dressing room with him, but at the same time it seemed cowardly to leave him alone, as if I were deserting him. I knew, and he knew too, that somehow or other I could bring him round, just by sitting with him, saying nothing. So that is what I did.

I felt so terribly sorry for him, he looked so upset, in his sheer frustration and despair: so famous and so beloved and yet unable to charm the entire world.

He danced *Le Corsaire* with Maria Aradi in America as well and it was she, the unfortunate, who danced the matinee with him following the review. From the wings I observed how in a wholly self-destructive way he reduced the pas de deux to a parody, making faces, uttering noises, cursing, and meantime glancing all around him like one possessed to be sure everyone in the wings had seen what he was up to.

I could bear it no longer and vanished. Back in his dressing room he said curtly, "You had to leave? Was I too much for you?"

"Yes, what was I supposed to have watched?"

A short while later, all friendliness once again, he was dishing out autographs to eager, naive schoolgirls.

He was acutely aware of the orchestral accompaniment to the performances and would always comment, "What were the oboes doing tonight?" or "Was the maestro hungry, did he want to go to a pizzeria quickly?" even when they were ballets or passages he was not dancing in himself.

That amazed me, as I was often so absorbed in watching a performance that I was only aware of the music if it interfered or went completely haywire.

He often became embroiled in hefty discussions with our young conductor, Adam Gatehouse: "Tell Rudi that Janowitz is not singing in tune in that first song. He doesn't believe me, he is too obsessed by her."

Adam reluctantly admitted that he, too, thought she occasionally sang Strauss's notes off-key, but later he said equally reluctantly, "I didn't want to disagree with him, but actually I think he's got it wrong."

Sometimes, even now, when I listen to Janowitz's performance, I wonder, "Who was right in the end?"

We left Chicago at last; a city that had seemed bleak and chilly and, above all, bereft of nature. We had felt landlocked among towering domestic and commercial buildings, even though our hotel afforded a view over the wide expanse of Lake Michigan.

I traveled ahead with Rudolf, Lilian Libman, and Luigi; our "young KGB agent" Franck preferring to accompany the dancers. At the airport, we were treated like VIPs and ushered into a visitors' lounge by an official, who plied us with refreshments and guided us on board the airplane.

Rudolf looked like a vagrant, unshaven, clothes wrinkled, deep furrows of fatigue on his brow, and Luigi and I did not bear scrutiny either: some down-at-heel pop group. Lilian, however, was every inch the efficient businesswoman, immaculate hairstyle, Dior suit, attaché case, cigarette holder, and sunglasses.

As soon as the airplane began to move, Rudolf dived down with his head between his knees. Strange phenomenon, the man who spent so much of his life in the air was still afraid of flying.

On arrival in San Francisco, we were greeted by friends of Rudolf's; Luigi was ordered to take the luggage to our hotel and we were bundled into a car—I protested, exhausted—and within the hour we were on board a large yacht in San Francisco Bay: a surprise arranged by the friends.

Shattered, I lay on board, longing for a hotel room, peace and quiet, and a book. Rudolf laughed and made small talk, strolling around, sipping champagne. He was nothing short of a miracle.

We were to appear at a theater on the Berkeley campus of the University of California, a beautiful park of rolling hills and winding streams, and strewn with colossal trees. There were sloping grassy meadows as far as the eye could see, with students thronging there at midday and in the evenings, who would read, make music, or merely lounge around.

Every day a regular theater came to life on the squares between the college buildings, an American *Petrouchka* of singers and illusionists, orchestras, onlookers; wild horses could not keep me away and I spent every free moment between rehearsals and classes out there in the sun. On several days in a row, one boy would appear and throw himself into his dancing with abandon, not caring for money and oblivious to the world. He seemed to be there solely for himself and his motion, undulating, jerking, freezing, spinning, and gliding along to the obsessive throbbing of a steel band farther along.

If anything was dancing, I realized, then this was it. And that boy was a born dancer, if anyone was.

Strange world: people pay a hefty price to see a ballet star in a performance that may or may not be good and yet they walk right past this hypnotic and highly original performance, which does not cost a dime.

I plucked up courage and went up to the dancer.

"That was lovely, what you did."

"Yeah?"

"Would you like to see one of our performances? We're appearing here." I pointed toward the theater. He roared with laughter at the joke and pointed at the poster of Rudolf, larger than life.

"With *him,* are you dancing with him? You're kidding."

"I work there, I can take you along."

"To see Nureyev, the great Nureyev?" When it really dawned on him he nearly jumped a mile high.

Ivan Katz was his name, lean and agile, with a spiritual head and luminous eyes.

"I live in the park," he told me. "There's food enough to be found on campus."

In the theater he could hardly believe his eyes and grabbed hold of me: "This is unreal."

"Rudolf, this is a boy I met on the street, he's a wonderful dancer. I'd really like him to see you dance."

I planted Ivan on a chair in Rudolf's dressing room and went on stage, as our matinee was due to begin in a half hour. Before I left the room, I glanced round and my eye fell upon a familiar scene: Rudolf, applying his makeup, foxy eyes taking in his visitor from top to toe, and firing short questions or remarks at him now and then.

A few minutes later one of our dancers came up to me: "There's a weird boy in the hallway, a sort of vagabond. He's asking for you."

Clearly upset, Ivan stood looking forlorn in a corner on stage.

"What's the matter, what happened?"

"Awful, he began making passes at me straightaway. How can he *do* that?" In his own familiar, direct way, Rudolf had got down to business and inquired whether his new and unsuspecting visitor was in for an amorous adventure. "I don't even know the man. I admired him, but now . . ."

I persuaded Ivan to stay and watch the performance with me from the theater, but I could see the miracle had more or less faded for him.

"Try to forgive him," I tried. "He is spoiled, but when you know him better . . ."

After the performance, Rudolf stalked right past Ivan and me with a haughty expression and a significant smile playing about his mouth. Offended.

We went downtown; I treated Ivan to a substantial meal and talked him in to going to see the evening performance, as well.

"I can't look at him objectively anymore," he sighed. "He has spoiled a dream."

It was our final performance; the tour was over. A Russian lady, Armin Bali, and her daughter Jeanette treated their friend Rudolf and our whole company to a fantastic party. Ivan went along; it had taken all my powers of persuasion, but our friendship was too unreal to let it end just like that.

"If you don't go I won't go either," I blackmailed him. I wanted him to enjoy himself a little and hoped to meet someone at the party who might help him on his way.

"Fate has brought us together, let's accept that." And he went along.

It was a fantastic evening. All around me I saw radiant dancers, a perfect ending to an unforgettable chain of experiences.

For me, the highlight was Kyra Nijinsky, the daughter of Rudolf's illustrious forerunner, who was among the guests. A remarkable, highly strung woman; as quiet and introverted as her father must have been, so excited and garrulous was she. She was wearing a pathetic little sequined hat, large, gold shoes and her lipstick painted her teeth red, as well. Sixty-four she was, and undaunted.

Rudolf invited her to join our table—treating Ivan as though he were thin air—and fired a barrage of questions at her about her father.

"Kyrotchka, please show us how he danced."

And right there, in among the tables, off went the golden shoes, and tossing a laugh in Rudolf's direction that was somewhere between madness and ecstasy, she raised her heavy, rounded arms.

She could no longer dance, but took on the poses that were familiar from her father's photographs, flirting coquettishly and shuffling among the tables on her stockinged feet. At first, the onlooker felt like a voyeur, but as time went on that feeling gave way to poignancy, enchantment.

"Look," said Rudolf, "look at her hands and how she curves her arm around her head. Nijinsky must have done it just like that in *Spectre de la Rose*. And those shoulders, the way she moves them, so soft and supple."

She was sensual and seductive, tragic and fascinating.

"No, you're not going back to the park tonight." It was unthinkable, after a party so full of brotherhood, to take our leave of Ivan out there in the night on a street corner in San Francisco.

He shared the room with Wade and me, dived into the bath and, while we began packing, leaped about like a boisterous puppy on the beds. At last he was himself again, I thought.

The next morning I got up at the crack of dawn, ordered an enormous breakfast—Ivan must eat well, for as long as possible—and then left with him in a taxi to Kyra Nijinsky's house, eager to hear more about her father.

It turned out that she lived in some dreadful condo in a remote part of town and was waiting impatiently. The only photograph she had of her father was torn from a book: "Voilà Monsieur Nijinsky," she said triumphantly.

"My father was not mad." (Nijinsky suffered from schizophrenia for much of his life.) "He was wiser than most people, but interested in other things. He chose to live in another world."

She showed me her paintings: "Father in *Spectre*," "Father in *Giselle*," "Father in *Petrouchka*," and begged me to find a publisher for her autobiography: "No one in America is interested."

After about an hour I had to leave; time to continue our travels. I filmed Kyra, taking on her *Spectre*-pose at the top of the staircase, her arms waving and gesturing: "Au revoir, au revoir. Bon Voyage." A forlorn girl.

Sadness of time, bitterness of memory.

The company flew back to Holland, Rudolf traveled on to Los Angeles with Alexandra Radius for another week of *Corsaire* and Valerie Valentine, Wade and I left for Hawaii, where we were to give a number of lecture-demonstrations on dance in Holland. The tour burst apart in all directions like the seeds of a pomegranate. In my bag I had with me the book that Lilian gave me at the last moment, *The Last Years of Stravinsky*, memories of their collaboration that she had written following his death.

I gave Ivan my address. "Please, keep in touch," I said, because he hardly had an address to give me: Ivan Katz, Bench no. 12, Campus Park, Berkeley, California.

"Keep in touch with the Balis," I tried to impress upon him. "I've told them about you, they want to help you."

In the months that followed, I wrote to Jeanette several times because I would have liked Ivan to come to Holland to work on *Life*, a new Dutch National Ballet production. "Did you hear from him? Try to find him. Is there no way?" And so on. To no avail.

On our return home from Hawaii we learned that Olga de Haas, once such a poignant Giselle, had died of a chronic illness.

Sadness of time, memory tinged with bitterness.

12 ✑ Farha

"Schmuszeldorf, Knuszeldorf, all your shitty little one-horse town tours,"[1] was Rudolf's reaction to a series of appearances a German agent, Frau Melsine Grehfesmuhl, had arranged for us in 1978. "is there nothing better to offer?"

Maybe the series of performances ahead of us was not all that grand, but Frankfurt, Cologne, Stuttgart and Dusseldorf hardly deserved the label "Schmuszeldorf"—Ludwigshafen at most, but even then, although it was no large city, it did boast a marvelous theater and a really grateful audience.

Whatever Rudolf thought of the German performances, he apparently had "no better fish to fry" at the time and accepted the offer.

The tour took place during a severe winter and Rudolf gave the impression he was suffering from the bleak weather, coughing and spluttering and feeling bad, constantly swathed in shawls and cardigans, woolen berets, and voluminous overcoats down to the ground. He scarcely danced to the full in any rehearsal, something quite unusual for him; he was short-tempered and gave the impression of being exhausted, hardly surprising with a diary like his.

Often, his voice would be hoarse, fading to a feeble, colorless whisper, indicating only the essential with a single word, "tea," "shoes," "taxi," "towel."

During performances as well, it was clear he was not on form and—in contrast to America where the audiences adored him—in Germany there was also jeering audible during the applause, or the audience's response would be shorter and cooler than he was accustomed to. He scoffed at the tour organization, the quality of the German theaters, and the German press: "They tear me to pieces just because they are jealous. And what in the end do they have themselves? Their dancers can't even move on two feet."

1. "Clapville, Crapville . . . all your shitty little one-horse-town tours!" (Schmuszeldorf rhymed with Dusseldorf in Nureyev's original words.)

Difficult times.

On arrival in Stuttgart, he called me (the agent had housed him in a another, better hotel than our dancers) and asked me to come over as quickly as possible: "I have a fever, I need a doctor."

A bundle of misery, he lay there in his disheveled bed, hidden under a mound of blankets and sheets. Motioning weakly with his hand toward where his diary lay, he asked me to dial the number of one of his most devoted friends, Douce François in Paris.

"Douce, listen, I am ill. Can you come to Germany and fetch me?"

Fetch him, what did he mean? Besides two performances in Stuttgart, we still had Frankfurt ahead of us.

In reply to my anxious question he declared he could not possibly go on like that.

I felt his forehead, which was clammy and feverish, but he always drank such enormous amounts of hot tea that it was unclear what caused his overheating.

"Go to sleep, I'll get a doctor."

Back in our own hotel, a girl who worked in the cloakroom clamped on to me: Are you with the ballet company?" She had read that "*ein Art Wundertanzer*"[2] was appearing with us and she would do anything to see a legend like that, only the tickets, "*leider*,"[3] were too expensive and sold out anyway.

I promised to try to arrange something for her—the agent was not so generous with complimentary tickets—then went in search of Clint Farha, and explained that Nureyev was sick and might not appear.

There was an understudy present for all the ballets Rudolf danced, except for the *Corsaire* pas de deux he danced with Radius.

"If he doesn't dance I'm counting on you." I knew Clint only had to see a ballet once to know it and I also knew that if he applied himself, he could give something special to *Le Corsaire*.

"Me? Dance a pas de deux with Lex? Have you taken leave of your senses?"

Clint had the technique, the powerful leap and exotic feline quality for the piece, I was certain.

2. A miracle of dance.
3. "Unfortunately"

"But Rudolf will dance. Ha! just you wait and see," were Clint's last words in my direction.

That evening there was an icy wind and snow was falling. I had received word from Frau Grehfesmuhl saying that a doctor had indeed diagnosed Rudolf as having a fever, but that he would dance nevertheless. Was it the idea of the loss of thousands of Deutsche marks if Rudolf did not appear that lent wings to her powers of persuasion? Had she dangled threatening clauses in contracts before his eyes? One way or another, Nureyev was going to dance but, as though she were not entirely reassured, she urgently requested me to escort him to the theater in person. I would be his warden . . . a good moment to ask for an extra complimentary ticket for the fan in the hotel!

"It's all taken care of, wait for me at the corner of the theater," I had said to the cloakroom girl. Like a mole, swathed in layer upon layer, only a strip of his face visible, Rudolf appeared in the hotel lobby far too late. "We have to hurry, the performance is about to start." He put his arm through mine and together we dived into the snow storm; we still had to make a small detour to the front of the theater to pick up the girl.

"*Schnell, wir sind ziemlich spät.*"[4] We hurried through a small park to the artists' entrance. On the way, the girl on my one arm and Rudolf like some crooked, wheezing granny on the other, I said to her: "And this is Rudolf Nureyev, the dancer you so wanted to see."

She bent forward incredulously to get a good look at Rudolf, laughed out loud, and said, "*Ach Mensch, quatsch!*"[5] Rudolf, who had understood the gist of our conversation, exploded: "That bitch, get her out of my sight."

Fortunately her ticket was at the rear entrance; she vanished into the theater and I did not see her after that to hear her comments on the "*Wundertanzer.*"

He traveled on to Frankfurt with us but, later in the day, he let me know he would not dance anymore: it was foreseeable.

An emergency meeting was arranged for the theater manager, our agent, Anton Gerritsen, and myself.

"Performing," said the manager, "was futile"; after all, the audience had

4. "Hurry, we're rather late."
5. "Oh, bullshit, man!"

come especially for Nureyev. We'll have to give them their money back." He wanted to put up notices in the theater foyer instantly and have an announcement broadcast on the radio.

Only come for Nureyev?! As though the Dutch National Ballet were hot air! I felt an icy loathing come over me. Our agent was sweating—the loss of money—and groping around for a satisfactory solution.

"*Könnten wir nicht versuchen ein anderes mal mit Herrn Nureyev und Ihre Gruppe nach Frankfurt zuruckzukommen? Falls wir das dem Publikum versprechen durften.*"[6]

I had had quite enough of being wedged between the lady and gentleman and their business interests like a worthless white elephant.

"It's not our fault Rudolf is sick; that's *your* risk. I'll help you and agree to promise the audience to return, on condition that our performance tonight goes ahead as planned."

"That's quite pointless," said the manager. "As soon as the audience hears that Nureyev is not dancing, the theater will empty."

I agreed to speak to the audience in person and guaranteed no one would leave. (And if they do I'll make sure it'll be a long time before they forget it. I'll rub their noses in it, I thought to myself.)

Radius and Farha and the whole company were waiting anxiously in the dressing rooms; what was going to happen?

"We're dancing. Lex and Clint will appear in *Corsaire.*" Rehearsals began immediately.

That evening, in the vast and entirely sold-out theater, I appeared before the curtain.

"*Damen und Herren, Rudolf Nureyev wird heute Abend nicht auftreten können.*"[7] Agitation.

"You have come here to see a world-famous star, someone who's a success, from whom you know what to expect. There is a rising star within our company, someone in whom I have utter faith. The choice is yours: to leave because the old star will not be dancing, or to witness an adventure, be here

6. "Couldn't we ask you and your company to come back to Frankfurt with Mr. Nureyev some other time?" If we could promise that to the audience.
7. "Ladies and gentlemen, Rudolf Nureyev will be unable to appear this evening."

to herald the debut of a new, young star. I guarantee that you will not be disappointed."

Twenty people at the most stood up and left the theater, and the Dutch National Ballet danced. Clint was cheered fittingly, the agent and manager were positively radiant, and I was satisfied because I had been able to show everyone what the group was worth, even without the decoy bird.

That same evening Clint was promoted to principal in the company. Rudolf had already left; in the panic of the day I had not seen him again, or even taken leave of him.

As it turned out, "Crapville" would be Rudolf's final tour with us.

The events in Frankfurt had given me food for thought. I had begun to doubt long beforehand whether it was so healthy for the group to continue performing with Nureyev, or with guest dancers in general: were we not making ourselves too vulnerable that way?

When Rudolf appeared with us, he demanded all the important male roles in the repertoire, more or less at the cost of our own male soloists.

For our ballerinas, dancing with Rudolf was stimulating and a challenge; for the group it was a chance in a million to see a star at work close up, to be offered tours at the drop of a hat, and to be seen by large numbers of people in a large number of countries. His appearing mainly in work by Dutch choreographers was unique, too. It was like a seal of approval on the creativity of dance art in Holland. But for our male soloists, standing on the sideline, it became more and more difficult to accept.

The company developed splendidly; the lower ranks were full of interesting young talent, especially owing to Nureyev's presence. It was time we put that talent to good use and assured ourselves that the audience came to see *us*, not a temporary magnet.

I decided to decline Rudolf's offers of collaboration, for a number of years, at least. Our own dancers needed the opportunity to dance everything, everywhere we went. We had done it all before, and we had to do it again—only this time even better.

In *La Bayadère*, around 1959, with the Kirov—now Mariinsky—Ballet. Photographer unknown.

Nureyev, van Dantzig, and Toer van Schayk at home in Amsterdam, looking at pictures of the Diaghilev Ballet, 1968. Photo by Bob van Dantzig from the author's private collection.

Maude Lloyd and Nigel Gosling on their wedding day, 1932. Photographer unknown.

Wallace Potts and Nureyev, around 1969. Photo from the author's private collection.

Douce Francois and Nureyev, 1979, on a Greek/Turkish holiday. Photo from the author's private collection.

First rehearsal of *Monument for a Dead Boy*, with Yvonne Vendrig, 1968. Photo by Siegfried Regeling.

Rehearsing *Monument for a Dead Boy*. Toer van Schayk and Christine Anthony demonstrate parts of the choreography for Rudolf Nureyev and van Dantzig, 1968. Photo by Bob van Dantzig.

Rehearsing Balanchine's *Apollo*. *Left to right:* Hélène Pex, Sonja Marchiolli, Olga de Haas, and Rudolf Nureyev, 1969. Photo by Ger van Leeuwen.

Leningrad (now St. Petersburg), 1971. *Left to right:* Nureyev's niece Gouzel, his eldest sister, Rosa, and his mother, Farida. Still photo by Bob van Dantzig from a film; from the author's private collection.

In Rudolf's garden at Richmond, outside London. *Left to right:* Nureyev, van Dantzig, and impresario Sol Hurok discussing a tour of the United States, 1971. Photographer unknown.

Rehearsal of *Blown in a Gentle Wind*. Rudolf Nureyev *(center)* with Wade Walthall *(left)* and Clint Farha, 1975. Photo by Jorge Fatauros.

Wade Walthall at Nureyev's house in La Turbie, France, 1975. From the author's private collection.

Nureyev opening exhibition by Toer van Schayk *(left)* in Amsterdam. Sculptures in front of *The Rolling Stones*, 1969. Photographer unknown.

Monument for a Dead Boy. In performance in Amsterdam, 1968. Photo by Hans van der Busken.

Nureyev, van Dantzig, and Sonja Marchiolli *(left to right)* taking a bow after *Blown in a Gentle Wind*, Minskoff Theater, New York, 1978. Photo from the collection of Nancy Sifton.

Costume design for "the Boy" in *Monument for a Dead Boy* by Toer van Schayk.

Four Schumann Pieces by Hans van Manen. *Left to right:* Rudolf Nureyev, Alexandra Radius, Henny Jurriëns, Sonja Marchiolli, and Wade Walthall. Photo by Jorge Fatauros.

Aboard the *Aspasia*: Nureyev *(left)* and Toer van Schayk, 1978. From the author's private collection.

Greek/Turkish holiday. *Left to right:* Govert van der Linden, van Dantzig, Nureyev, and Robert Tracy, 1978. From the author's private collection.

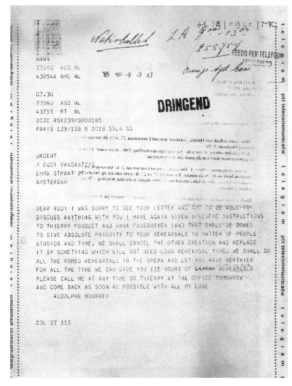

Telegram from Nureyev to Van Dantzig, concerning rehearsals for *'Sans armes, Citoyens!'* 1986.

Poster for the Paris Opera by Toer van Schayk, for *"Sans armes, Citoyens!"* 1987.

Maria Aradi *(left)*, Alexandra Radius, and Nureyev in *Afternoon of a Faun* by Toer van Schayk, 1978. Photo by Jorge Fatauros.

Le Corsaire pas de deux. Nureyev with Alexandra Radius, 1978. Photo by Jorge Fatauros.

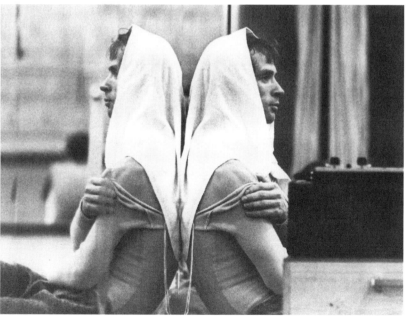

Nureyev taking a break during rehearsals in Amsterdam, 1978. Photo by Jorge Fatauros.

Rehearsal for *About a Dark House*. Nureyev with Sonja Marchiolli, 1978. Photo by Jorge Fatauros.

About a Dark House. Nureyev with Karin Schnabel *(right)* and Henny Jurriëns *(center)*, 1978. Photo by Jorge Fatauros.

The last role Rudolf Nureyev hoped to dance: *Man Caged in Water*. Here with Leon Pronk *(left)* and Gertjan Evenhuis as the "caged man." Performed in Amsterdam by the Dutch National Ballet, 1991. Photo by Bob van Dantzig.

About a Dark House. Left to right: Joanne Zimmerman, Nureyev, and Wade Walthall, 1978. Photo by Jorge Fatauros.

Rudolf rehearsing *Ropes of Time* with the Royal Ballet, London, 1970. Photographer unknown. Photo from the collection of Nancy Sifton.

Picture on the beach of the Lido, Venice, Italy, ca. 1928, a present from Boris Kochno. *Left to right:* Serge Lifar, Enrico Cecchetti, Serge Diaghilev, Mme. Cechetti, Lord Bernes, and Boris Kochno. Photographer unknown.

Vienna, State Opera Ballet: Nureyev and "three youngsters" in *Ulysses*, 1978. Photographer unknown. Copyright from Palffy, Vienna.

Nureyev in rehearsal, with Wade Walthall *(left)*, 1978. Photo by Jorge Fatauros.

Nureyev in *Faun* by Toer van Schayk, 1978. Photo by Dirk Buwalda.

Rudolf rehearsing *About a Dark House*, 1978. Photo by Kors van Bennekom.

Faun enjoying his "coffee break": Nureyev eating grapes during rehearsals for *Faun*, 1978. Photographer unknown. Photo from the collection of Nancy Sifton.

Nureyev and Van Dantzig *(right)* aboard the *Aspasia*, 1978. From the author's private collection.

Summer in Turkey, 1978. From the author's private collection.

Enjoying freedom, silence, and peace. At last. Photo by Rudi van Dantzig.

13 ⟳ *Ithaca*

The State Opera in Vienna had requested me to make a ballet to a piece of music, by Haubenstock-Ramati once again, called *Ulysses*, a work for which Gerhard Brunner, the director of the Viennese ballet, had great expectations.

He rang to warn me that the music was extremely difficult and might cause me many problems, but (as though to sugar the pill) Nureyev had agreed to dance the title role. It was not hard to guess whose idea the whole project had been.

Indeed, a few days later Rudolf telephoned me, inquiring when I had time to discuss the new project with him. I mentioned that I planned to spend my holiday in Greece that summer, with Toer and a friend of mine, Govert van der Linden.

"Wonderful," Rudolf answered. "I think I'm there at the same time."

That summer, Govert and I were first to leave; Toer would join us later. Govert was unfamiliar with Greece and we roamed the mainland together, alternating our sojourn in mountain hamlets with days on secluded, rocky beaches. When Toer arrived, we would try to find a few small, unspoiled islands.

Back in Athens, we went to the airport, where Rudolf and Toer were due to arrive on the same day, but on different flights. Rudolf turned up first, a bevy of photographers in his wake, even on holiday. It was a strange confrontation: Govert and I looked as though we had just emerged from the youth hostel, but Rudolf still appeared to be on tour, with as much luggage as ever, in as much of a hurry as ever, and with as much of a following.

Since we intended to stay at the airport until Toer's arrival, he called out to us, halfway into a waiting car, "Come to Piraeus, our yacht is in the harbour there," and someone thrust a slip of paper into my hand with the exact berth. "The name of the boat is *Aspasia*."

As soon as Toer had arrived, we bore him off to our hotel, Attalos, in our beloved Odos Athinas, a street in a workers' district full of stalls piled high with meats, fruits, and herbs; whores and their passing clientele, street vendors on the corners of narrow, derelict alleys, and the view of the Acropolis high above us.

"Must we?" asked Toer when I wanted to go to Piraeus straightaway. "We're on holiday." But I had promised to talk to Rudolf about *Ulysses* and had no idea how long he would be staying in Athens, so we jumped into the small train that led us through shabby neighborhoods with an oriental air on the way to Piraeus.

"But where is your luggage?" asked Rudolf, when we had discovered the yacht in the harbor area seething with people and cars, and walked up the gangplank. "You are joining us, no?"

It was the last thing to have occurred to me and, as far as I was concerned, it was never agreed upon; I had planned a trip with Govert and Toer and the idea of some sort of cruise did not fit in with that in the least.

He was amazed at our doubtful faces and said, hesitantly,: "Join us, for a while anyway; it will be fun."

He insisted on having his way and the prospect of seeing the Greek islands in relative peace, without having to traipse around on overfull boats, made us yield. After a short deliberation, we rushed back to Athens like lightning, this time in the car belonging to the owner of the ship, Perry Embirikos, to fetch our bags from the hotel and, a few hours later we saw the Piraeus quayside receding, small and hazy in the distance. Out on the open sea, the expansive, sprawling view of Athens, its hills full of dusty roofs and factory chimneys, hotels, temples, beaches, all in miniature and the surrounding mountains bathed in gentle ocher filled us with anticipation: we were footloose and fancy-free and bound on a glorious journey.

The *Aspasia* was a large yacht with every comfort; besides the crew of about eight, Rudolf's friend, the faithful Douce, and Robert Tracy, an American dancer and would-be writer were on board. With the three of us, we made up a commune of fourteen men and one woman who would have to get along together for a while. An adventure in itself . . .

Rudolf's reaction to Govert was distant; he greeted him rather haughtily and otherwise remained silent and aloof. Had I known we would be taking a trip with Rudolf I would certainly have prepared Govert better for the encounter.

A strange atmosphere hung in the air, a number of people not having met before; Rudolf was the linchpin around whom we were gathered. We were shown around the boat, cabins allotted, and the living quarters explored. The "master's cabin" a large, luxurious salon full of photos of Maria Callas, a frequent guest on the ship, had not, to my amazement, been annexed by Rudolf this time, but remained the domain of Embirikos himself.

When everything and everyone had more or less fallen into place, we gathered on deck and sat gazing as we sailed along the coastline, rocky islets, colossal tankers passing by, and seagulls keeping us company with their screeching. "That over there is Sounion," Embirikos pointed out to us. "After this we'll head out for the open sea."

I gazed longingly at the coastline bathed in the golden light of evening and realized what a landlubber I was.

For days on end we sailed around from island to island. For Govert, Toer, and me, it was an unprecedented way to reach unspoiled places; when we found a beautiful spot, a speed boat was lowered, provisions loaded on board, and we would head off for a deserted beach, nestled between towering cliffs, and there we would while away the hottest hours of the day, bathing or venturing a little way into the hills. Sometimes I took a small tape recorder along with me and Rudolf and I listened to the music for *Ulysses*, but, in spite of the title, the sounds were so discordant with the surroundings that I soon dropped that initiative. Rudolf did not protest.

"He looks like Maria Schell," Rudolf had said at table about Govert on one of the first evenings. "Where did you find him?" It sounded as though we were discussing a stray dog I had found on the street somewhere. It shocked me and Govert, already unsure of himself, stiffened.

I had gotten to know Govert in Amsterdam. He was a medical student and the theater world, fortunately, was unfamiliar to him. He reacted coolly and with reticence to Rudolf's extravaganzas, an attitude that irritated Rudolf in the extreme. As our voyage progressed, he began to ignore Govert increasingly and became irritated if he and I went off together when we alighted on an island. Mostly he referred to Govert in the third person, never addressing him directly: "What is the matter with Maria Schell? Does Schell not want to swim?"

Although he was young, a mere seventeen years old, Govert could take care of himself, ignoring not only Rudolf's barely concealed hostility, but Rudolf himself, a state of affairs which, in the fairly small space at our disposal, became more and more tense as time went on.

"Talk to him, ask him about his work, then he'll thaw out a bit," I tried to urge Govert, but he merely became more grimly determined in his manner. In my heart, I felt he was right and admired his independence.

Fortunately, he made friends with Robert Tracy, who was nearer his age. When the ship dropped anchor in a small harbor in the evenings, they would hire mopeds and, while we went in search of the sights or a restaurant, they would streak off like wild men around the hills on the island.

One evening I brought up the matter with Rudolf, saying that it disturbed me and I found it really unpleasant for Govert and for him that they continued to ignore one another, day in, day out.

"Unpleasant? For me?" he feigned, somewhat offended. Then he grinned: "I recognize the situation."

He told me of a trip he had taken on Onassis's yacht while Callas was on board as well. "She absolutely didn't like me and ignored me. So I ignored her, too."

At table she had said to Onassis, pointing at Rudolf, "Why does he look at me like that the whole time?"

Upon which Rudolf hit the ball back: "Because she happens to sit opposite me and she somehow seems familiar to me."

Occasionally, to escape the monotony of existence on board, we would ramble through the small towns or around the countryside. On one of the islands we were strolling along the beach; it was late in the evening, the surf drew glistening lines in the dark, and here and there were pools of moonlight. Suddenly, there was a shadowy figure crawling awkwardly over the sand on his arms. I started and shrank backward in a vehement reaction: "Let's go back." It was a badly misshapen man, probably seeking silence and darkness to be by the sea undisturbed and not to be gaped at.

Rudolf responded sharply to my reaction. "Is *that* your human interest, you shy away when someone looks a bit different?" he chided me. "I thought that was against your philosophy. In a situation like this your own emotions are of no importance."

In the dark, I saw only the look in his eyes, searching and critical, as though he had weighed me and found me wanting. I was ashamed; he was right.

The daily swimming, sunbathing, and lazing about did Rudolf visible good. He seemed relaxed and apart from the repressed friction with Govert was in a fine mood. In the morning, he dutifully—and with some exaggeration—did his barre on board the gently swaying ship and we spoke—more and more sporadically—about the Viennese project.

Each evening we would interrupt our reading, sleeping and writing and all gather at the bow to gaze at the contours of yet another new island looming ahead. After that the bell rang and we would gather round the table for yet another meal.

"If we have watermelon for dessert again, I'll scream," Govert whispered in my ear. I, too, began to tire of the gourmet meals and yearned for a simple inn.

We went on a long hike across Santorini, climbing the hundreds of steps to the village and then, with the entire company, roamed the hills from coast to coast. Everywhere, even in the tiniest hamlets, someone would recognize Rudolf. He seldom got any real peace, for there was always a mother who sent her small daughter for an autograph, or a tourist angling to take a photograph of—or worse *with*—him.

The journey back was unforgettable, in a small fishing-boat gaily painted in blue, we sailed from the farthest tip of the island back to the harbor where the *Aspasia* was moored.

The heat and deathly calm of night were stifling. The boy at the helm sang Greek melodies and somewhere in the dark, high on the edge of the craterlike wall of rock, the lights of a faraway village were twinkling. Now and then, the water would splash against the bow, a stray insect would zoom by, and a long way off a dog barked in vain for the moon.

Lying on my back, I saw a sky laden with stars, glowing, glistening, or draped in soft gray veils. Not a soul spoke, an occasional whispered word at the most, we were languid from our long walk in the scorching sun and overawed by the benign calm and the beauty all around.

Something that should never end, a vessel sailing on forever, where it took us of no concern.

"*Is dies etwa der Tod?*"[1]

In Turkey, the trip seemed to acquire an extra dimension for Rudolf; at small ports he showed us around down tiny, shabby alleyways and would suddenly halt and sniff the air with pleasure: "This smells like home, I feel that this is where I come from. My roots are here."

He told us what it meant to him to be a Tatar, to have a Muslim background: "I smell it in the air, even in the dirt, in the rubbish. The food here is better than anything I know, it heals me."

He purchased jangling ornaments, chains, bracelets, mounds of kelims, headcloths, and burnouses which he donned in the evenings on board, a warm-blooded hero from *A Thousand and One Nights*. On occasion he was wont to lure those heroes on board too: swarthy, Gypsy-like figures with war-like mustaches and tremendous muscles: one—or more—of the seven robbers, gathered round an Ali Baba yearning for adventure.

And yet, we began to tire of cruise life, being together on board for days on end, breakfasting together, having lunch, dining, days overflowing with champagne and sophisticated feasts that had everything to do with Paris and nothing with Greece: I yearned for the rough Greek peasant life, simple fare in taverns lit only by a bare and poverty-stricken bulb hanging from the ceiling, where we would fade into the murmur of the villagers around us.

"We want to go our own way," I managed to say to Rudolf one evening. "We have to continue our own lives."

He exploded in irritation and protested, considered it bad-mannered of us to withdraw in the middle of the trip. Even though I pointed out that this holiday had never been agreed upon, that our presence was to have been a temporary one, it made no difference.

Two evenings later we found ourselves sitting on the deck of a fishing boat, on our way back to Greece, and that same night we slept under the scaffolding of an unfinished house, in among the sacks of cement and piles of wood. It took some acclimatization but we were free once more.

1. "Could this be death somehow?"

14 ⌒ *Salo*

I had begun work in Vienna before Rudolf arrived there. The casting had to be worked out—*Ulysses* was to be a piece for some forty dancers—and I wanted to become familiar with the company and the theater's way of working beforehand.

The Viennese Opera: throughout the world, its name has the sound of radiance, imagination and color. Nothing could have been farther from the truth. The State Opera turned out to be an inflexible, colorless organization, housed in a somber building with an oppressive atmosphere. Perhaps it was me, my state of mind at that time, for, to be honest, I found the whole of Vienna oppressive.

I was struggling with an extremely demanding score and foresaw a new, difficult period of work with Rudolf, a period due to last for at least two months.

The Vienna State Opera Ballet was housed on the top floor of the building, with long, dark corridors lit only by one tiny lamp; there were somber cubbyholes for offices and the studios, too, had only emergency lighting. As in Germany, the dancers' working hours were divided into two blocks, one in the morning, from ten until one in the afternoon, and then in the evening from seven until ten. It was a working schedule I found a great hindrance, because if there were an evening performance then an important rehearsal block was simply abandoned. And, although the Vienna State Opera Ballet gave but a few performances, it danced all the more frequently in the operas.

The music for *Ulysses* was composed of strange, discordant, and scarcely appealing sounds, lasting for some forty-five minutes. I had to dig deep into my imagination to come to terms with it.

In my version of the myth, Ulysses was still the Greek hero, but strayed into a modern world; he was roaming around on his way home to Ithaca past airports, mythological spots full of tourists, and found Penelope as Molly Bloom,[1] vacuuming her house and meddlesomely tolerating the bevy of male tenants—I called them "*Teppichfresser*"[2] for their aggressive-hysterical manner.

When Ulysses finally returns to the spouse he had feared dead, on his beloved island, the spot he had yearned for desperately for all those years, Ithaca has become an urbanized, over-populated island, on which he can barely grasp a foothold, suspended as he is half over the water.

On arrival, Rudolf appeared to be plunged into a deep depression, I was shocked by his cynicism (and I was used to a great deal from him) and his complete lack of energy; he seemed mentally drained. My attempts to cheer him up were to no avail; I had more the impression he had been sentenced to two months' imprisonment than that he was ready to embark on a new venture. Since I found the atmosphere in Vienna so oppressive, I tended to blame Rudolf's mood on the same problem, but he denied that the city had anything to do with it.

"It's not easy being a hero all the time," he sighed by way of explanation in his hotel room.

Rudolf had three partners in the new ballet: the nymph Nausicaa, the goddess Circe, and Penelope, the wife he imagined he had lost. The three personified the images of the future, resignation, and disillusionment, respectively.

Pas de deux play a prominent role in dance, revealing facets of the state of mind between two people and the emotional color of their relationship. The fusion of two or more figures affords potential for intriguing, dynamic forms: emotions are echoed, reflect one another or merge from double into single forms; partners fold into a seemingly infinite sequence of sculptural variations, curved around one another, split up, close in, uplifted or oppressed.

I enjoyed exploring this material, but Rudolf did not care for partnering; he was a soloist first and foremost and wished to be confronted with others as

1. Molly Bloom, leading lady in James Joyce's novel *Ulysses*.
2. "Carpet-eaters"—impatient, would-be suitors wearing the carpets thin as they pace up and down.

little as possible, wanting no concern with the—dance-technical—problems and shortcomings of his partners. Those problems might then indirectly become his own and, besides, they required time and energy, needing painstaking repetition, the search for solutions and of attempts—sometimes in vain—for which he appeared to have no patience.

In my ballet version, Ulysses was a man wending his way home, all the way back to square one, and as in the previous work I created for Rudolf, he was in action from beginning to end, for a full three-quarters of an hour. This meant he would be the central figure in nearly every scene, with barely a moment to recover in the wings. Seeing Rudolf's condition, I doubted whether I had found the right concept: a forty-five-minute dance marathon would be too much for him. And, besides, I had again committed myself to him—or his presence—in almost all the rehearsals.

The starting times of the Vienna company deviated from those in most others, with warm-up starting at nine in the morning and rehearsals at a quarter past ten. That was far too early for Rudolf, who usually appeared in the building only around half-past ten, upon which, right in the middle of my rehearsals and, agonizingly slowly, he would begin his barre exercises.

His late arrival did not cause any problems for the first two weeks, as I had more than enough material to work out and arrange with the groups. Toward the time when Rudolf had finally warmed up, I would slot him into a scene like the final piece in a puzzle; a roundabout way of doing things and often very irritating for the corps de ballet, but there was no other option. Rudolf's manner of working was familiar to the Viennese anyway and, happily, there was still an air of newness about the venture, so the mood among the dancers was still one of goodwill and forgiveness.

My apartment was near the theater where Mozart's *Magic Flute* had had its premiere and Rudolf was staying at the Sacher Hotel, in rooms directly opposite the theater's ballet studios. Sometimes, when our activities were already in full swing, and Haubenstock-Ramati's cacophonies filled the air, I would see his pale, tousled head appear at the hotel windows across the road, casting a gloomy eye over "*Wien, Wien, nur du allein.*"[3]

---

3. "Vienna, Vienna, you alone." "Song of Praise" by Rudolf von Sieczyniski describing Vienna as the city of his dreams.

The moment had come when I needed Rudolf immediately after class; his absence now began to mean a tremendous loss of time and an exodus for the dancers. "*Machen Sie eine kurze Pause bis Rudolf fertig ist.*"[4]

I implored him to manage to arrive on time one way or another, because otherwise the work would stagnate. I asked the company secretary to call the Sacher at half past nine ("*Uns ist unbedingt gesagt Herrn Nureyev nicht zu stören*")[5] and sometimes, in sheer desperation, I would throw open the studio windows and yell across the street, "Rudolf, rehearsal!"

But the curtains at his window would remain drawn.

Outside the studio we saw a fair amount of one another. We were both alone in a strange city (for him, I realized, every city save the distant Ufa was strange), but time was limited, as he rested in the afternoon hours while I sweated on with *Ulysses*. After evening rehearsals, he would insist I accompany him to a restaurant. Often, all I longed for was to withdraw after yet another enervating day, but he would not hear of it.

"It's alright for you," I said. "If need be, you'll arrive late again tomorrow. I can't afford to."

But it was amazing how amiable and open he was in those hours, seeming to understand my creative dilemmas, how I was wrestling with the music, the large number of dancers, the laborious arrangements at the Opera which caused me to suffer from a constant lack of time, and he even seemed to understand my displeasure at his own early-morning whims. After every talk I thought, "Tomorrow I'll see a difference in him during rehearsals," but when day dawned he would be as obstinate as ever.

It remained difficult. The dancers were ready to work after class, but Rudolf, who did eventually appear at rehearsals a little earlier, was often so tired and apathetic and bad-tempered to boot, that all the work achieved in the studio seemed a waste of time. It was irritating for the dancers, but for me it was sheer torment: I was burning to see how the work was coming along and whether what I had assembled thus far had any value at all. I was uncertain enough as it was.

---

4. "Take a short break until Rudolf is ready."
5. "We have received strict instructions not to disturb Mr. Nureyev."

But Rudolf marked out most passages with a poker face, giving the impression that what I had made did not interest him in the least—fatal when, unsure of yourself in the first place, you have to conduct a rehearsal.

"I'll just have to grin and bear it," I thought to myself, "wear blinkers, ignore his whims and not let any of it get to me. The main thing is that the piece should be more or less complete. I can always change what I don't like later."

By the evening rehearsals, he was usually in a far better mood and his physical condition was up to the mark, as if he finally came to life: he was energetic, enterprising, and cheerful. The frustrating part, though, was that most of the company were less motivated in the evenings—surely in part owing to the music: being immersed in that noise twice a day meant enhancing my powers of persuasion to involve them again. And, besides all that, I got the impression that some of the male dancers had dined substantially during the lengthy lunch break, had a few drinks as well, and would now like nothing better than to sleep it off.

To regain lost time, Rudolf again requested private weekend sessions, hours alone in the deserted studios. That may have given him satisfaction, but for me it meant I was hardly ever free of the project or able to keep a distance from it all.

In order to go on working undisturbed in Rudolf's absence, I had finally taken on an understudy again, a pleasant young soloist, although not an awesome dancer, no competition for Rudolf in any way at all.

My decision brought relief; Ludwig Musil worked hard and well, so that even the several pas de deux that went so awkwardly with Rudolf soon turned out well.

"Impossible," he would say, on seeing a newly formed piece danced by Ludwig. "I can't do that, I am too tired. Can you change?"

"But if Ludwig can do it?" It was an unfair ruse, because it would pique his pride to admit that his understudy was better than he was, and so he applied himself once again.

It was painful to see how his technique had deteriorated. He no longer stretched his knees in leaps and, when landing, would slam down on the floor, his face betraying considerable effort. Sometimes he would ask me anxiously whether I had corrections for him but, if I indicated anything specific, he would react in irritation: "What do you suppose, that I am eighteen?"

"No, but that's exactly why you must start working differently and be more careful with your body." But it seemed to be too late; he was like a rocket launched, not to be halted in his lethal flight.

When he applied himself, however, he still managed it all and without our wasting too much time. That whole tiring process of repeated giving up, starting again, discussion and occasionally even sabotage was quite unnecessary. If he had put his all into it, the choreography would have been completed in half the time.

In Vienna he had acquired a penchant for trout and, every afternoon, he would take himself off to the Imperial Hotel to partake of his favorite dish. Around lunchtime the restaurant was usually peopled by a coven of dignified, elderly ladies adorned with bonnets and jewels, who would sit spying on Rudolf and discussing him, as if in a scene from *Macbeth*.

"Doesn't it bother you that people are always staring?" I asked him. By way of an answer he swung round like an adder hissing in the direction of the tables where the "witches" were spooning their gateaux. He made faces, stretching his mouth open wide with both hands and waggling his tongue in lightning fashion like a whore in a Fellini film. The court was in great dismay.

No, being a hero was not easy.

In the evenings—although usually it was night—and on Rudolf's initiative, we strolled through the town after dinner; it was as though he were afraid of returning to his hotel. He resembled some boyar, clad in voluminous overcoats and large fur hats. It had grown bitterly cold, the sidewalks were slippery, snow had fallen, and there was seldom a passerby. We would amble from square to sqare, with him leaning on me heavily.

"I don't know what it is, I sometimes feel desperate. You know, I just want to jump out of the window, to get it all over with." It was no game, he meant every word and it made me fearful and somber.

What was wrong with him, he who appeared to have the whole world in his hands? What was it that was tormenting him?

The lonesome beings we encountered on the street at night, a corpulent sergeant or a couple of unsavory looking drunkards, he would observe closely.

"How nice," he mumbled, as though of an appetizing dish. "Would be good to take to my room." On occasion he would pause for a moment, gaze after them, whistle.

I was astounded at his annihilism; had he lost every iota of discernment, had he become so lonely that each passing male held the promise of attractive company for him?

Naturally, we went to the theater, too, and the Vienna Opera as well. *Lucia di Lammermoor*, so exquisitely rendered by Edita Gruberova, was unforgettable for me, but Rudolf wanted me to accompany him to Wagner's *Lohengrin* as well, music which held no appeal for me at all in my difficult Haubenstock-Ramati process.

Our box was directly above the orchestra and Rudolf hardly glanced at the stage, hanging forward over the rail to observe the conductor, Karl Böhm, instead.

Böhm was already very advanced in years. He appeared to have been suspended in some kind of standard and there, leaning over backwards, he conducted with minute and barely visible gestures. I wondered what purpose he could possibly serve for the orchestra.

When the performance was over, Rudolf seemed quite enchanted by what he had heard and insisted on speaking to Böhm.

"*Was wünschen Sie von mir, junger Mann?*"[6] It was a shock to see Böhm at close range; he seemed like one no longer in the land of the living, fragile, gray, and speaking as though his spirit were already sojourning elsewhere.

"What would you advise me if I wanted to become a conductor?" Never before had I heard Rudolf express the wish to become a conductor.

Böhm gave a glimmer of a smile and murmured that he would be pleased to speak to Rudolf another time. "*Aber Sie sollen tanzen, junger Mann, nur tanzen.*"[7]

"That's what I really want, to conduct," said Rudolf. "Music is the most fabulous thing there is, much better than dancing." At the time, I wondered whether it was an opportunist remark, knowing his dance career was coming to an end (but he would dance for at least another ten years!).

6. "What do you want from me, young man?"
7. "But you should dance, young man, only dance."

I was mistaken; his interest in music, in studying the scores of great composers, Bach especially, cropped up time and again in conversation: without doubt, his musical wish was in earnest.

A few days later, Böhm did indeed grant him an audience and Rudolf was as elated as a child about it. Later, somewhat crestfallen, he acquainted me with the outcome.

"He told me I should study with one teacher for at least one year. It means that I have to give up everything and stay in one place all the time. I wonder if I am able to stand that." The thought of staying in *one* place for a year, was that so terrifying to him? Was he continually on the run from himself?

In his hotel room, he showed me a collection of old coins from the time of Rudolf the Second and Rudolf of Austria, laying them out before me lovingly and examining them carefully, one by one.

"I bought them for you," he said, "as a present after *Ulysses.*" Again, he pondered the solid, circular objects, weighing them in his hand. "But I like them so much, I think I'll keep them for myself. So better take a good look at them."

That was typical of Rudolf, an utter, quite unnecessary and almost hurtful honesty.

"I'll get you some Mozart and your Gruberova, instead."

The coins would doubtless vanish beneath the enormous piles of curios he carted around with him to his various houses and rarely set eyes on afterward.

"Shall we run away for a few days?" he asked me during a public holiday break. "What about Berlin?"

I would far rather have gone to Warsaw, Prague, or Budapest, but that was out of the question on his passport in those days, and I had an idea those cities did not offer what Rudolf was looking for, either.

"Would you mind if I didn't go with you?" But he did mind, and so off we went.

On arrival in Berlin, he immediately wanted to go to Pasolini's *Salo, or the 120 days of Sodom*, a film I found hard to swallow and this was probably not made easier by the German dubbing, either. In the sounds of the Italian original, the scale of perversity and horrors might have retained some sense of mockery and distance, but the German merely seemed to rub our noses in the excrement.

After *Salo*, Rudolf was keen we should visit a sauna: "They seem to be very exciting in Berlin." But with the aftertaste of Pasolini that seemed to me far from pleasurable.

I saw Rudolf disappear cheerfully into the steaming masses and return again an hour or so later: "Well?" What I had seen had reminded me of Fellini's *Satyricon*: hazy tableaux with numerous naked limbs looming out of the murky gloom and, beyond, a maze of darkened hollows, where strange beings seemed to have withdrawn, gargoyle shapes with glistening eyes, grimacing, grinning mouths, slithering away into the cracks and grooves like lizards.

But Rudolf's experiences were different: "They have such nice skins, the Germans. Like silk. Do you think it is because they eat so many potatoes?"

"It's probably all that beer," I suggested.

During the Viennese period, he imparted more about his early life in Russia, his father with whom he went hunting or fishing as a small boy, the dog they had had of which he had been so fond, the poverty at home—"But it was nice, it did not matter"—his early dancing lessons in Ufa, and about the feeling that he was never really accepted anywhere, that he had always been a loner but also that he had had that solitary existence forced upon him.

"I had that feeling all my life. People were jealous of me because they thought I knew what I wanted. But I wasn't so sure about what I wanted, I only knew I didn't want to lose."

In Leningrad, the dancers thought him arrogant because he hardly said a word to his colleagues. "But I was simply too damned insecure. I listened to them and learned that way."

"I learned what *not* to say and how *not* to behave," he added with sarcasm, a moment later.

His teacher, Alexander Pushkin, tried to engineer a liaison between the young ballerina Gabriela Komleva and his promising pupil: "We went out on Sundays, we sat under a tree. She badly wanted me to take action but I didn't know what to do, I was just intimidated and scared as hell. I just knew how to work, I worked and worked, I was in the studio working until I could not speak from exhaustion and fell down."

Was he intimidated by Komleva because a young woman appeared farther in her sexual development than he was himself, or because he felt he was a provincial boy?

"I had no idea about homosexuality at that time, it never entered my head. I discovered things in East Germany, when we gave guest performances in Berlin. I met a very gentle boy in the school there, good-looking too. He took me around the city and showed me many interesting things. I was very grateful, and I was also impressed. For me, Germany was already more or less the West, even if it was the East part. At the end we kissed, but I don't remember who took the initiative."

He threw me a mocking glance. "Don't look so worried, it must all sound familiar to you. By the way, you know that boy from East Germany very well; he is a teacher in your company now."

Nureyev dealt with his homosexuality in quite an emancipated way, an emancipation free of coquettishness or pamphleteering, merely assuming it was the most ordinary thing in the world. It was scarcely a matter for discussion with him—why discuss something so obvious? He would walk into a shop selling male pin-up magazines with the same ease as he would remark to a French minister at an awesomely grand banquet on how much he should like to take the waiter home with him: "Such a delicious piece of meat."

When I heard him in that depressing Viennese period, talking so passionately about his parents, his sisters, the snowy forests of Ufa, his dog and his first impressions of Leningrad and the Kirov Ballet ("The culture there was unsurpassed, they had everything worked out in such detail"), I could not avoid the impression that he was suffering, understandably, from homesickness.

"Why don't you try to get permission to go home. I can feel that you miss your family, your friends, the memories of your youth."

Incensed, he retorted, "Don't put things in my mind that are not mine, these are *your* ideas. I am perfectly happy here. I don't miss anybody or anything. Life here has given me everything I want, all possibilities."

In the rehearsals the following day, he made a deeply frustrated, embittered, and disillusioned impression.

During the premiere, I saw Ulysses return home, staring at the transformed Penelope and the Ithaca that was no longer *his* Ithaca. And I remember that

I then regretted that the dog Argos, the only one to recognize Ulysses on his homecoming, was missing from the ballet.

The next morning I tore back hell-for-leather to Holland, *my* Ithaca, before I might find that that had changed too.

Rudolf was to remain in Vienna for another two weeks, to complete the series. I did not envy him.

15   Bourgeois Gentilhomme

Over the following four years I saw Rudolf only sporadically; most of our contact was by telephone. It was he who rang and he who spoke; I would listen and say, "Oh" and "Yes?" and sometimes "Good," while he regaled me with stories of his travels, contracts, projects, and the latest real-estate acquisitions. Talking to him on the phone was not easy for me.

He had bought a large ranch near Washington and an apartment in New York, a city where he loved appearing, and invited me to come and advise him on "something that is right up your alley, a movie about Nijinsky."

I left for New York with a leaden, sinking feeling, because my first task would be to tell Rudolf that his guest appearances with the Dutch National Ballet, something upon which he was always insisting, were to become a thing of the past.

I had broached the matter with him more than once, but he waved it aside grumpily, as though it were a whim of mine that would eventually pass. However, for a number of reasons, I knew for certain I would not ask Rudolf to appear as guest soloist with our company anymore.

The first reason was that his dancing had deteriorated to such an extent that I no longer felt I could defend precisely why Nureyev should appear as guest soloist with the group, except for selfish reasons: the tours and publicity for the company.

Besides that, I considered the sums of money that went with such guest appearances exorbitant and they stuck in my gizzard. I felt that the relationship between superstars and their super salaries had become inflated beyond all proportion in the artistic world and I had no wish to go along with that. On top of this, and perhaps most vital of all, I believed we could develop best if we did so on our own. I had come across the dovecote system of guest soloists flying in and out in New York, London, and Paris and I loathed it; it gave rise to a system of states within states, and very egocentric and materialistic states at that.

Rudolf's new apartment in the Dakota, on Central Park West, was more than impressive. It might still resemble a warehouse—the many vast rooms chock-ablock with half-unpacked furniture, statues, paintings, musical instruments, and enormous rolls of ancient leather wallcovering from China strewn around the place—but I could see what he had in mind and it was quite something.

Our first talk was quite something, as well; my painful announcement lay leaden in my heart and I wanted to get it off my chest right away.

"So, you mean you sacked me," he sneered. "Am I too old, or what?"

I explained all aspects of the problem to him, pointing out that it could hardly make much difference to him whether Holland wanted him or not as, after all, the rest of the world was at his feet.

"You are just plain provincial."

"Yes, I know I am," I agreed, adding, "Thank God," for I was often nauseated by the exclusive, pretentious, and like-knows-like small world that was founded on protectionism.

"I think I'd better try to find a hotel," I remarked at the end of our conversation, almost positive I had brought our friendship to an end. But yet again I found I had underestimated him as a person. He grinned a trifle sheepishly: "Of course not, you stay here."

Did he agree with me, deep down in his heart? After all, where dancing was concerned he was a purist and professionalism itself.

The following day he pushed a thick pile of paper across the breakfast table at me: "Read this, it is script for Nijinsky film. I hate it."

Rudolf as Nijinksy? It was mind-boggling.

Nijinsky was a myth and a mystery in the world of ballet, a dancer around whom legends had been woven. His contemporaries saw him as one of the wonders of the world, a dancer who arose from the earth with ease, like a bird, an artist who did not interpret the role he was dancing, but became one with it. He brought phenomenal technique and a wondrous expressive quality to a role, seeming to transform his identity by magic from one ballet to the next.

Nijinsky retained his mystique because only stories about him had survived, eye-witness accounts; not even the briefest fragment had been captured on film.

Maybe Rudolf had had a few of his qualities when he was younger, the technique, for example, or the agility maybe. But beyond that, they seemed to me two extremes, Nijinsky, utterly intuitive, losing himself, oblivious in his dancing, accountable to nothing and no one; Nureyev, aware of himself and his surroundings down to the last detail, calculating, lord and master on stage (and off) but harnessed tightly into classical technique.

Nijinsky, it is said, was an exceedingly modest, uncertain, and reticent man with a mystic leaning; Rudolf was the opposite in every respect.

During the talk we had with the film's scriptwriter later that day, it suddenly dawned on me that, without my knowledge, Rudolf had suggested I should create a choreography for the film for *Jeux*—Nijinsky's second choreography, which was later lost.

"Tell him your ideas about *Jeux*, and how it should fit in the film." It was easy for Rudolf to talk; for me it was rather a shock.

I suggested that it might be interesting to incorporate Diaghilev's original idea, in which he had *Jeux* danced by three men, intended to represent Diaghilev and two of his young protégés—a ball game in which envy, ambition, protectionism, and power games formed the basis. (Nijinsky had finally made it into a flirt between two women and a man on a tennis court.)

But the mere hint of a possible relationship between men was not appreciated, making the film too problematic and distracting, in the eyes of the scriptwriter.

Rudolf supported my idea and kept putting forward arguments to sustain it, at least as a suggestion in the script; perhaps the producer would see something in it, but, scrutinizing the man, I already knew the answer.

The film was never discussed again, but shortly afterward, a film about Nijinsky and Diaghilev was launched, with an unknown dancer in the main role. Whether or not it was the same project was unclear.

"Balanchine is doing a ballet for me," he confided in me, glowing with happiness and pride, "finally."

Nureyev had danced choreographies by the great choreographer with a number of companies in the world, but never with the New York City Ballet, Balanchine's own company.

Over the years, Rudolf had come to look upon Balanchine as a father, or an older brother, with whom he tried to curry favor. Like Nureyev and Baryshnikov, Balanchine, came from the Petersburg school and, with his abundance of genial choreographies, had influenced Western dance greatly, as had his two younger fellow countrymen in another way.

"He is doing *Le Bourgeois Gentilhomme* for me. It will be very exciting."

I asked him when the premiere would be, since I wanted to come back and see some performances by Balanchine's company.

"But it will not be for his company; it is with the New York City Opera," he admitted, adding hastily, "I am sure he'll let me do it with his company too, if it is a success."

In the studio I saw a tableau unfolding between two men who seemed to have little to say to one another. The conversation was occasionally in English, but far more often in Russian and from their tone I deduced they were treating each other politely but heeding a certain distance: the venerable, elderly teacher and his youthful student.

Balanchine seemed to me to be absent-minded and uninspired that day; he tried out some steps and asked Rudolf, "How would you do this?" "Does that feel right to you?" or "Don't make this too complicated, it should be simple, just a little joke, a little nothing," then nosing around like a mouse and coming up with a few weird little moves.

Rudolf copied the master, but the essence was gone; all that seemed natural and obvious by Balanchine gained an unnatural emphasis when Rudolf tried it out.

Frighteningly little else happened at all. It saddened me. Was this Rudolf's great dream?

"Show me what we did yesterday, or are you tired?" But the rehearsal had begun not an hour earlier.

"Ah," Balanchine leaned on the piano and sighed, "maybe this is not good idea," and he began again.

Suddenly he stood up: "I have rehearsal at other side. Susie will take over." And he disappeared, leaving the rehearsal to the ballet mistress, Susan Hendl.

Rudolf took daily classes at the School of American Ballet, which was linked to Balanchine's company.

Like many dancers, Rudolf also had his favorite teachers, the dancers' chosen ones, who might drift in and out of favor from one moment to the next: one day teacher X was in fashion and *his* studio was full, and teacher Y the next.

Stanley Williams was a Dane by birth and had belonged to Balanchine's school for years. He was a master at teaching exercises in which the dancers' legs seemed to become supple, pliant lianas during the class and their feet small animals of prey moving like greased lightning.

No profession displays the artist's capacity so ruthlessly as the art of ballet: all dancers, from world-famous star to budding corps de ballet girl, practice together, as parts of a cooperative, under a teacher's supervision. Often there are choreographers, ballet masters, artistic directors and other interested parties following the dancers' achievements from the sidelines.

And so, too, that morning, a small audience had gathered in Stanley Williams's class and, naturally, Rudolf received his share of curious glances, even though he was a regular visitor to the studio and there were other well-known dancers at the same lesson, mostly from Balanchine's own company.

After the barre, during the floor exercises, there was a young boy of about fifteen or sixteen years old standing next to Rudolf. While Rudolf turned two pirouettes, he effortlessly spun eight, eliciting "Ahs" and "Ohs" from his colleagues; while Rudolf wobbled and tottered shakily on one leg, the boy stood beside him, motionless, balanced on his toes at the end of a perfectly extended limb, straight as an arrow.

Toward the end of class, Rudolf fell onto the barre, huffing and puffing noisily after a combination of leaps; the boy followed effortlessly and without a sound, agile and light as a feather.

Everyone in the studio—dancers, teacher, and audience alike—followed this unintentional and unwanted contest with open admiration for the young virtuoso, but Rudolf ignored it, plodded on, and acted as though there were only air around him in the studio.

It hurt me to witness the ruthless struggle taking place under my very nose; I would rather have left the studio.

"Well," he said later as we crossed a sun-drenched Broadway, "they can turn pirouettes, they can jump, but it doesn't mean they are artists."

We walked along together in silence for a while, entered a bookshop only to emerge again hastily—"too many people"—and ended up in the sunny park.

"You know, this is not easy for me to say," he looked away from me, his eye trailing a boy cycling by, "if you want to see Nigel, you'll have to do it soon. He is dying of cancer."

He stood up and went on talking, his back toward me: "It's like losing my father; *more* than that." He snatched up his bag: "Let's go," and, at the park gate: "As long as Maude survives. She means home to me."

In the fall of 1982 I traveled to New York once again, to prepare a series of performances the Dutch National Ballet was to give that same winter at the Brooklyn Academy of Music. A few informative talks had been arranged with the press and I would use the remaining time to scout around for some new dancers for the company.

Nureyev turned out to be in New York then as well, and it was soon decided I should stay with him. "We don't see each other that often," he said.

But even though I was staying with him, we saw little of one another; Rudolf always seemed to be even busier in New York than anywhere else, his telephone was constantly ringing, he seemed to tear from studio to theater to museum to restaurant. No wonder he made an overreactive and highly-strung impression.

"He's burning himself out," I thought.

"I have two free periods in my season," he mumbled over breakfast, "and I need to dance. Don't you do one of the classics later on in Amsterdam? I want to stay in shape." Sometimes he gave me the impression he saw our company as a fitness center.

What it boiled down to was that he had two short periods, each about eight days, for which (as yet) he had no performances and those gaps must be filled, whatever happened. But we were not dancing any evening-length ballets that year and, besides, he knew of my resolve not to allow him to guest with us anymore. Was he putting me to the test?

"Why not take a holiday? Go to Egypt or Morocco." I'd seen some Paul Bowles books lying on his table and hoped to spur him on that way.

"Margot will soon stop dancing, that will mean my work at Covent Garden is finished. When she's gone I'm sure they kick me out." He was still in mortal fear that the rug of certainty would suddenly be pulled out from under his feet.

Fonteyn was over sixty; it could hardly come as a surprise to him that the moment when she would say farewell to dance—as far as I was concerned the reverse had happened long ago—was approaching.

Again, I was amazed and touched by the deep respect and the love and admiration with which he spoke of her, not merely as a colleague, but particularly her achievements as a dancer. He knew I did not share his opinion, and he would sometimes launch a bitter and hostile attack on me for my dissident view.

Now we spent an entire evening watching videos to sustain his argument, numerous films with Fonteyn and one or two of Galina Ulanova, the Soviet dancer I respected most. Ulanova had ended her career long before, aged around forty-five—"A decent age," I added to Rudolf. There was no grand farewell organized for someone considered by many the most gifted dancer of the post-war generations; Ulanova had decided overnight that the time had come to leave the stage to younger dancers. For the rest, she would share her experience and insight with them as répétiteur in the studios.

We pored over passages from tapes, ran them in slow motion, and for me the result was crystal clear. Ulanova had such subtlety, such animation and refinement in her interpretation and, at the same time, she displayed a uniqueness, a faith and purity that, if this were vocal art, could be compared only to Kathleen Ferrier.

"But Margot is not the right dancer to see on film," Rudolf objected. "Alive, on stage, she is a different story."

"Unstretched toes are unstretched toes. That has nothing to do with film."

And I *had* seen Fonteyn on stage, and for me she had remained a lovely but expressionless dancer, one who made a pleasant impression on the audience, but who danced all her roles in the same way. Her technique was limited and so her movements remained static, imprisoned in a taut and often rather awkward form.

One evening when I collected him from Lincoln Center after a performance, I saw Rudolf in conversation with Martha Graham, standing in a deserted corner outside the theater. Both were shrouded from head to toe in identical cloaks of black mink, an exceptional sight even in wealthy midtown New York.

They had been allowed to keep the coats as a gift following a photo campaign, "The stars also wear mink," in which Fonteyn had taken part as well. It was a ludicrous sight, the two forlorn figures in their oversized, costly coats, as though they belonged to some sect or other.

Rudolf had himself immortalized by the painter Andrew Wyeth in that same coat, hanging nonchalantly around his quasi-naked, bodystockinged body for the occasion. I wondered what was supposed to impress the person viewing the painting more: the flamboyant garment or the celebrated emperor.

During the weeks when our group was appearing in the Brooklyn Academy of Music, Rudolf would not be in town, but he offered Toer and me the use of his apartment for the period: "Here, take the key and enjoy the place."

The Dakota, dating from the beginning of the twentieth century, was a fortresslike building inhabited mainly by successful artists, painters, writers, and singers.

"The place is crawling with millionaires," as Rudolf put it and, for this reason, the entrance was guarded day and night by a couple of security guards, as well.

One morning, when we looked out of the window, we observed small knots of people standing everywhere around the building in the snow, straggling along the fences of Central Park, sitting and standing on low walls, on the steps opposite the house and on windy street corners. Many had burning candles with them, or a photograph in hand, indiscernible to us. All eyes were on the the Dakota, creating an eerie spectacle, as though a ghostly miracle were about to happen.

"What's all the crowd for? Surely they're not fans of Rudolf's." I asked Toer, for in New York everything seemed possible.

"No," the porter explained to us later. "John Lennon lived in this building. It's two years ago today that he was shot down outside the door."

16 ⟶ *Palais Garnier*

"Maybe I'll be director of the Paris Opéra next," he had confided in me during a conversation in New York. "What you think?"

I told him what it meant to *me* to be the artistic director of a large company, all the pros and cons, the ups and downs. "But it's all on a far smaller scale in Holland and I think our dancers and the management have a closer bond with one another."

"But dancing is the same everywhere; you always come up against the same problems, don't you?" He was probably right, although I soon discovered that dancers in Paris behaved very differently from their Dutch colleagues.

"If you take on a position like that, of course, you won't be able to travel so much, you'll have to spend most of your time with your dancers."

"Well, that's to arrange."

"And do you want to go on appearing with the Opéra, or are you going to stop that?" For he would have to quench his insatiable thirst for appearing on stage.

"Of course I dance there, that is one of the big attractions for them, I can dance, give them my ballets, everything."

"But, as director, you have to want your own dancers to appear on stage in the first place."

"Well, they can dance, too."

To be honest, it seemed an ideal solution for Rudolf, who still led a nomadic existence, rehearsing his choreographies here and there, frequently traveling around the globe with a small and ever-changing troupe called "Rudolf and Friends," and dancing in ever less cosmopolitan cities and in ever smaller and lesser-known theaters.

Not that that was a scandal, on the contrary, but it seemed to me a waste of his energy. His body was clearly responding with more and more difficulty and he was generally sapping his strength. That life of airplanes, hotels, and suitcases, ever-changing faces, different theaters, new choreographies, to the tune of an ever more scathing press: how did he keep going and why did he do it?

If he worked in Paris he would have a base, a company to belong to, and a place to call "home." Personally, I felt that that must be a relief for him.

But over the years I had heard him unfold other great plans, all of which he dropped: "I need my freedom, I need to perform."

"It's done, I signed my contract in Paris," he told me on the telephone some time later.

"You sound as though you've sold your soul."

"Well, in a way I feel like that. They are a tough lot at the Opéra, I tell you." But he had often guested there, so he knew what to expect.

"I want you to do ballets in Paris. They should get confronted with different things, the situation there is sort of inbred now, nothing new."

I laughed: "But I doubt if they are waiting for my work."

Several years earlier, he had bought an apartment in Paris, in a magnificent spot on the Seine, overlooking the Louvre. The Tuileries were nearby and he was enmeshed, as it were, in a web of cozy streets full of antique shops, galleries, bookshops, and small restaurants, to revel in to his heart's content!

It was the first time I saw him decorate a home with the utmost care and with the guidance of interior decorators. In a way I regretted that; I loved his nonchalance, it gave his art treasures an extraordinary appearance. His Paris house breathed the excess of an Eastern palace, overflowing with exotic colors and shapes, no nook or cranny left unturned; at long last, he was able to provide a home for a part of his collection.

Rooms were crammed full of paintings, ancient prints and drawings, heavy damask curtains, gobelins, and, in among the colossal, late medieval furniture, a slender, seventeenth- century, finely-enameled harpsichord: Ioannes Ruckers, 1627.

Outside, the gray Seine hurried by, flanked by towering trees, which first bare, then in full green ornate or showers of ocher leaves, were always a tranquil sight.

It could be a paradise for him.

In 1984 I went to Paris with an assistant, Merrilee Macourt, an Australian dancer who had studied a dance notation system called choreology in London and now worked for the Dutch National Ballet. Together we were to rehearse one of my most recent ballets, *Niemandsland,*[1] to music by Sytze Smit, with the Opéra, and the prospect of several weeks in Paris twinkled before our eyes: besides working we were going to enjoy ourselves, too!

Without Merrilee's score, I thought I might be unable to recall the details of my latest works, which had often been created when I was very pressed for time.

No Man's Land was a challenging test for the dancers, but also for the two of us, full as it was of demanding, intricate group passages, in which each dancer often moved individually *and* divergently. Besides this, a large part of the choreography went at an incredible speed.

A year and a half earlier, before Rudolf had taken on the directorship, I had been invited by Rosella Hightower, then director of the Paris Opéra, to sit on the annual examination board. Each dancer in the company who wished to be promoted in rank (the hierarchy in the French institution was amazing, with its seven ranks) was required to enroll for an examination. Each rank had to meet certain requirements; there was an obligatory classical variation prescribed and a free solo, but selected from the Opéra repertoire.

The jury consisted of the management, several ballet masters, representatives from the dancers, and a guest from outside the company.

The examination system for professional dancers customary in Paris is not, I believe, to be found in any other ballet company in the world. In many ways, it seemed to me to be a just and satisfactory system for all concerned, although my doubts arose later as to its democratic quality. It was certainly interesting; the Paris Opéra is descended from the first official school for professional dancers in the world, founded by Louis XIV in 1661. Some of the customs and traditions date all the way back to that dim and distant past.

1. *No Man's Land.*

The exams were held on stage, usually that of the Opéra-Comique, which had a smaller stage than the Palais Garnier, the official home of the Opéra.

Before a candidate came on stage—in order of rank, from low to high—someone appeared from the wings with a little basket containing a small bell. He approached the footlights, rang the bell, and announced the victims in a loud voice: "Mademoiselle X," "Monsieur Y."

Afterward, a meeting was held and the members of the jury cast their votes for the dancers: teachers fighting tooth and nail for their pupils, dancers for a colleague and the management, too, seemed to have its own esoteric insights that often seemed to be based on internal politics: "A good exam, but he is undisciplined" or "He will never develop farther than this level."

A young dancer with an athletic, open face had immediately taken me under his wing to explain the workings of the evaluation system and to give me a reassuring wink when members of the dancers' committee became aggressive toward Hightower: "*C'est une comédie, pas plus.*"[2] He introduced himself as Patrick. I later found out that that was followed by Dupond.

In those days I was not acquainted with a single dancer at the Opéra personally, but I had been impressed by the performance of one young dancer from the lowest echelons, with a splendid leap and a dynamic and tense interpretation of the variation from *Le Corsaire*, which had remained in my mind.

I fought for him and went on voting for him with grim determination at every new voting round, but to no avail. I think I amazed the other jury members with my unrelenting faith in that one dancer. Was I blinded by the fact that he had been the first candidate on stage and there had been no one to compare him with later on? That question continued to plague me.

My jury membership unexpectedly came in handy when I was fixing the cast for *No Man's Land*; a number of faces must already be familiar. I attended class after class and, exam list in hand, I tried to put names to the faces of the 150 dancers who made up the company.

During that first year of his leadership, Rudolf was actually absent for lengthy periods, owing to a number of tour obligations that had to be met; my queries, he had instructed me, I could take to the *régisseur géneral*; Anna Faussurier. Anna, I later found out, was heavily overworked and tormented by the company's internal problems, but she was a straightforward and ef-

2. "It's a comedy, nothing more."

ficient woman all the same, who helped me with advice and assistance wherever she could.

"I recall a boy from the exams whom I considered very talented." I hunted through the list, Delormes, Philippe Delormes."

Anna shrugged her shoulders: "I don't know that name, never heard of him."

"But he must work here, in the corps de ballet. He wasn't promoted then."

She left her office to inquire of the ballet masters, but came back without any luck. "Unknown."

Two days later I stumbled across him on a staircase in a corridor backstage, smoking a cigarette.

"Aren't you Philippe Delormes? Didn't you dance the *Corsaire* variation in the exams?"

He looked at me in amazement: "Yes." I'd found him!

Later, when he saw my cast list, Rudolf confessed he had instructed Anna to prevent me from choosing people whom he did not consider talented. Which explained it all.

But then I just happened to think Delormes *was* talented.

The Opéra ballet was a remarkable institution in those days; there was no one, not even Anna, who could tell me which dancer I would find where and when in the building. I wandered from studio to studio but could not make heads or tails of the groups of dancers constantly traipsing back and forth throughout the vast building.

This Opéra building, too, like the one in Vienna, seemed unappealing and oppressive on first sight, but—maybe because this was France—there also hung a titillating air of mystery in the rabbit-warren of corridors, archways, connecting hallways, and staircases. The company with so many dancers had but two, fairly small, round studios on the topmost floors and one more rehearsal location in the public area down below, where a somber foyer without any light had been turned into a makeshift studio. A number of teachers preferred to teach in studios belonging to the ballet school, also housed in the building, small rooms often barely larger than a living room.

It could easily take ten minutes to reach the various rehearsal rooms, wandering up and down attic floors, in and out of lifts, through foyers, or in between the piled-up scenery backstage. A hint of romanticism appealed to me, but this was rather too medieval.

Rudolf called me up regularly to ask if all was going according to my wishes and whether I was sure I had chosen the most promising dancers.

"I never see all your dancers together; I get the impression that I haven't seen half of them yet so I can't tell you anything."

The company had marvelous young dancers, talent in abundance. Something that had never occurred before in my career happened to me there, during a class in which I saw two dancers go through the same sequence of steps together. What they did was so perfect, so incredibly beautiful it brought tears to my eyes just to see a simple exercise; both seemed to be unadorned perfection personified.

One was Elisabeth Platel, first soloist with the company, and the other Sylvie Guillem, only two years out of school and yet soon to be first soloist and—inevitable with her stunningly refined body and dazzling technique—a world-famous star. To my surprise, when we became better acquainted, I learned from Platel that she had been the last pupil of Sonia Gaskell who, after leaving the Dutch National Ballet, had taught in Paris until her death.

Rudolf had offered me a place to stay in his Paris house but I thought it better and more amicable to share at a hotel with Merrilee. We had a huge amount of work to do together, outside the studio as well: going through and dividing up the choreography for the following day, how many hours for the boys, who would rehearse with the girls, and when we would sort out the pas de deux sections for the solo couple.

As is usual almost everywhere in the world of dance, rehearsals took place under pressure for lack of time. On paper, the time allotted seemed fairly reasonable but, in reality, hours were lost all round and sometimes even whole days.

"On Tuesday and Wednesday most of the group are rehearsing on stage for Friday's performance, so you can work with the dancers who are free." That turned out to be two or three dancers with whom we could hardly achieve anything substantial on their own.

Or there was a meeting of the *syndicat*, the dancers' union, "to see if there would be a strike the following week." A strike? Nothing like that had ever happened to us in Holland! And sometimes I would receive announcements like "Patrick Dupond absent for four days due to guest appearances in Marseille."

"But how can he? After all, he has the leading role in the ballet and Sylvie needs the rehearsals with Patrick very badly. How on earth can you give him permission to leave in such a pressing period?" I asked Anna.

"At the Opéra *étoiles* always have the freedom to guest when and where they please," Anna explained to me, patronizingly.

I exploded, the *étoiles* came and went as they pleased while people were hardly aware of the existence of the corps de ballet members.

I rang Rudolf: "I can't work like this, it's driving us mad."

"But what do you want me to do? I can't help that."

"You're the boss, you should be here. Or send Patrick a telegram saying he has to come back."

"Impossible, my dear, just work with the others." It was easy for him to talk.

We opted for emergency measures: in order to get ahead, Merrilee rehearsed in the studio with the boys, while I taught the girls their steps in the corridor at the same time (as there was a shortage of studios). They were rehearsals without music, as a tape recorder was forbidden in the corridor. I sang and screeched Smit's uncountable music so that passing stage technicians thought madness was rife in the building. And it rained comments.

I had given Sylvie Guillem, with her unprecedented potential, the role that had been created by Valerie Valentine in Holland; Patrick Dupond, the friendly, virtuoso free spirit who had guided me through the past exams, took on Farha's role. In the ensemble, I had a number of wonderful dancers, some of whom would later become *étoiles* in the Opéra, or whom I encountered later as soloists abroad: Manuel Legris, Kader Belarbi, Laurent Hilaire, Wilfrid Romoli, Guillaume Graffin, Marie-Claude Pietragalla.

Our experiences with the dancers, certainly that first week, were sheer hell. We were unable to get a grip on them and the boys, especially, drove us to desperation, behaving like a bunch of spoiled children, laughing at the drop of a hat and talking continually through it all. They showed no concentration or, it seemed, the least modicum of respect at all. I felt like some tormented high school teacher; while I yelled for silence, the conversation between the two dancers right in front of me continued loudly.

"*Silence, nom de Dieu! Pourquoi vous êtes tellement emmerdant?*"[3]

3. "Silence, for God's sake! Why are you so annoying?"

I had worked across the entire world, from Finland to Japan, and wherever I had been, the dancers behaved the same, working hard, with concentration and with interest. Never before had I encountered behavior like this; the Parisian dancers were a different species altogether, as though they hailed from another planet.

Even the pleasant types like Belarbi, Romoli, and Delormes larked about. What was going on? Was this their way of showing me that they thought *No Man's Land* was useless?

"It's a disaster," I said to Rudolf, again over the telephone. "You'd better send us home, my ballet will not work, I'm telling you."

Often when we went back to our hotel exhausted, Merrilee would be crying and I was unable to utter a word, so humiliated and broken did we feel.

"I hate them." I said to her in the evening. "What a disgusting lot."

Even the easygoing and unsophisticated way of life in the rue de Seine where we had chosen our hotel could not improve our mood.

"Next week I'll be back," Rudolf let me know.

"Too late," I thought, "we'll have gone by then."

"What's got into you all?" I asked Philippe. "Why do you behave like a lot of impossible children? I constantly feel I'm a kindergarten teacher instead of a choreographer."

He was astounded and said that everyone enjoyed doing the ballet.

"Well, you could have fooled me."

"It's because the movements are so different from what we are used to, they are contrary to our classical schooling. And it is because we have all known each other since we were eight years old. We came together as children at school; it's like being with your brothers and sisters all the time."

I realized that they were indeed all no more than seventeen or eighteen years old. How did I behave at that age?

"The discipline at the Opéra ballet school was dreadful. We were oppressed in everything there, and now, at last, we can let our hair down." Philippe tried to explain why he and the group behaved the way they did.

Guillem worked brilliantly; nothing was too difficult for her. The line and interplay of her limbs, the pliancy and utter refinement she showed, were such as I had not imagined possible for the human body. She was still young, a mere slip of a girl, and *No Man's Land* was one of her first important roles.

Dupond, slightly older, had already been promoted to *étoile* and was a dazzling virtuoso. During the rehearsal period I had christened him *monstre sacré*, a title of honor to which he found it hard to respond. When he turned up again after two days' absence I greeted him with *"Ah, voilà notre monstre sacré. Quelle honneur!"*[4] But, since the exams, we had become good friends and I enjoyed working with him. I saw a great deal of Farha in him—but he did not make me forget Clint.

On Rudolf's return I told him the studios were too small to rehearse the ballet properly and to gain an impression of how it was going to look.

"I arrange other studios for you," and the very next week found us in a suburb where the Opéra apparently had scenery storage space and where a couple of large rehearsal rooms had been built as an extension.

It was a relief to me, so much space; but what misery it was for the dancers: after practice and a rehearsal in the Opéra they had to change and travel by car or métro to the new studio. After the rehearsals, there was the changing ritual once again and, by the end of *No Man's Land*, everyone was wet through with perspiration. Then it was often back to the theater for other rehearsals, a very roundabout way of working.

The mood, which had lifted considerably (or had Merrilee and I become inured to the Parisian mentality?), plummeted again from the tiring journey, but *No Man's Land* improved by leaps and bounds now that the dancers could move with ease and without any hindrance.

"Tomorrow I will come and watch," Rudolf announced.

"At last," I said to Merrilee. "If he comes, at least the kids will work with as much discipline as possible." But that was an illusion: the Big Boss's presence had little effect on their monkeyish behavior.

"It's fine," he said, "don't worry. They know the ballet now. Just wait till they dance it. They will astonish you."

"Mais je ne suis pas un chien. Je suis un être humain,"[5] the man in the métro had called out in despair. He walked up and down the aisle between the seats in the compartment, clamoring for a few francs, but no one responded, everyone kept staring ahead, as though the beggar were thin air.

4. "Ah, here's our sacred monster. What an honor!"
5. "But I'm not a dog. I'm a human being."

At moments like that I thought Paris was a far tougher city than New York and that the Parisians seemed more frustrated and heartless than the citizens of that other cosmopolitan capital.

In front of the window of a large store near the Opéra, I had seen a young girl, sitting on the pavement, with downcast eyes. On a cardboard sign it read: *"J'ai faim."*[6]

"Here, too?" I thought. It was 1984 and sights like that were still fairly rare in Europe; they shocked me.

In the studio, I mentioned the two incidents to the dancers as examples: "That's what *No Man's Land* is about. The ballet might not have a narrative, but the atmosphere is very important to me. The anger, the frustration in the movements has everything to do with situations like that. It's a ballet about a lost generation, with no work, no hope, without illusions. It could be about you, because it's *your* future, even though you have a job now."

They looked at me blankly, as though wondering what on earth had got into me: ballet was just ballet. What could that have to do with unemployment and poverty?

When I swung round I saw some of them snickering a little at this strange confrontation.

When I told Rudolf of the dancers' response, which had quite shocked me, he was silent first and then said, "Why on earth tell them such stupid stories?"

Merrilee returned to Amsterdam, where she had work to do with our company which could no longer wait; I was sorry to see her go. She, however, was relieved. *No Man's Land* was as good as finished and she—the fortunate one—could leave the daily pressure of the studio confrontations behind her.

"Good luck," she said, "and don't let it get you down." Our fear of the French went very deep!

After Merrilee left, I moved in with Rudolf; he had a studio next to his apartment on the same floor, overlooking a courtyard. It was a peaceful place, with every creature comfort.

The feeling of having a home of one's own made life far more pleasant: no more restaurants and hotels. I could leave books and notes lying around and no one laid a finger on them.

6. "I'm hungry."

When I encountered Rudolf at home each day, I began to notice great changes in him, changes that were sometimes amazing, but also pleasing. He suddenly enjoyed being at home, took far more notice of his surroundings, read more and studied music: he could spend hours working on the Bach suites on his harpsichord.

Sometimes, out of the blue, he would say, "Let's go see a movie," or he wanted to see a play, but he was most contented when he could stay home for an evening.

He asked me a great deal about his own company and discussed the dancers, their capacities, the talent, the mentality; sometimes he made me feel I knew more about them than he did himself. We were of one mind about Guillem; her talent was beyond all differences of opinion but, if I mentioned my enthusiasm for Dupond, he would say with a sly grin, "Too modern" and "No style." But Dupond was the dancer who enraptured the audiences.

Rudolf had great plans for the company. The repertoire he wanted it to dance in the future would come from all over the world, from the hand of dance celebrities like Balanchine, Graham, Jerome Robbins, Paul Taylor, Merce Cunningham, row upon row of icons.

His Paris household was run by two people. Douce François went there every day, more than once. She was a comely young woman with striking features, raven black hair cropped short and a deep, husky voice, a *gamine*.

She had the capacity to go about her business, whatever dilemmas arose or unpleasantness occurred in Rudolf's apartment, to go on with what she was doing and to see it through to the end—silently, and with a taut face, but she *did* it. If Rudolf were in a fine mood, Douce would be radiant.

She would appear at his home early in the morning, go through his mail, and check whether the housekeeping was "running." Mountains of mail arrived daily from all over the world, but also the bills and the taxes that seemed a special torment to Rudolf.

Although Douce said she also had her own work, she would often appear in the theater during the day as well, armed with thermos flasks of soup and sandwiches for the master, and was usually there in the evening as well; her energy was almost comparable to Rudolf's.

Manuel Fuente, a Chilean, was Rudolf's help in the house, a kind of gofer, who was supposed to take care of everything: shopping, the preparation of copious meals, cooking, washing, vacuum cleaning, polishing. He was a gentle and somewhat reticent man who entered the house at the crack of dawn, even before Rudolf awoke, only departing when the remains of the last meal were finally cleared away, rarely before one o'clock in the morning.

He often clocked up a fifteen-hour day and, he confided to me later, "Mister Nureyev does not pay me much."

When I dared, one day, to say something about that to Rudolf, he remonstrated, "But I'm often away and then he has an easy job."

It was a mystery to me how two people could spend so much time together in one house in such a manner: I had the impression that Rudolf never addressed *one* personal word to Manuel. When he arrived home, he greeted him barely or not at all, or curtly demanded the things he wanted: "No newspaper?" "Can we have wine?" "Not risotto again tonight, I hope."

Manuel was the silent witness of Rudolf's bouts of rage, his "one-night stands," his whims and inner turmoil, and the controversies that flared up now and then with Douce or with the Opéra.

"*Qu'est-ce que ce passe?*"[7] he would sometimes ask me worriedly. "I read in the newspaper that Monsieur Nureyev and the Opéra . . ."

If Toer or I complimented Manuel on a meal, then Rudolf might agree gruffly: "Yes, was not bad," but otherwise he treated his helper more or less as part of the furniture, while their lives were linked for five years and they spent hours alone in that house together every day. "He does not have an easy life," Manuel would say graciously. "Monsieur Nureyev has no time for other people."

During one of the final rehearsals, Rudolf entered the studio with an older gentleman: "Do you mind Monsieur Kochno to watch for a while?"

Boris Kochno had been Diaghilev's last secretary and right-hand man; he had written scripts for well-known ballets and a number of beautiful books on dance in the Diaghilev period.

Kochno shuffled into the studio between Rudolf and a beautiful woman—the former ballerina Hélène Sadowska—and sat down on a bench with difficulty. When I shook hands with him and afterward, too, he continued to gaze at the ceiling as though he had no wish to see today, and was searching

7. "What's going on?"

for images from days gone by. His face was familiar to me from old photographs and from a drawing by Picasso: an angular, aristocratic head with finely drawn features. But he seemed to have turned into a rather crotchety, walruslike old man, with quite a mustache and a sultry glance.

The rehearsal had not yet begun and the dancers were making a great deal of noise; the studio seemed more reminiscent of a playground.

"Listen," I said, "we have a visitor, he is part of our dance history," but the illustrious past seemed to make little impression on the dancers and the noise droned on.

"Monsieur Kochno worked together with Serge Lifar," I tried. "They were friends."

Lifar—Diaghilev's last discovery in the Nijinsky-Massine line, and the original interpreter of Balanchine's *Apollo* and *The Prodigal Son* among other ballets—had been director of the Opéra Ballet for a long time and was still hallowed as a saint by many in the building.

At the sound of Lifar's name it became a little quieter in the studio and Kochno, whose gaze was still directed at the dome, was regarded in awe.

Only at my words "They were friends" did his glance fall on me fleetingly. Had I said something wrong?

I switched on the music and Sytze Smit's shrill sounds unashamedly took possession of the room. While I had nearly forgotten our illustrious visitor in the heat of the rehearsal, I suddenly saw the procession had moved slowly toward the studio door.

"*Très intéressant,*"[8] Kochno mumbled, but I had the distinct impression that he was fleeing our contemporary chaos.

I used Rudolf's dressing room, which was next to his office, but when he was really busy or receiving important visitors, then I would change in a small room in a really somber darkened hallway backstage. To my surprise, I shared that space with Michel Renault, a former star of the Paris Opéra, who now worked as a teacher for the company and the school.

Long ago, around 1956, on holiday with Toer, backpacks on our backs, I had caught sight of a young man standing on the sidewalk in a Parisian avenue whose face I recognized from photographs.

"Toer, that's Michel Renault!"

8. "Very interesting."

The man had looked at me with a gleam of triumph in his eyes: "*Oui, c'est moi.*"[9]

Now, the beautiful, vain boy had become a rather sulky and sarcastic gentleman.

"*Ah, vous-êtes d'Amsterdam, invité par Monsieur Nureyev,*"[10] and then he promptly began reviling against the new director with quite some scorn and singing Lifar's praises.

"In those days dance had its own image, Lifar style. There were no foreigners in the Opéra, everything was French. French and excellent. But now . . ." He gave a demonic little laugh. In his eyes, I was clearly part of the Nureyev camp and he did all in his power to convert me.

A few years later I heard that Rudolf had slapped him in the face at the studio, a scandal that threatened to become a court case.

"Lifar is my evil spirit here," he growled, "and many of his disciples are still here in this building."

But there was another teacher, also dating from the Lifar period, Alexandre Kalioujny, whom he adored.

"His classes are heaven. You *have* to go and study them. His exercises are choreographic masterpieces and they are like balsam for your body. However tired you are, in Kalioujny's classes you feel reborn."

He confided to me that Kalioujny had cancer and did not have long to live. "Is it possible for you to send Merrilee here, or another notator? His classes should be saved for future generations, they are such jewels."

It seemed to me rather far-fetched to have a choreologist come over from Holland to do work like that: "Don't you have notators yourself?"

"Ah," he shrugged, "they don't care a shit, here."

Reinbert Martijn, a young dancer from our company, and Clint Farha came over from Amsterdam for a few days and stayed with me, curious to know how the Parisians would dance *No Man's Land*.

I knew that Rudolf had a weakness for the lively and good-humored Reinbert, but I was curious to see how he would respond to Clint this time, now no longer an irritating adversary but a guest in his house.

The whole stay passed in an amiable atmosphere of great friendliness, with

9. "Yes, it's me."
10. "Ah, you're from Amsterdam, invited by Mr. Nureyev."

Rudolf taking on the role of a somewhat amused papa, beaming goodwill on his two sons; he teased Clint, who was already intimidated, went out of his way to cause small skirmishes and let them both admire the museum pieces in his house, not showing off, but with clear satisfaction: "Look, *that*'s what I've achieved with our profession."

The premiere was a great success, but it was bound to be. The dancers performed so that the sparks flew and Guillem and Dupond were supreme: she cool, vulnerable, and technically perfect; Dupond a lithe, impetuous animal.

"This is the hardest part I ever did," I heard him saying to Clint afterward.

For me, perhaps the greatest satisfaction came from the fact that I had succeeded in giving Philippe Delormes, the almost forgotten dancer, a clearer place in his own company, no one could now say they did not know who Delormes was! Maybe I had been somewhat fanatical at the exams, but he was surely a dancer with great potential.

Afterward, Rudolf held a supper-party at the Quai Voltaire; Sytze Smit and his wife Ella were there, Douce of course, Boris Kochno (the guest of honor as far as I was concerned) and a number of friends.

"Manuel, arrange a separate table for the boys," because there was not enough space for everyone, even though the table was large. And although we would dearly have loved to watch Kochno (for he did not speak, only an incomprehensible grunting was audible when Rudolf was looking after him), we joined the "boys" Clint and Reinbert, at their table; after all, it was a Dutch National Ballet party, too.

Two days later Rudolf handed me an envelope: "Kochno says thank you."

In the envelope, I found an ancient, sepia photograph, taken at the Lido in Venice: *Serge Diaghilev, Serge Lifar, and Boris Kochno and the teacher Cecchetti, posing on the beach.*

An unforgettable gift.

17 ∽ *The Youngsters*

A few months later, Rudolf arranged a Stockhausen evening and asked me to rehearse the composer's *Gesang der Jünglinge*[1] for the occasion with his dancers; I was beginning to feel I had a season ticket to Paris.

Rudolf had seen the piece by the Dutch National Ballet before and enjoyed it, able to relate to the schoolboy world the ballet portrayed. He had also seen instantly which works had served as a source of inspiration for *Jünglinge*, something no critic in Holland had noticed.

"Well, I see you love Fellini and Kantor," he had said and, indeed, Fellini's *Amarcord* and Tadeusz Kantor's *The Dead Class* had made a great impression on me and certainly played a part in the creative process.

I was unsure whether I could leave for Paris again so soon; there was enough work to be done in Holland and my *No Man's Land* experiences had not been all that great, either.

"It would give such a good balance to the program, the other works will all be abstract."

I had made *Jünglinge* in 1977, some seven years earlier, and I wondered how much I would remember: the ballet had not been notated, so now Merrilee was unable to reach out her faithful, helping hand. This one I would have to do on my own.

It was reassuring to feel I was now more familiar with the Opéra dancers; I had made a number of friends there and, besides, I could now see their unnerving behavior was merely a mask, a facade of which they were scarcely aware.

Springtime in Paris; once again I moved in with Rudolf, who left me to my own devices for the greater part of my stay, having guest appearances to carry

1. *Chants of the Youngsters.*

out here and there. And so, somewhat dazed with elation, I strolled beneath the budding trees in the Tuileries in the direction of the Opéra.

I soon awoke from my dream and had my nose rubbed in the reality of that strange institution once again.

Passing the concierge of the building was a happening in itself. At almost all hours of the day, the odor of meals wafted out of his abode just to the rear of reception: celery, garlic, fried apple, and onion aromas engulfed the passing singers and ballerinas. The poetry of cuisine!

Once into the wide and rather shabby corridor, and all around and inside the lifts, the visitor would often be overwhelmed by a plethora of posters and pamphlets, many hand-written, pasted all over the walls: "Summons: Strike!" "Show your solidarity," "Calling all personnel to a protest meeting at 12:00," and "The management has betrayed us again."

I had never before encountered a temple of art so driven by politics and, I must admit, I found it adventurous and exciting at the start. There were no wimps working here!

Sometimes, once every two weeks, the broad corridor would be transformed into a marketplace, merchants positioned everywhere behind their stalls laden with pots of honey, pullovers, shoes, and cheeses, toiletries, sweetmeats, and delicatessen wares. *Bon marché*, artist's prices.

One might catch a glimpse of opera stars, stage personnel, *étoiles*, seamstresses and chorus singers; all would nose around among the desirable wares and then disappear, clutching a package under their arm in satisfaction.

The two faces of France.

When I turned up for my first rehearsal, the studio was completely deserted; in a corner, by the tape recorder at the back, there was a somber-looking man whom I recognized as I approached him to be the company conductor, Michel Quéval.

"I beg your pardon, I thought I was rehearsing in this studio, but I see I'm wrong."

"No, Stockhausen is being rehearsed here."

"But then why are you here? *Jünglinge* is done to a tape; there is no conductor necessary."

He laughed a bitter laugh: "I have been commissioned to work the tape recorder for you."

I froze, a conductor—or anyone—who was to switch the tape on and off hundreds of times at my request?

"I always do that myself, I don't need anyone for that." But Quéval had to stay there; it was part of his work agreement, he said.

"I conduct in Tokyo, in Moscow, in London, but here I have to work the tape recorder, too," he sneered.

"And where are the dancers?" I wanted to change the painful subject.

"On strike, I think. Or preparing to go on strike. And so they should." It sounded vindictive.

In the evening, I persuaded Rudolf not to have Quéval serve as button-pushing gofer in my rehearsals anymore: "I find it frustrating and I really can't work like that."

"But you'll create a precedent," was the reluctant answer. "If he doesn't have to do it for you anymore then he won't do it anywhere."

"That's the Opéra's problem, then; I want to be able to work unhindered."

And Quéval could put his time to better use and study scores to his heart's content.

I soon noticed, however, that more than half my rehearsal time was lost to political campaigning. I was making *Petits Gosses*,[2] as I had christened the youngsters for the French version, at a time when the whole of the Opéra was fairly seething with displeasure, not only among the technical personnel, but the dancers, as well.

What especially amazed me was that nearly all the dancers joined in the meetings. In the dance world to which I was accustomed, only three or four dancers at most would concern themselves with matters beyond dance steps, casting, or sore toes.

I often had little option other than to wait patiently until the meeting fever had ebbed. Still, it was a lovely springtime and I climbed out of one of the rotunda studios onto the roof, edging my way along wide gutters to a comfortable spot, and sat there majestically on the monumental roof, flanked by Garnier's gigantic groups of statues. Way below me were the hushed noises of street life: cars, passersby, buses and a panoramic view out over an ocean of roofs in all sizes and shades of gray—sheer enjoyment.

2. "Young boys."

No matter how insurmountable the difficulties might seem, the sight of Paris made it all worthwhile, each day anew.

Chants des Petits Gosses was about a class of growing lads and their dictatorial schoolmistress. In among the nervous swarm of small boys and their military-drilling matron, a group of youths, four nearly adults in white sports clothes, advanced in a slow but insistent tempo in long, linear movements and a single gloomy adult wandered around among the groups, a loner in a shapeless rain-coat, dilapidated hat, attaché case. The small schoolboys protested against their dictatorial warden. In the background the adolescents raised a blood-red flag in a gesture of solidarity, but the *putsch*[3] was quashed with a single gesture by the fundamentalist teacher, the revolutionary elan sagged like a soufflé. What remained was a drab, disillusioned, middle-aged man.

For the two boys giving vent to their first sexual curiosity together, an alliance that was instantly and roughly exposed by the schoolmistress, I had chosen Philippe Delormes and Kader Belarbi, and it was a pleasure to work with them. Now and then they would slip away from a meeting, so that we could rehearse undisturbed in the empty studio and add the finishing touches.

I realized that there had been no dissonance during rehearsals this time. Had I become accustomed to their behavior, or the dancers to my method of working?

It was a strange sensation to live in Rudolf's apartment alone; I slept in the "studio" but Rudolf had given me the key to his house, instructing me about all I must do, and not do, to guarantee the security of his domain.

"Don't let strangers in. If you have friends over, then stay in your own apartment." It was never really clear what the risk of visiting friends could be; he knew most of my friends, so they were hardly "strangers," and they would not steal! There *was* one Russian character, someone I had become acquainted with earlier in Canada who had turned up again, a fanatic ballet-lover, or so he maintained.

One evening I came upon him out of the blue after a rehearsal, outside the Opéra, where he clamped onto me: "I read you were working here and came to France. Could I attend some rehearsals?"

What he really wanted was to get in touch with Rudolf: "We knew each other a long time ago."

3. A coup.

When I told Rudolf, he reacted with extreme agitation: "He is dangerous, never ever let him come near me, it's Russian mafia. And you, too, stay away from him."

Sometimes, on my way to work in the morning, I would see "the mafia" walking back and forth on the Seine quayside opposite the house and I would hasten in another direction.

There was an intricate ritual that had to be enacted before the gates to Rudolf's realm would open: a security system that was timed to the second and consisted of turning a number of keys, rearranging of figures, and the pulling of levers: if I made a mistake, then the police would be on the doorstep within minutes.

Before I set foot in his part of the house or took my leave, I always concentrated and went through the maneuvers in my mind: first, I had to turn the little right-hand key, then that small handle, the left-hand button, another little key, that should be the figure and, when it appeared, pull the door closed and shut to the count of four.

Each time it gave me the unpleasant sensation of being an intruder in the deserted house, but Rudolf's enormous collection of books, video films, and long-playing records was beckoning and, besides all of that, I used his video-recorder and, with the aid of the Dutch National Ballet recording, I checked the parts I wanted to rehearse with the "petits gosses" the following day.

As soon as Rudolf returned from abroad, another meeting was arranged, to which he was "subpoenaed"; in the morning he spoke disdainfully about the imminent event: "Come and see how they treat me."

The company's complaints were mainly about his regular absence and his own appearances with the company: the principals complained that he stole the artistic bread from their mouths. It sounded familiar to me.

The gathering was hardline: without beating about the bush, it was made clear to him that he should spend more time with the group, not merely to rehearse his own ballets or when he himself was to perform but, in particular, during the other company activities, which might not serve his personal interests, but were essential to the dancers and the staff.

"I am a dancer," Rudolf snapped at the assembled gathering, "and, if you don't allow me to dance here, I will have to go elsewhere and be absent, so . . ." and he made a guillotine-like gesture, "take it or leave it."

It was an embarrassing spectacle: a room full of people united against one individual, even if that person did seem equal to the challenge.

The most painful moment was when one of the dancers stood up ("That bitch," Rudolf said later, "and she is a lousy dancer, too," as if that had anything to do with it) and said, "*Monsieur Nureyev, on vous respecte comme danseur mais on trouve que l'Opéra n'a pas besoin de vos choréographies,*"[4] a remark that must have been a dreadful slap in the face for Rudolf; he had produced his versions of *Raymonda*, *Swan Lake*, *Don Quixote* and a number of other evening-length productions plus four works of his own, and they were dismissed in a few paltry syllables.

I was not looking forward to encountering him at home that evening, imagining that he would be like a bear with a sore head. Initially, however, he approached the affair quite matter-of-factly, which was even more disturbing; I would have preferred him to react with one of his familiar outbursts of rage.

Naturally, he was bitter and his comments were scathing, but he remained aloof, as though the whole occurrence really did not affect him.

"Small thanks one receives for one's pains. Even the people I support, whom I help to become soloists, were sitting in the meeting and no one uttered a word in my defense. Not a soul."

There had also been members of the Opéra management present: "Larquié was there, Martinotti; they listened but no one intervened, so for me it was as if they had chosen the side of the dancers. Cowards."

"Politicians," I supposed.

And yet, he had changed over the years. Even if he did persist in reverting to the matter for days on end, his anger was less destructive, did not endure as long, and so he was able to keep it under control.

"I'd so much like to read Bulgakov's *Teatral'nyi Roman*, do you know it? About a playwright who is pestered out of a drama company."[5] Was he searching for a comparison with his own situation?

I had once read that book in Dutch, *Black Snow*, about the fortunes of

4. "Mr. Nureyev, we respect you as a dancer, but we do not believe the Paris Opéra needs your choreographies."

5. Adaptations of Mikhail Bulgakov's *Teatral'nyi Roman*, a theatrical novel, were published in English as *Black Snow* by Keith Reddin and Keith Dewhurst.

someone who can see through the two-faced vanity of the theatrical world, but is rejected by it and attracted to it at the same time.

"But the man in the book is eliminated by the management and you *are* the management, Rudolf. Surely that's a difference."

"Me, the management?" He gave a lascivious laugh: "You should meet the people above me, the ones that decide. A whole political party!"

Since he wanted to read Bulgakov in Russian and could not find it in Paris, I managed to unearth it at Pegasus Books in Amsterdam and, on my following visit, I was able to surprise him with Bulgakov's collected works in his mother tongue.

His Paris house had become a gathering place for his friends. Maude was often there, Wallace, Robert, and many other people I had met with him in various parts of the world. Marriage to a Chilean student had provided his niece Gouzel with the chance to leave the Soviet Union and she had arrived on Rudolf's doorstep. She astounded me, not only because that small girl from St. Petersburg had become such a self-assured young woman, but especially because of her attitude.

I had seen her circumstances in St. Petersburg, the dire straits, but in Rudolf's house she seemed to find everything perfectly ordinary, or not good enough. She criticized Manuel's cooking continually, and he suddenly had to obey two masters. Nothing was to her liking and she treated him quite clearly like a servant, a low-ranking person to be ordered about; did she come from the land that considered solidarity of such paramount importance?

Gouzel's mother, Rosa, had also gained permission from the Soviet government to go to Paris for Gouzel's wedding and refused to return to St Petersburg.

"But where is Rosa living now, then?" I asked him.

"I sent her to La Turbie; if she were here we would fight all the time." Fight, after a separation of eighteen years?

I wondered how someone from a completely differently functioning society, who spoke no French either, would manage in that vast and isolated house in the hills.

"Serge is there, they can speak Russian together." But the situation must have seemed very like *Huis Clas*[6] to Rosa.

---

6. In translation, *No Exit*, a one-act play by Jean-Paul Sartre

To afford his sister an official opportunity to remain in France, Rudolf persuaded Douce to have her brother enter into a marriage of convenience with Rosa. How Douce managed it I do not know, but it happened as Rudolf wished. The fact that Douce's brother, an extremely pleasant man, already had another marriage in mind seemed irrelevant, a matter which only arose when Rosa, having become more or less paranoid, later refused to go through with the previously agreed upon divorce.

There were other, daily, visitors, as well; Rudolf's secretary, for example, Suzanne Soubie, came to his home each morning to go through the daily work schedule with him. While Suzanne arranged appointments and I had my breakfast, Rudolf lay on the massage table, where his masseur kneaded him from top to toe.

Meanwhile, Rudolf would answer the telephone which rang continually—Los Angeles, Sydney, Toronto, Berlin, Copenhagen—instructed Madame Soubie, asked Manuel, hovering silently during these séances, for "more tea, and toast, warm toast," and inquired whether everything was going according to plan in my rehearsals.

I had noticed that a doctor would arrive at the house nearly every morning, even before Rudolf rose. He would leave his case on a table and vanish into Rudolf's bedroom with various medications, ampules, hypodermic syringes, and rubber gloves.

It hardly disconcerted me at all, really; Rudolf led an abnormal life, did the work of four people and, despite swollen ankles, injured knees, and strained Achilles' tendons, danced, albeit no longer every evening, but more than was good for him or anyone else.

As he stumbled around the room in the morning, he had the appearance of an invalid and gave the impression he could hardly climb two steps. He slept badly as well, and I hardly ever received a positive answer to my standard question, "Did you sleep well?" He suffered from insomnia, woke up several times a night wet through with perspiration and then drank liters of water or tea—one of the few things he made himself—"and after, I worry a lot, till I sleep."

"But what do you worry about then?" for there seemed to be little in his life that could really go wrong.

A lifeless little sigh escaped from his chest. "I don't know, I just worry," even though he was by no means a hypochondriac.

A daily visit from the doctor thus seemed fairly reasonable: cortisone injections for the pain, or vitamins for his immense tiredness. There were reasons enough.

Douce (it was hard to imagine Rudolf without her) usually appeared in the course of the morning rituals, and a subtle contest evolved between the two faithfuls, Suzanne Soubie, secretary by profession, and Douce, adoring helper: who would do what for Rudolf, who took which papers, who answered the telephone while Rudolf was taking his bath, and who would have the honor of driving him to the Opéra.

Gouzel, whom he had installed in an apartment on the top floor of his house, would occasionally sail in and suddenly *she* would behave as the lady of the manor toward the other two women. She would order coffee, enthrone herself upon a chair, survey the room, and give rise to frosty silences.

It was like the court of Louis XIV, a court bending over backward to compete, a family member behaving more regally than the monarch himself, and His Serene Highness taking a bath in princely fashion, lathering himself, shampooing and blow-drying his hair, an agonizingly time-consuming affair for those hovering in the antechambers to pay their respects.

Water seemed to hold a magical attraction for Rudolf, especially hot water. He could while away the hours veiled in steamy vapour, philosophizing or merely relaxing; occasionally, his visitors were invited to take a seat on the edge of the bath.

He had taken great pains with his choice of music (almost always Bach) in order to make the pleasure as exquisite as possible. The bathroom he used most frequently was decorated like a print gallery, as well, hung from top to bottom with fine drawings of male nudes, studies in the style of, and sometimes also by, Géricault, David or Delacroix.

Along with the dinners, the bathtime conversations were among the most relaxed and agreeable moments of the day. It seemed like a return to the womb: with safe, warm water all around him, he felt freed of all obligations.

However much visible pleasure he took in lathering himself in the mornings, it had more to do with caring for a beloved instrument—oiling, polishing, lubricating—than with vanity. He was by no means vain, in the ordinary sense of the word. In the theater, he studied himself in the mirrors as an object, coolly and with distance; whether it was his dancing, his costumes, or his makeup, it was all part of the task in hand.

In his private life, as well, he was beyond vanity, quite the opposite, in fact; he might appear as though he did not have a dime to his name and, while his cupboards were overflowing with brand-new clothes, his favorite attire was trousers, jackets, and boots I had seen him wearing ten years earlier.

Sometimes he would suddenly squeeze himself into a tight pair of trousers from the flower-power era and say in dismay, "I can't get in anymore."

"But you used to wear that when you were dancing *Monument*, didn't you?"

Ornaments did not interest him. I do not believe I ever saw him wearing rings, chains or bracelets. At one stage, he appeared with a massive gold watch on his wrist that he also wore to rehearsals. When he was very tired, he would come over to me and slip it onto my wrist: "If I put it down it disappears." The weight of the enormous timepiece made my arm sag instantly; wearing a gold Cartier was rather like weightlifting.

He did dress up on special occasions, but with such fantasy and imagination that it seldom looked "official." I remember one occasion, lunch with a wealthy baron and wine producer, when he suddenly cast a critical eye over my apparel and suggested that maybe I could put on something from *his* wardrobe.

"If I'm not good enough for those people like this, then I'll just stay at home."

He tilted his head to one side, then took off his jacket and pulled on a wide and multicolored pullover: "We'll show them solidarity."

The host and hostess received us on the balcony of their "chateau" in blue jeans, woolen sweater, and open-necked shirt.

"They tried to outdo us in simplicity," Rudolf joked on the way back. "That's because we are only artists."

At lunch he had pulled off one of his strange, impulsive stunts. "Show Rudi your hands," he said to the hostess, who happened to be of Dutch extraction, and took her by the wrist and held her arm above the table. Her hand was deformed and bent by arthritis.

"You see, they are just like Martha Graham's hands, in a contraction." I was at a loss how to react, but the woman courteously took the incident in her stride, looking at me agreeably and said, "It's not a beautiful sight; I keep them out of sight as much as possible. Those are the impediments of growing older. *C'est embarrassant.*"[7]

Despite his fame and possessions, he never became a snob, remaining the contrary rebel with no regard for convention, a vagabond who would not be out of place in Genet's oeuvre, an antihero straight from the pages of books by Aldo Busi or Edward Limonov. It was no wonder he had the greatest admiration for Chaplin, the cheerful rover who, with many ups and downs, weaves his way in and out of one society scrape after another.

Before I returned to Amsterdam—how beautifully my *petits et plus grands gosses*[8] had worked!—Rudolf asked me to accompany him to the offices of the Opéra management.

There, in the den of the lion—André Larquié, a distant, polite diplomat—Rudolf proposed that I should make a ballet for the company, so a new creation rather than a restaging.

What he really had in mind was a piece for a large cast: "You have such ease in handling masses." I would have complete freedom, with one exception: the music was to be by a French composer.

"The whole organization is at your disposal," the king of the animal kingdom, Larquié, deigned to add.

What was I to do? Bow out of the room gracefully?

7. "It's embarrassing."
8. Young and older boys.

18 ∽ *"Aux Armes, Citoyen!"*[1]

My mood was one of profound depression when I left for Paris with Toer in spring 1985 to begin rehearsing the new piece.

The unexpected death of one of our young dancers, Sjoerd van den Berg, was still strongly affecting my way of thinking, and all the fuss and excitement that was part and parcel of the ballet world was distasteful to me, seeming quite irrelevant. I was not looking forward to the new Parisian period at all.

Why did I accept? I wondered. Why did I allow myself to become involved?

Some six months earlier, I had traveled to London to discuss with Rudolf his choice of music for the new piece. He had a number of suggestions, which was a great help to me as, owing to an enormously busy period at the Dutch National Ballet, I had scarcely got around to listening to French—or any other—compositions.

Rudolf was staying in his flat in Maude Gosling's house and it was his intention that I should spend those few days with him. When I arrived, however, Rudolf was in such a dreadful mood that it seemed wiser—and quieter!—to move in with Maude.

Maude informed me that Rudolf had just learned that Gorlinsky, Rudolf's manager who also managed his finances, had taken the initiative of selling Rudolf's Richmond house. Since Rudolf hardly ever went there, the house had already been let to an American family several years earlier, and as he already had five or six other real estate properties, Gorlinsky had imagined, I assume, that one (gigantic) plum on a tree would not be missed.

---

1. "To Arms, Citizen!"

A miscalculation: Rudolf had reacted furiously and, in his rage, even broke a window in his flat at the Goslings.

"He is very unpredictable, these days," Maude whispered.

His flat was now transformed into a regular warehouse; had I wanted to stay there, I would not have fitted in!

All the rooms were crammed full of trunks and boxes, mounds of carpets and oriental fabrics everywhere; pieces of scenery from productions were lying in the hall. One room was stacked high with costumes from various ballets that belonged to him because he made guest appearances everywhere and these were never allowed to vanish into the theater costume storage.

"Many of them are still wet with perspiration," Maude said, "and he doesn't clean or dry them, he just piles them high."

Those were difficult days with Rudolf; he was going through a period of deep gloom and often seemed inaccessible, his voice either sounding grumpy or inaudible from fatigue.

"I'm always upset when I'm here," he managed to say with effort. "The Royal Ballet doesn't really want me anymore, so I wonder what I'm doing here, I feel out of place. And I'm constantly reminded of Nigel's death. I miss him terribly, he was of such guidance to me."

On one occasion I remember from that time, he wanted to take his daily bath in the flat and found that the hot water from the boiler had given out. After a spurt of swearing and cursing about the pleasures of British life in general and bathing habits in particular, he simply sat there, plaintively, in the half-filled bath and seemed inconsolable, deprived of the wallowing he so loved. There was nothing else to be done: I should have to traipse back and forth from Maude's home with buckets of hot water to fill the bath to the desired level. While I emptied the plastic buckets over the grumbling figure, I was shaking with laughter inside at the absurdity of the situation: his admirers should see their idol now!

"Can't you do me a piece on Rimbaud? I think his way of being goes very well with yours. Imagine what possibilities there are."

In reply to my inquiry whether he was familiar with Rimbaud's work he admitted he had tried a few poems, the simplest. Rudolf had fared the same way as I had.

"But think of his life, the things that happened."

"Oh, Rudolf, but I know I'm not ready for that; a project like that needs some years of preparation."

"Now, anyway, listen to this. This is something exceptional."

The music he played for me was the *Symphony Funereal and Triumphal* by Hector Berlioz. In 1840, at the first performance, in commemoration of the French Revolution, the music was played by two hundred marching musicians.

Performed solely by wind instruments—plenty of brass—and percussion, the music had a hallucinating, ominous sound, like the trumpets sounding the Last Judgment and, even in the apotheosis, when large choirs sang "*Gloire, gloire et triomphe,*" the piece still seemed infused with eerie echoes, as though the victory were occurring in Dante's inferno.

It was an interesting, if not particularly danceable, piece of music; I had made my choice.

Toer and I arrived at the Opéra by station-wagon, and in the back there was an enormous model of the stage set that Toer had produced.

He had an appointment with the stage and scenery technical services at a particular time to discuss things but, as it turned out, the Paris traffic was so stifling and clogged up that we drove round and round the building in vain, arriving only just in the nick of time. There was not a parking space to be seen, of course!

"This is ridiculous. Leave the car in the theater courtyard," I said to Toer. However, we had hardly emerged from the car when the concierge ran squawking out of her abode:

"What are you doing there? That's a management space!"

"That's good, because we have an appointment with the management and, besides, we have a large model with us that is expected here." I motioned toward the colossal box in the back.

"None of my business. Go on, get out of here, now," was the gracious and courteous response.

There was the theater trouble again. I exploded: "If you send us away we won't come back. Tell the management that!" I was shaking with fury.

"Come on, we're going." I said to Toer, who had already gotten into the car again, white as a sheet.

At that moment, Rudolf appeared on the scene, chauffeur-driven by

Douce. Like Peter the Great, he surveyed the battlefield, dismissed the concierge, who was suddenly all smiles and service, and helped us unload the model.

That afternoon I had an appointment with Anna Faussurier to show her my casting for the new ballet and to plan the first rehearsal week. She looked at my list: "You must be mad! So many people?"

"That's what Rudolf wanted, a big ballet. Didn't he tell you?"

"We know nothing at all." Her tone spoke volumes. "We're only allowed to pick up the pieces."

"For most of the rehearsals, I'll need everyone, especially the first few weeks. After that I think I can divide up the ballet into groups."

Anna laughed: "Everyone? I can't give you even a quarter of an hour a day with everyone; that's out of the question." She called over a ballet master, Serge Poliakoff, and repeated my rehearsal wishes: "This is absolutely impossible to realize with all the work we're doing. *C'est ridicule, ça.*"[2]

Poliakoff perused the lists and, shaking his head, agreed with Anna. She told me that Jerome Robbins was working there, as well, and was on the warpath every day for more time, "and you'll never beat him, you can forget that."

It seemed to be a battle lost, and my mood plummeted steadily. "I shall put it to Rudolf tonight; *he* wanted the ballet, *he* knows how much work is involved and he will have to solve it."

But Rudolf was rather nonchalant about the matter in the evening: "It should be possible. Tell Anna she just has to find a way for you. I'm not going to do her job for her." And that was that.

The next day I bore the great news to Anna. "It's up to you, you have to give me the time and space according to your boss," I informed her with a measure of sarcasm in my voice.

Once again, we went through the lists and my wishes.

"I'm sorry, it's impossible. The most I can try is to give you an hour a day. But you know that Denard and Platel are away for two weeks, too?"

"How on earth can that be? Rudolf himself asked me to use Denard!"

"*C'est un désastre.*"[3] Anna told me how the previous months had passed, that a week earlier, the English choreographer David Bintley had boarded the

2. "This is ridiculous."
3. "It's a disaster."

airplane back to London, two days before his premiere, because he had been unable to finish his ballet. *"Deux jours avant la première nous devions trouver un autre ballet, imagines-toi!"*[4]

For the next day, as if by way of consolation, Anna wrote on the list: *"Répétition nouveau ballet Van Dantzig. Tout le monde disponible."*[5]

Everyone who was available, I knew from experience what that meant: a handful of people with whom I could do nothing at that moment. But in David Bintley's example she had given me an idea.

I paced through the blind corridors of the building in a daze; what was I to do? Should I descend into that hell of hopeless daily battles? Would I have to go on mixing water with the wine? I was inured to that, from the bitter experience of years and years gone by, but now the dismal prospect overwhelmed me.

I sought my way through the maze of halls and floors to the costume studios, where Toer was working, surrounded by bales of material and wardrobe-mistresses leafing their way through piles of drawings.

"How long are you going to be?"

Toer glanced at my somber face and then at the clock: "There's a break at twelve."

I waited for him, pacing up and down a dark corridor.

"It's over, Toer, I'm not doing it. Having to work like this will break me."

I told him the situation as Anna had explained it to me and which, blatantly clear from the work schedules, was hopeless. "How can Rudolf imagine an enormous work can be crammed into such an overloaded agenda? He simply hasn't left me an inch of space."

We walked back to Rudolf's house; Place Vendôme, Tuileries, the Seine. An unbelievably warm and carefree day, but I was laboring under a ton of bricks.

"I'm leaving. Now, right away. Get your stuff together."

Toer was aghast: "But you can't do that, talk to Rudolf."

"Toer, I did that yesterday. All he'll do is persuade me to stay after all, but he can't alter the situation. Unless he cancels performances and other choreographers."

4. "Just imagine, we had to find another ballet, two days before the premiere."
5. "Rehearsal new ballet Van Dantzig. Everyone available."

From a strategic point of view, retreat is maybe not the most honorable weapon in battle, but I was not keen to perish prematurely on *that* of all battlefields.

We packed our bags, loaded them into the car and disappeared; *Symphony funereal*. I could forget the *triumphal* for the time being.

Back in Holland, I was plunged into a depression; it was as though I had been preparing for a birth that was suddenly aborted. For months on end I had listened to Berlioz, worked out ideas and wrought plans together with Toer, who had come up with heaps of wonderful costume designs and brilliant sets worked out in minute detail on a scale model that was standing in his studio. It was for him that I found the whole affair most distressing.

Naturally, I doubted whether my decision to flee Paris at the drop of a hat had been the right one. In retrospect, safe home again, I wondered whether the most wretched circumstances do not bring about the best results. Deep in my heart, however, I knew that was nonsense: the situation at the Opéra had been one of utter deadlock; there was nowhere I could turn and, in the rehearsal time available, I could only have created a ballet with a small cast and lasting a quarter of an hour at most.

Naturally, Rudolf called me up time after time, imploring me to return, main-taining he was simply going ahead with the production of the sets, as he was sure I would change my mind and continue with the work.

"It's impossible for me to have two works cancelled in one season, first Bintley, now you," he said. "They'll throw me out, my career with the Opéra will be finshed." Moral blackmail?

"But I feel betrayed. How can you invite me to come under such impos-sible circumstances? If I come back I want a guarantee, on paper, of how many hours a day I can work, and with my whole cast. No *étoiles* away for two weeks, no *tout le monde disponible*,[6] none of all that. *Tout le monde*, full stop."

But I knew he could not give me that promise.

"Come and do something else instead, anything, as long as it is a new work. I need a world première."

6. "Everyone available."

Is that what Toer and I had been preparing for, for six long months, for "something else, anything?"

When I failed to answer the telephone after that, he sent me lengthy telegrams, pleading and threatening: breach of contract, financial demands, damages.

But my spirit was broken and I did not reply, legal proceedings it would have to be.

"Now it's really over," I thought once again, "the end of the friendship."

I tried to see it as matter-of-factly as possible, but it hurt.

19 ∽ *Serge Lifar*

The affair continued to nag at me, for months on end. After six months, I had had enough: I could not bear to go on with that vague, unsettled feeling inside me. The matter would have to be broached.

I decided to return to Paris unannounced. If I had called him, the discussion would most probably have been conducted over the telephone. And besides, I was not too good on the telephone: conversations tended to come from one end of the line, and not mine. The most important thing, however, was that I wanted this conversation to be face to face and I was ready for anything he might do: he might slam the door in my face, he might be very curt and address me rather haughtily, or he might curse and swear at me.

When I arrived in Paris, I took a long walk from the Gare du Nord, strolling through noisy districts and ending in the relative peace of the banks of the Seine. Rudolf opened the door himself. He uttered a yell, "Ruditchka," pulled me inside, and would not hear of a serious talk.

"All that is past, let's forget. You can start next season, I will make sure that you get all the time you want. And we will have two new studios then; that will make all the difference."

Manuel was listening just outside the kitchen. "Are you coming back?" he whispered later. "That will be nice."

"I think I will." To be honest, I could still not believe it yet.

The new studios were, indeed, a relief. On Rudolf's initiative, the space above the auditorium had been entirely rebuilt. One part of the colossal loft had always been used to haul up the enormous chandeliers that hung in the theater with a pulley, in order to polish the thousands of crystals when distinguished visitors were expected. How the chandeliers were kept gleaming now was not wholly clear to me but, for the company, the two new rooms were like a land-slide: for the first time in history I could *see* the group and each individual had the necessary space needed to work in. No more canned-sardine scenes.

The Opéra *étoiles* each had their own dressing room in the building, *"ma loge,"*[1] a status symbol.

They were fitted out like small apartments, with a divan, a shower, and even a small kitchen nook, a welcome luxury, as the Opéra—where hundreds of people worked on a daily basis—did not have its own canteen in those days.

On previous occasions, I had either shared a dressing room with Michel Renault or changed for rehearsals in Rudolf's room, but as I would now be in the building for more than two months, I needed my own dressing room, where I could withdraw undisturbed. The rehearsals were scheduled for ir-regular hours of the day and sometimes evening; in the "lost" hours I could continue working on the ballet in peace and leave my notes, tapes, and scores there, as well.

The space I had been allotted was Noëlla Pontois' loge: *"Tu peux prendre la loge numéro x, quatrième étage."*[2] Anna gave me the key and, when I in-serted it in the lock on the fourth floor, it turned out that Pontois was chang-ing there.

"Pardon, ça doit être une erreur,"[3] but it did not appear to be a mistake.

"Noëlla's contract is ended," Anna said, when I asked for a different key, "she no longer has any right to the loge. Just go inside and say the room has been allotted to you."

"But it's not my job to show your soloists the door." The situation was painful enough. In 1969 I had met Pontois as a young ballerina and partner to Rudolf in Antwerp and now, seventeen years later, her career had come to an end; she would have to take her things and leave the loge. I could imagine what that must mean to her.

"It's Rudolf's job," Anna complained, but Rudolf looked aghast and obvi-

1. "My dressing room."
2. "You can take room x, fourth floor."
3. "I'm sorry, there must be a mistake."

ously did not intend to burn his fingers on such a thorny question. The lion was rather timid!

"Then give me another room." But Pontois' loge appeared to be the only one available, and it was up to me to solve the problem.

On the first day of rehearsals, the dressing room was vacant, but clothing and toiletries left behind clearly showed that Pontois was still attending practice.

The loge was frightful; I renamed it the "*chapelle ardente*";[4] the room was swathed from top to bottom in heavy, crimson velvet; the windows, doors, mirrors, washbasins and couch and the few decorations were in a matching style; heavy engravings, depressing fin-de-siècle lamps and furniture. A chamber of death, in short, that would have suited Sarah Bernhardt.

The start to my first rehearsal day was anything but promising. Outside, it was a bleak winter's day and the building was somber and oppressive. The narrow hallways brought out my inclination to run and the "*chapelle ardente*," where I was an intruder, seemed to be preparing me for an imminent catastrophe.

Philippe Delormes had come from Amsterdam to be there on the first rehearsal day of his new chief (me) with his old company and his old colleagues: he had left the Opéra the previous year and followed me to the Dutch National Ballet in Amsterdam.

He found me perched on the wine-red couch in the half-dark room where, from sheer misery, I had just thrown up in the washbasin.

"*Mais qu'est-ce-que tu as?*"[5]

"Nothing, I'm looking forward to my first rehearsal with your colleagues," I tried to joke.

"But they'll enjoy working with you again, believe me."

I wanted to believe Philippe, but it was to no avail.

Noëlla later asked me whether I would mind if she used her room in the mornings; she still wanted to take classes in the morning and would otherwise be obliged to change in the corps de ballet dressing rooms, quite a demotion.

For different reasons, we were both a little uncomfortable and nervous,

4. Funeral chapel.
5. "But what's wrong with you?"

like timid animals, during the first few days. After a week she no longer turned up and I missed her.

I used the first rehearsal mainly to become acquainted with the people—some fifty dancers—with whom I would be working.

I had chosen many older and "so" apparently seldom-used dancers, because the ballet, which had the French Revolution as its point of departure, had no need of refined ballet types.

Sans armes, citoyens! began in the belly of Paris, in a métro station named "*Liberté*." The train moved toward *Egalité* and, in the background, a corridor could be seen to the station *Fraternité*, the three revolutionary principles.[6]

The crowd waiting for the train was a free, but not equal and by no means fraternal group of individuals, ranging from wealthy down to poor as a church mouse. The passengers in the Paris métro had always fascinated, depressed, and amazed me; nowhere had I seen more embittered and disillusioned faces than underground in the City of Light.

In the ensuing scenes, the same characters became the masses in the 1790s rebellions, scenes intersected by a procession of victims, citizens, and soldiers from both the world wars and by a cluster of modern tourists who were admiring the Revolution scenes like ancient tableaux in the Louvre.

In the euphoria of victory, a genuine fraternity springs up between rich and poor, black and white, men, women, and children: "Gloire, gloire et triomphe!" the choirs of Berlioz rejoice.

Following the glow of contentment when everything seems attainable, complete acceptance, the crowd disperses into groups and single individuals. There is a *Dallas*-like tune, and the same soap opera is seen everywhere on the lowered screens: the end of the euphoria.

It was difficult to gauge what the assembled company thought of my story, but we had made a start. After an initial confrontation like that, something I always dreaded (in Holland, too) the real work could begin.

The previous evening, I had had another altercation with Rudolf. He pushed a piece of paper across the dinner table with a series of dates on it: "These are the days when I'm abroad, you can't rehearse with me then."

6. The names mean liberty, equality, and brotherhood.

I looked at him, astonished, and somewhat concerned. Had he counted on a role?

"But I don't need you, you're not in my new ballet."

He had informed me that, after that certain meeting with the group, he had agreed not to dance any more premieres: first performances would be reserved for the company dancers.

"But if *you* insist on having me in your ballet it is different," Rudolf tried. "A visiting choreographer is another story."

But I still did not intend to use him in my ballet. Working with Rudolf had never been simple, but to have to cope with him, the director of the company, as a dancer as well, seemed to me to be impossible. I would feel terribly limited in my freedom and everything would revolve around one person again.

"You shouldn't compete with your dancers, Rudolf, not in any way. You should create a distance there."

A year earlier, I had seen him appear in a ballet he had made for the Opéra, *Washington Square*, a period piece in which he had danced the part of an older man, attired in a three-piece suit, with a mustache and gray sideburns.

I was seated beside a group of American tourists in the theater and one of them whispered, "That one there is Nureyev."
"No, come on," was the chuckling commentary, "that can't be him."

"Yes, look, it's in the program." The booklet was passed along as evidence.

Large sections of the public would not accept him any other way than as a beautiful youth and virtuoso dancer, the perfect picture in a schoolgirl's book. For them, this gray-whiskered Nureyev in pants meant the curtain on the fairy-tale world they believed they were visiting.

Afterward, when Rudolf approached the footlights, a loud booing sounded from the auditorium; some Parisians did not hide what they thought of his activities. He looked up, laughed bitterly, and stuck a meaningful finger in the air: "Fuck you."

In spite of everything, it did me good to see him make that gesture in that bourgeois palace, to that oh-so-respectable, smug, and self-satisfied audience. A confrontation with contemporary language and gestures would do no harm, I felt.

Was it his obsession that he was loved nowhere? On the way home he told me that, behind him, too, from the rows of bowing dancers, he had heard booing as well. "The bastards, they hate me. All they can think of is their Lifar. They'll do anything to get rid of me."

During the months when I was rehearsing *Sans armes*, I often saw parts of performances that the company gave from the wings, productions by Rudolf, such as *Raymonda* or *Don Quixote*. When Rudolf was dancing his variations, a group of mainly older soloists, ballet masters, and staff would gather there, in the first wing, where there was most space.

There was an aura of the French court about it all, the whispered remarks, the glances exchanged between lackeys, the significant smiles and, when Rudolf ran into the wings after bowing to the audience, the etiquette of stepping aside to allow his passage, whispered and insincere "bravos," friendly gallantries. Sugar-coated bitterness.

Louis XIV's French court from the days of yore, or simply the reality of today?

I also worked with a group of eleven children from the school, who came marching into the studio after school hours—half-past five!—three times a week, under the strict guardianship of a pair of teachers. As they were not allowed to do every performance, (they were only ten years old), each child had an understudy and so there were actually twenty-two children; *French* children, who sometimes chattered like eager little parrots! But I enjoyed working with them; after a time they were open, without reserve, to any suggestion.

Initially, they were amazed at the freedom that I gave them and had no idea how to cope with that freedom in their dancing; I felt the drilled, strictly regimented background of their training in everything. But the group of street urchins they were supposed to portray appealed to their imagination and they achieved the most fantastic and frequently quite moving interpretations. Often, I simply sat still, open-mouthed, watching and enjoying them.

Occasionally, while he was waiting to go home with me, Rudolf would come into the studio to see the progress. Then there would be enormous excitement among the children and, instead of the shy and rather awkward behavior I usually saw in Dutch schools on such an occasion, everyone would exaggerate, each trying harder to be more expressive and daring than the other.

At the end of the rehearsal, and in spite of the protests from the guardian teachers, they ran to Rudolf and thronged about him to obtain the coveted autograph in their exercise-books.

With them, he was beloved in no uncertain terms, respected and admired, they left no doubt about that.

One evening, watching the news with Rudolf, we heard that Serge Lifar, eighty-one years old, had died. He was to be buried in Paris.

On the morning of the funeral, I said I wanted to attend the service at the Russian church in the rue Daru. "You're going too, aren't you?" But Rudolf showed little enthusiasm. "And what on earth does he mean to you?" he inquired scornfully.

Lifar was a part of history for me. In my early days as a dancer, I had devoured books on Diaghilev's Russian ballet, and Lifar had been one of the legendary names. But I also wanted to see the mourners, among whom there were bound to be a number of old Russian émigrés, sure to provide quaint nostalgic little groups. Often one seemed to be attending a family reunion; conservative, official-looking gentlemen chatting confidentially together, moving from one circle to another, and ladies breathing a dated aura of standing with their coats redolent of mothballs and wearing ancient, but imposing headgear.

"Rudolf, you *have* to go, it'll only give rise to comment otherwise." But he donned a mask: "You go and represent me."

During the service in the dark church, where many (ex-)dancers, particularly the older generations, and teachers were present, someone suddenly tweaked me in the neck: Rudolf was standing behind me with a little grin on his face. He paced up and down, whispering with the odd person here and there, and after the service was one of the first to disappear from the church that was wreathed in clouds of incense. "They don't want me here."

I stayed and observed a number of historic dance and theatrical personalities jostling one another for pride of place on the sunny vestibule steps, in front of the clicking and whirring cameras. Lifar no longer seemed so important.

"*Il était un vrai maître,*"[7] said Elisabeth Platel, with whom I returned to the Opéra to rehearse. Coming from her, it seemed utterly sincere.

---

7. "He was a true master."

20 ⟶ Tout le Monde

Nureyev was forty-eight, and for the first time in his adult life, he had a permanent base; his abode in Paris had become his home and it was evident that he enjoyed it. He felt less need to travel; if he went, he longed to be home again right from departure, and once he was home, he seemed less inclined to go out during every free hour he had.

To my amazement, I sometimes heard him saying, "Shall we skip this?" or: "Why don't we stay home!" when we had made plans to go somewhere.

And yet, he still occasionally felt a need to be out on the street: a breath of air, people, a rendezvous, maybe.

In the rue de Seine, I showed him the building where, long ago, Toer and I had met Isadora Duncan's brother, a gray-haired man with locks down to his shoulder blades and robed in quasi-Greek garments he had hand-woven himself. He dwelt in a studio-cum-small-theater, where people from the neighborhood were given the chance to display their talent on Saturday afternoons.

Rudolf reveled in the stories of the old ladies who conjured up Debussy on the out-of-tune piano in the Duncan theater or their yells of disgust, "*Ah, c'est elle. Je la déteste!*"[1] at the sight of a militant woman about to recite poems by Li Tai Pe in French. "You have to write that down," Rudolf would say.

Or we would walk to the Saint Sulpice, where he showed me the rather disappointing mural *Jacob and the Angel* by Delacroix. "I should cut out those two figures and take them home," he said covetously, peering around the darkened church as though he were really considering doing so!

On one of the trips, he confided a new dilemma to me: one of the ballerinas in the troupe was related to the Minister for Inland Revenue. "The entire family is very fanatical about her career, they sit in the audience and call out

1. "Ah, it's her. I detest her!"

173

"bravo" whenever she appears. If I raise her to *étoile* position it could mean they will help me to escape my taxes. Now the French government charges me millions, every year. What do you think?"

I could only laugh: "If you start doing that kind of thing you are lost, believe me." But I could hardly imagine he would seriously consider entering such a hornet's nest.

In Paris, he seemed to have discovered the medium television as well, watching all manner of programs fairly indiscriminately, sometimes keeping an eye on the moving pictures while trying to conduct a conversation at the same time, in a childlike and almost irritating way. Then, when he burst out laughing or uttered a strange remark, it was occasionally unclear whether his response was to our conversation or the screen, leading to somewhat schizophrenic situations.

Evening meals at home with him never began before ten in the evening and, often, afterward, at midnight, he would say, "Shall we look at my ballets?"

He never watched his own films—he had two to his name. His dance films, on the other hand, he watched all the more. I never had the courage to say they really did not interest me, complete performances of *Don Quixote*, *Swan Lake*, *The Nutcracker* or *Raymonda*, but he appeared fascinated, gave a running commentary on his own dancing, and seemed thrilled with all he saw.

I would stifle a yawn and await an appropriate moment to withdraw. When I left around two, he would still be in front of the box.

He trained faithfully, every day. Sometimes, as he stumbled around his house in the morning, he sighed, "Everything hurts me, why don't I go back to bed?" But he hardly ever did, even though I readily advised him to do so.

When I had time, I went with him and watched class, as I was always fascinated by dancers at work and certainly such virtuosos as those at the Opéra. Rudolf did the practice with incredible vigor; scorning danger, he threw himself into high leaps, dotted with double turns, as though he were in competition with the soloists in the class who were so much younger. Often he would land with a dull thud, because his knees and ankles could scarcely take his weight. What happened to his painfully swollen and nearly deformed feet at those moments, I dare not think.

Once, he saw the tortured expression on my face and walked over to me. "Kerdoing! Old frog jumps," he grinned. But on the way back in the car, he confided to me, "Tell me, I do those jumps better than the other boys, don't you think? More correct?" He asked a question, although with the intonation of an answer. But for me to find an answer that was at all honest was by no means easy.

At home, he would often play his harpsichord, slowly, huddled over the score, eyes pinched tight into slits. An unforgettable scene, twilight falling through the high windows onto his bent shoulders, his hands feeling their way over the keys, and the thin, needlelike sounds he brought forth, often with long and concentrated silences between them, as though he were jumping from stone to stone in a stream.

Toer sometimes came to Paris from Amsterdam and, one evening, while Rudolf was playing, we caught one another's eye at the same moment.

"Did you see what I saw a while back?" I asked Toer later. Rudolf looking like an aged Greek peasant, a fatigued and rather neglected farmer, a sight that moved us and of which we were both acutely aware. Toer drew a sketch of the musician Rudolf and though the likeness was uncanny, it seemed wiser he should not see Toer's interpretation. He might be painfully hurt by what we considered striking.

Mikhail Baryshnikov had come over from New York, where he had become artistic director of American Ballet Theatre, some years after his flight from the Soviet Union in 1974. On holiday in Paris, he took daily classes at the Opéra.

"Did you see Moshe?" Rudolf asked me mockingly; switching Misha's name into "Moshe" did not, alas, signify anything very positive. And yet, he still invited him into his home—they were old acquaintances, after all, and had often worked together in the West. Despite the air of camaraderie, I felt the rivalry Rudolf unconsciously radiated: he made scathing comments, played down Baryshnikov's work in America very subtly, and tried to provoke him in a pseudo-playful way. It was a game between two male animals, one still in his prime, the other on the wane but defending his territory in advance all the same.

Their common past was not mentioned, as though it were taboo. Leningrad, the Kirov Ballet, Pushkin, it all seemed far behind them and, instead, they boasted—rather transparently—of their productions, their guest appearances and their possessions.

"I'm in Paris to look for a pied-à-terre, I sometimes feel I've had enough of New York." Baryshnikov looked around Rudolf's room. "A little larger than this, perhaps, and a bit lighter. A view of the Tuileries would be nice."

Astronomical real-estate prices were bandied about as though they were at a roulette table, a tough, capitalist game. Each trying to outdo the other. I recalled the tiny room in Leningrad and Xenia Pushkin, touching the divan: "This is where they slept."

Later they took turns on the harpsichord, Baryshnikov playfully and with a nonchalant ease, Nureyev seriously, with more devotion but less ease. It was marvelous for me to watch them: both of them world famous dancers, both artistic directors of large companies, both had produced ballets and appeared in films, only Baryshnikov with more success than Rudolf.

Rudolf had always had a burning desire to work with Balanchine, as had Baryshnikov, but the latter's wish had been realized: he had danced in Balanchine's company for two years, a matter that possibly disturbed Rudolf most. Their lives had followed similar lines, sometimes moving in the same stream, sometimes colliding momentarily, a meeting accompanied by creaking and sometimes flying splinters. And yet, *still*, Rudolf remained the undisputed and absolute star.

When Misha had left, Rudolf snarled, "Did you hear that? Why does he want a house in Paris, all of a sudden? He wants my job. I'm sure he is already negotiating with the Opéra."

Rudolf was very keen that Toer and I should see his new production of *Swan Lake*; his version had caused quite a stir within the company, because the version the Opéra had been showing for years, created by the Muscovite Vladimir Bourmeister, was much loved by the dancers and audiences.

"There are lots of new ideas, you'll see."

I was working out plans for a new *Swan Lake* with the Dutch National Ballet myself and so, on the one hand I was really curious to see how Rudolf approached certain things but, on the other hand, still frightened of possibly being influenced as well.

Unfortunately, the new ideas in Rudolf's *Swan Lake* were mainly ornamental ones, the whole production taking place in a boxlike form with painted screens, which were pushed into place to indicate a change in setting, endowing the whole with a Kabuki theater-like perspective. Since the basic color of the decor was white—right down to the floor!—the all-important white scenes gave no contrast and were lacking in atmosphere. Every attempt at enchantment failed in the white-on-white spectacle evolving in the glaring light.

"Why have you allowed the designer to make such ill-conceived sets?" we were brave enough to ask. "They murder the production."

"But that white box is just what it's all about. The prince is held captive in a cage of ideas of purity and innocence, he hides himself away in an aesthetic, immaculate white space, which is a prison at the same time."

He was quiet for the remainder of the evening, because we could not come round to his way of thinking at all.

Working with the group went more smoothly than I had expected. I had made sure by now that I knew most of those taking part in *Sans armes* by name, something for which the corps de ballet, in particular, showed their gratitude.

A number of nondancers were added to the cast, some twenty-five people, students, older women and men, among whom were a number of blacks taking on character roles in the crowd scenes. In the mass gathering scenes, I did not want the extras to stand on the sideline, but to move with the occasionally fairly intricate choreography. This required a great deal of rehearsal time and was initially viewed with some scepticism by the dancers—"professionals," after all. Breaking with social convention was not always simple either. The aristocratic lady (but she really *did* imagine herself to be from a "better class") and a black street-cleaner (who actually carried out that profession in daily life), whom I wanted to embrace one another at the fulfillment of the revolutionary ideals as living proof of equality and fraternity, had strong objections toward this at the beginning. Integrating the black group was a challenge altogether and they remained a separate island for a long time, even when the "whites" made occasional strained social overtures.

But there were other social conventions to be broken with, as well. If I had announcements for the group, changed a rehearsal, or wanted to rehearse a new scene for which not everyone was needed, I hung up a note with the names of the people concerned. Amazement all round: no one ever seemed to do that. The dancers, "*tout le monde*," were expected to find out for themselves in the studios what was happening; so, often a great number of people sat around for hours, waiting unnecessarily.

"We don't exist here," the dancers from the corps de ballet said to me frequently, "The *étoiles* have a name, Monsieur L., Mademoiselle G., but we're just '*tout le monde*,' nameless."

"*Révolution, tout le monde!*" I would then sometimes call out with a wink when one of the étoiles showed up late for a rehearsal—Lormeaux and Denard were masters at that. "*Sans armes, contre la classe privilégée.*"[2]

Even if *Sans armes* was not destined to be a successful ballet, it had certainly been a fine exercise in fraternity; in two months' time I saw the group, consisting of fairly indifferent individuals at first, transformed into a unit: children, "*tout le monde*," extras, and *étoiles*, all merged enthusiastically into one.

"How do you do that?" Rudolf sometimes asked me a little suspiciously. "They all seem to trust you."

"But Rudolf, you know how it works. When you're a guest somewhere for a short time it's easy to whip up enthusiasm. But long term, that's when the trouble starts."

Sometimes, when he was still watching television eagerly, long after midnight, and I said, "sorry Rudolf, I'm going to sleep," he would glance up in amazement, as though he were puzzled that I might be tired or bored.

"Okay, you sleep."

As I left the vast and sumptuously decorated room, I would see the silhouette of his small head projected starkly against the lighted screen. It seemed as if he was afraid to go to bed, afraid to lose a minute of life. I had the feeling he did four or five times as much with his life as other people did, as I did.

He had once told me he had never cooked a meal in his life: at school, after leaving home, he had eaten in the theater canteen and, in the West, after living in hotels for a short time and eating in restaurants, he had soon had

---

2. "Without weapons, against the privileged classes."

admirers and, later on, people working for him who took care of all the day-to-day worries that got in the way of his dancing.

"I can boil an egg, that's about it. I never had to buy my own food, never cooked it, and I never washed anything but myself. And I never ever made my own bed." But I could refute that. On one of the very first days when he was staying with us during the *Monument* period, Toer had found him upstairs, busy making his bed. Toer had laughed and pointed at our unmade beds, meaning to say, "Leave it, we don't do it either."

Rudolf had misunderstood the gesture and nodded: "Yes, I'll do them, too."

"But he has nothing else to worry about," I sometimes thought, when I withdrew to sleep, far earlier than he did. "He has no day-to-day worries, he doesn't have to shop and cook or keep his house clean."

What his greatest daily worry and obsession must have been in those days, I still had no notion.

One Sunday morning, Douce was standing in the doorway to his bathroom in desperation: "Rudolf, it's half past ten. You should have checked in by now."

We had already put his baggage into the car, Manuel had breakfast waiting on the table and Rudolf was drying himself painstakingly and with infuriating care; he was due to depart for South America that morning.

"He'll never make it." I wondered how Douce kept going under the constant nervous strain; the more excited she became, the calmer Rudolf seemed to be.

"If you miss this plane, you'll have to wait six hours." Rudolf drank his tea calmly and, eating a piece of toast, took his place in the car next to Douce.

"Don't drive too fast." Throwing caution to the wind, however, Douce tore along the boulevards, ignoring traffic lights and speed limits.

"They'll wait, don't worry." Rudolf appeared to be certainty personified. "I'm sure you will fix it." With those few subtle words, he seemed to lay the responsibility for the expedition's success on Douce's shoulders. Turning around, he said to me, loudly, "Late or not, Douce always finds a way."

Douce's only answer was to put her foot down hard on the gas pedal. Attired in a multi-colored poncho, a folkloristic cap on his tousled hair, he strode into the departure lounge and up to the desk where Douce had gone ahead of us.

"*Je regrette, vous êtes trop tard.*"[3] The girl shrugged; the airplane doors had already closed, fifteen minutes earlier.

Cursing, Rudolf threw his bag down on the ground and, looking daggers at Douce, assumed an expectant air.

"But he has to be in Buenos Aires tomorrow morning, it's terribly important, do you hear? He *has* to be there," Douce tried to bend the iron rules of the airport. Her final, well-aimed shot would achieve the miracle: "*Vous savez, c'est Monsieur Nureyev! Il a son spectacle, demain!*"[4]

The girl looked at the sulking man beneath the woolen hat and smiled somewhat condescendingly: "*Et alors?*"[5]

Despite the race—Douce ran from desk to desk through the lounge—Rudolf did not board that airplane. In haste, an emergency route was mapped out that would take some hours longer and Rudolf disappeared through customs, greeting me curtly and Douce not at all, as though we had caused his delay.

Sans armes was nearing completion. In Elisabeth Platel, Marie-Claude Pietragalla, Annie Carbonnel and Denard, Romoli, and Belarbi, I had a group of soloists who worked brilliantly, and in the groups, many dancers gave beautiful and expressive performances as well.

The poster and program went into production and that provided Toer and me with even more surprises yet.

Toer had produced a fine design for the poster, a figure advancing with a burning torch and a sword in hand. The drawing lay awaiting approval in one of the management offices and, one morning, Toer was called onto the carpet. To be on the safe side, I accompanied him and asked Rudolf to be there, as well, as I had little faith in the judgment of the top brass.

"But that figure's only half on the page," commented one of the members of the management. "It gives the impression the drawing is only half-finished, or that it's accidentally been cut off."

A remark like that in the country of Matisse, Picasso, and Delaunay! It hardly amazed me when I saw what was exhibited in many Paris galleries, the sorry arrangements of kitschy prints and expensive baubles.

3. "I'm sorry, you're too late."
4. "You know, it's Mr. Nureyev! His show is tomorrow."
5. "So what?"

Toer refused to add the missing half-figure and we left it up to Rudolf whether the poster would go ahead or not.

I wanted to dedicate *Sans armes* to Rudolf, for the confidence he kept placing in me, but also to the people from Greenpeace, firstly, because of the subject of the ballet, but also because the French government had just had a Greenpeace ship sunk in New Zealand, leading to the loss of a human life.

Immediately after the text of my dedication became known to the organizations concerned, I received the announcement that the Opéra management refused to mention Greenpeace in the programs; it was, after all, an organization that was hostile toward the French state!

It was fantastic how people managed to twist things here.

Fortunately, though, Toer and I had made a number of good friends in the organization who did everything to help us with problems. Josseline Le Bourhis from the "Publicité" department winked at me: "Don't worry, the dedication will appear in the program the way you want it. I'll take care of it for you."

On his return from South America, Rudolf was tired and depressed. Now that *Sans armes* was almost finished, there was more free time and I tried to cheer Rudolf up as much as possible. We went to the *"marché aux puces,"*[6] an occasional film, or to Fontainebleau or Versailles on a Sunday afternoon, for a walk in the gardens. However, nothing really seemed to divert him: he remained distracted and appeared to have no real interest in anything.

"What's worrying you, Rudolf? Are there problems?" But he remarked scornfully that his life was always full of problems: the taxes, agents, critics, the ballet companies with which he had always appeared but which seemed to have forgotten him now, plummeting shares. "No one is interested in me anymore," he said one evening, "and not in love, either. I'm old. They all walk right past me. It's so degrading," he laughed bitterly. "Women I can get as many as I want. But I don't *want* them, they drive me crazy."

Douce often had problems with Rudolf, although—or precisely because—she tried to bring order and regularity into his life. From early morning until late at night, she flew and ran about for him, arranging the daily course of affairs in his house ("But she is not my boss," Manuel would often protest

6. Flea market.

to me. "I only take orders from Mister Nureyev"), and the maintenance or decoration of the various and ever-increasing number of homes, besides.

"Rudolf buys houses but never has time to do anything to them, so I'm the one who has to see that everything is restored and redecorated and who is responsible for how the houses look afterward. Naturally, I ask him what he would like, but he never answers. When he finally sees what I've had done, he's furious, nothing's ever right in his eyes. But if I do nothing he's furious, too; then he says that everyone lets him down. You can't win."

I understood her situation, witnessed it almost every day and often wondered what drove her to go on with her caring and arranging. But I understood Rudolf's reaction, as well; Douce's care, however well meant, was sometimes stifling and engulfed everything.

"Just stay away for a few days, until he *asks* you to come again." But Douce appeared morning, noon, and night, no matter what he said and however he behaved toward her. She cried sometimes, walked about the house in silence, sighed, but she was *there*.

"He needs me. If I don't come, his life goes haywire, someone has to keep his accounts, keep track of his contracts, run the house, the taxes, the paintings and furniture he buys all over the place and still has to pay for."

Sometimes, Rudolf's "business" did seem to have spiraled out of control, something set in motion and not to be brought to a standstill after that, a snowball grown into an avalanche on the hillside.

Douce was not welcome at the Opéra, either; the battle between the staff and her had flared up.

"*Rudolf est notre chef, pas Douce*,"[7] they mumbled in the offices. Where had I heard those words before?

But Rudolf refused to make a decision, allowing the two parties to conduct their battle under the surface, acting as if he noticed nothing or was not involved at all. Divide and rule. I saw the awful state in which Douce often was, in her lonely and determined battle of adoration and devotion.

Sometimes he would suddenly bring people home with him, admirers he had met, who had waited for him after a performance or approached him in the street. The German student, for example; a pleasant boy who was taken unawares by the keen friendliness suddenly displayed by the star he so admired.

"I asked for his autograph for my girlfriend in Germany," he told Toer and

---

7. "Rudolf is our boss, not Douce."

me, "and he immediately invited me out for a meal. I don't know what to do now. *Es ist sehr verehrend, aber . . .*"[8]

Rudolf was in another room answering the telephone. "*Und es ist zum ersten Mal in meinem Leben dass jemand Pupsie zu mir hat gesagt,*"[9] something the boy apparently considered a dubious honor: "Pupsie, can you pass me the salad?" "Can you give Pupsie some more wine?"

"Don't you think he is sympathetic?," Rudolf asked, when the boy had found an oportunity to leave, "and so good-looking. I fancy him."

A few mornings later, the boy was indeed sitting at the breakfast table; he grimaced when he saw us. Rudolf made a businesslike, but satisfied, impression.

The doctor had just left, after putting the hypodermic syringes and the rubber gloves into his little black bag.

"Are *you* afraid of dying?" he asked me one evening. I wasn't, not *really*, and I said so. But the question amazed me, it was not a bit like Rudolf.

"Me not either." The only thing he was unhappy about was the shape of the coffin, the cold, rectangular shape, the shiny wood. "One lies there so exposed, no intimacy at all."

I agreed with him, a round basket in which one could lie curled up might feel familiar and more secure. But Rudolf was more radical: "I would prefer to be burnt by my best friends, on a beach, like Shelley. Close to the sea."

"Do you want to see a bit of hell?" He put on a video of Maguy Marin's ballet *May B*, which I had already admired a number of times: a hilarious-pathetic and oppressive piece about a group of Breughelian characters.

"This is what I fear most, that my future will be like this."

To me, it did not seem such a terrifying vision of the future; there was a great sense of sympathy and solidarity among the half-demented souls in Marin's ballet that moved me.

"I'll make her do a ballet for me, but not like this," said Rudolf, "I can't watch such scenes night after night."

After the pre-dress rehearsal of *Sans armes*, Rudolf grabbed me by the arm: "Very good. You made me cry."

But he had not seen the whole ballet; problems had cropped up in the last

8. "It's very flattering, but . . ."
9. "And this is the first time in my life that anyone has called me 'Pupsie.'"

scene. I had wanted the overpopular *Dallas* tune resounding throughout the auditorium and video shots of the artificial *Dallas* stars projected onto a large number of screens. The rights of both the tune and the film shots, however, turned out to be so exorbitant that the Opéra rightly would not contemplate it.

Chiel Meyering, a Dutch composer with whom I had worked several times before, and who, I knew, could arrange a piece of music like lightning, helped me out of my fix. When I had rung him and explained my predicament, a short score arrived a few days later, which was copied for the orchestra on the very day of the pre-dress rehearsal.

A master in thinking up ambiguous titles, Meyering had christened the composition *Falla$*.

Sans armes, citoyens! was not a great success; public opinion seemed divided, with many jeers and somewhat fewer bravos, the sort of tumult I had become accustomed to with more of my work.

In the ensuing weeks, I did receive fan mail forwarded on, letters from people expressing their pleasure that a piece with socially concerned content had been shown on the Opéra stage. I saw a number of people again and again at subsequent performances, and, when I observed the look in their eyes, I knew the ballet had satisfied them.

When I thanked the dancers on stage for our two-month collaboration, the applause they gave me seemed to go on forever, and that made me really happy: working together had been a success, I could not have wished for anything more.

Fraternité!

No matter what happened, I was going to celebrate the premiere with the company; I would not have it any other way, because I regretted having to break short our bond.

We had not seen Rudolf any more, but when we arrived home to a house full of guests, he appeared to be in a very bad mood.

"How could you do that, dedicate your ballet to me *and* to such a criminal organization as Greenpeace? Everyone will think that there's a connection between them and me. You did me a lot of harm."

Rudolf, brainwashed by the petty French politics he so often complained about himself.

The unarmed revolution of Greenpeace still had a long way to go.

"Do you know we have all the sets and costumes for *Daphnis and Chloë* by Chagall in our storerooms"? he asked me, just before my return to Amsterdam. "What would you think of redoing that ballet?"

He proposed that I should return within the foreseeable future and he would then arrange for the backdrops to be hanging on stage and for me to see all the costumes. "Magnificent colors they have, every costume is a masterpiece, the whole thing belongs in a museum."

Just before I had started work in Paris, I had staged a large ballet in Holland, *To Bend or to Break*, with more than a hundred participants and, besides that, I had completed a book I had begun writing at Rudolf's house, during the *Petits Gosses* strike periods. After *Sans armes*, I stepped straight into a new version of *Swan Lake*; I felt utterly drained and had had more than enough of large-scale ballets for the time being. Much as I loved Ravel's score, I simply could not start on another evening-length ballet immediately. What I needed was rest.

"If I do something like that, you'll have to wait two years; I need to rest and do some smaller works first."

But he did not want to wait, it was now or never.

It would be never.

After I had told him, yet *again,* that I would not organize a guest season for him with the Dutch National Ballet—he kept on about it—I asked him whether he would be interested in making a choreography for our group. I had seen a number of his contemporary ballets, all narrative, and thought it was time he tried his hand at an abstract one. He pricked up his ears immediately: "What would you like, what should it be?"

He had said a number of times that he was so impressed by the men in our company—"so many talents"—and I knew he enjoyed dancers like Jurriëns, Farha, Walthall, and Martijn. But he had also discovered the younger talents in the corps de ballet, such as Lindsay Fischer, Alan Land, Wim Broeckx, Barry Watt, Bruno Barat.

"Make a ballet for our boys, you can teach them so much about technique and style. You could help them on their way."

For a year-and-a-half there was talk of its happening, but he never committed himself. If I suggested a rehearsal period, then it would transpire that he either had a tour ahead of him or was waiting for a new film contract *or* he had to stage one of his evening-length ballets somewhere in the world.

"Why do you have to know so far ahead if I am available?" he asked in irritation.

"Because we are a big company and we are planning ahead, just like all the others, and like you. You can't just walk in and expect us to be ready for you. We're busy, too."

21 ⌒ *Last Songs*

He seemed to have a constant appetite for new works for his company and I had hardly left Paris before he called me yet again with the urgent request to stage *another* work for him, *Vier letzte Lieder*.[1]

"Our girls will dance it exquisitely, you'll see."

Three months after *Sans armes*, I was standing in the Paris studios once more, this time with Merrilee at my side again, to prepare the ballet as soon as possible.

"A new rule has been introduced, on the initiative of the *étoiles*," Rudolf told me, when I put my cast list in front of him. "I'm sorry for you, but you can't use most of these people. The rule is now that the solo roles are to be danced by the *étoiles* at a premiere."

He was familiar with my enthusiasm for a number of dancers from the lower echelons and with my tenacity regarding casting. "But after the first night you can decide who dances what. Then you can do whatever you feel is right."

It seemed to me to be quite a ridiculous rule: so the stars wanted to take all the glory for the first performances themselves?

I had a long talk with him on the importance of giving the choreographer freedom of choice because it offered the opportunity for unknown dancers to advance. Someone from outside the company would see the dancers' potential through different eyes and might discover other things in them than would the staff, who were confronted with the dancers every day.

But the inspiration, especially, between the choreographer and the dancers of his choice, seemed to me to be of vital importance. Surely it was absurd to have people working together more or less by force and then expect inspiration? After all, creating a ballet together was rather like being married for

---

1. *Four Last Songs* by Richard Strauss.

a while! You exposed yourself and shared a number of your most intimate feelings with one another.

Rudolf agreed with me, of course, because he made ballets himself and knew how hard it was—and how important—to find a good cast for a choreography, the combination of personalities, the dramatic qualities, the contrasts, but above all the inspiration that one dancer arouses in the choreographer and another far less.

"But it's also simply a question of rank; people are not soloists for no reason at all, they've worked hard for years." Rudolf rejected my arguments. "It's my task to make sure everyone gets the work that is due to them."

I looked at him in amazement. "I can't believe my ears. Your socialist train is finally riding in time? Congratulations!"

He looked at me with fatigue in his eyes and sighed.

"Sometimes you have no choice, you have to take any available train to get to the destination."

I finally agreed to try to draw up a cast list according to the Opéra rules, but, if I did not succeed, then he would have to find another choreographer for his premiere.

"But you will not do that to me, you can't," he pointed out drily.

Another problem appeared to be that the company had to go on tour to New York in the middle of the rehearsal period available to us.

"Is it possible to finish the ballet within two weeks?" he inquired, donning his most innocent face.

Perhaps, with a concerted effort, Merrilee and I could manage to have the dancers learn the ballet in two weeks, but by no means would it be ready for performing: merely a rough sketch.

On top of that, again, the rehearsal time available was terrifyingly short, as the company would have to work hard on refining the New York repertoire, which had not been danced for rather a long time.

The only solution was that Merrilee and I should travel with the company and continue rehearsing with the dancers in America. This meant it was a problem with an appealing side to it, and Rudolf proposed it with enthusiasm: "Yes, come with us!"

I drew up a cast list that seemed acceptable, although certainly not ideal. I had worked well with a number of soloists in the past and developed a bond with them: Platel, Legris, Hilaire, Legrée, Denard, and Guillem, but the others were new to me except Kader Belarbi, who was lower in rank, but whom Rudolf "granted" me. I had no idea what I could achieve with the newcomers.

Once again, we had made our abode above the small market in our beloved rue de Seine and spent a large part of our time roaming around Paris: the group had so much to rehearse that we hardly stood a chance with *Vier Letzte Lieder,* especially now it had been decided we should travel with them. "You'll get time enough in New York." The whole business seemed to us a considerable financial squandering for the Opéra, but we decided not to become annoyed this time, but to enjoy it: Paris was always a marvelous experience every time.

Rudolf left for New York earlier than the group and, as we were not on the group ticket, Merrilee and I traveled separately as well.

There would be two weeks of performances at the Metropolitan Opera House and, for the occasion, the company had taken along a repertoire of mainly evening-length ballets. For this reason, nearly the whole company had made the crossing, some hundred dancers and an enormous staff of ballet masters, secretaries, and the press service; with our eternal but essential thrift on such occasions in mind, I feasted my Dutch eyes!

Finding the necessary time and concentration to rehearse *Vier letzte lieder* with the dancers, amidst that gigantic operation and such hectic events, was going to become a new problem.

For the first three days, indeed, nothing happened, at least, not for Merrilee and me. The company had dress rehearsals, but were suffering from jet lag and needed a long time to get started, to Rudolf's annoyance.

"What is the matter, you are all young and spoiled. Look at me, I travel around world and dance same night, I don't waste time."

It was all true, but there was only one person who worked the way he did and there was simply no way he could expect such efforts from others; not everyone had his iron will and a body of steel.

We saw most of the rehearsals and were repeatedly amazed at the high degree of virtuosity and technical ease in the dancing, but also at the apparent lack of discipline on the part of the French dancers. Many rehearsals were reminiscent of the disorganized topsy-turvy little market in the rue de Seine.

The remaining time I spent on showing Merrilee, in New York for the first time, all the places to which I had lost my heart over the years: the Staten

Island ferry, which offered the most fantastic view of the city skyline from the water, Central Park, the Metropolitan Museum, and the Museum of Modern Art, the Cloisters. We traveled on buses and in the subway and walked for hours, until our legs refused to carry us any farther.

"What are you doing all day, aren't you getting bored?" inquired Rudolf between the acts, but it did not seem to occur to him to give us rehearsal time. Did we look too happy?

Our life of leisure came to an abrupt end after all; on the rehearsal schedule we suddenly discovered two hours reserved, out of the blue, for *Quatre Derniers Lieder,*[2] as the ballet was called in a strange blend of tongues: someone had apparently realized that those two people from Amsterdam had come to New York to enjoy the city.

We had once cautiously tried to track down our dressing rooms in the enormous theater, but all the rooms appeared to be crammed full of costumes, dancers, extras, members of staff and of the orchestra; not an inch seemed to be unused.

Merrilee found herself a home with an English ballet mistress belonging to the company. I decided, having heard the dancers' frequent complaints about lack of space, not to cause any more trouble and to change somewhere in a corner backstage.

Our first rehearsal took place with all the dancers involved, as it seemed wise to see how much of the sporadic Paris rehearsals they could still recall and which couples would need the most rehearsal time.

The studio we worked in, the largest in the theater, was underground and had no windows; outside it was at least 104 degrees Fahrenheit but, in the practice room, where some sixty people took classes every day, it was even hotter and the lack of air almost unbearable. The air conditioning people swear by in America had been switched off because the cool currents of air gave the dancers muscle problems, so it was like working in a Turkish bath. To make things worse, the dancers were tired—no wonder—and arguments and disagreements arose at the drop of a hat, followed by floods of tears.

I could understand their frustration: after company classes, which ended at twelve, most rehearsed on until four o'clock, starting again at six with prep-

2. *Four Last Songs* was written in a combination of French and German.

arations for the evening performance. Besides that, there was a matinee twice a week. Most of them hardly had time to see anything of the city at all.

Before the rehearsal began, I spoke to the dancers, saying that I understood their situation and so I would not want them to dance full out during the first rehearsals. The main thing, at this stage, was for me to see whether they had remembered the steps, whether the partnering was going well, and most important of all, whether the ballet was musically correct.

I would only want them to dance full out on the final days, which was essential, as the premiere was due to take place in Paris a mere three days after our return. Insane planning, indeed; I agreed with the dancers on that.

Guillem—in the three years I had been working at the Opéra, she had shot like an arrow to become a true dance sensation—was visibly exhausted. She was *the* discovery of the New York season, dancing important roles constantly and hounded by the press. Her exceedingly fragile body appeared not to have an ounce of resistance left and seemed ready to melt like snow in the sun under immense pressure from high tension and the cruel heat.

Despite the fact that I forgave her a great deal, however, I found her manner of rehearsing rather shocking; she would chew gum during the marking-out of the third song, wore an enormous pair of sunglasses that hid the top half of her face, and responded to each correction that was made to her work with a grimace or a surly shrug of the shoulders.

At the initial rehearsal, I assumed it was only a matter of the first day, but when her attitude remained more or less the same on the following days, I commented on her behavior: what she thought she could permit herself toward me did not particularly interest me, I said to her, but out of respect for the music I expected different behavior; she was not dancing to pop music.

Sylvie had just discovered that, besides Paris, she had New York at her feet as well, quite a challenging experience for a nineteen-year-old; that I understood. It disappointed me, though, that such a discovery should lead to such coolness and aloofness.

Isabelle Guérin and Jean-Yves Lormeaux seemed to be infected with the long face "virus" as well, their mood surrounding them like a concrete wall. It was unscalable and, to be honest, I felt no inclination to try.

"I don't understand you. Rudolf has explained that the *étoiles* have demanded to dance all premieres. So why don't you work then, why do you spoil my pleasure and that of the colleagues who *do* want to? Be consistent and let me choose who I want to work with. I can do without you, really."

Those concerned listened, shocked: "It's not directed at you, or your ballet. It's the organization, the way we have to work here, the way we're treated."

A discussion arose among the dancers. One group was on Rudolf's side; they felt he had done a great deal for the company and that, without him, they would never have been invited to New York, while the others objected that he was only interested in his own performance and his own productions. "*Il s'en fiche de nous.*"[3]

Naturally, he *was* interested in the dancers, only in his own peculiar way.

The success he still had in New York—the audience cheered him evening after evening—was reflected onto the group. Conversely, a marvelous company like the Paris Opéra Ballet provided Rudolf with exactly the rich nourishment he needed for success: as a dancer, choreographer, and as an innovative leader most of all.

The arguing continued, the parties seeming irreconcilable. Lormeaux stood, bag in hand, ready and keen to leave, and an atmosphere conducive to work no longer seemed feasible. I was really gloomy.

"Okay, let's call it all off, not just this rehearsal but the entire thing. Working like this is quite ridiculous, a waste of time."

Since Rudolf was nowhere to be found, I rang Anna in the hotel and informed her of my decision. But during the evening performance, at the intermission, she came up to me and said that all was taken care of. The dancers would be paid extra and there would be no more problems; that she promised me.

It was a bitter lesson for me; never again would I allow myself to be forced to work with dancers who were not my own choice. I should have stuck to my guns from the start.

After one of the rehearsals, while I was changing behind a few scenery chests on stage, I saw Rudolf in his practice clothes, traipsing across the empty stage, shoulders hunched, head toward the ground, bulging bag on his back.

I whistled and when he discovered me in my hiding place came to a halt, amazed: "Ruditchka, what on earth are you doing in such a strange place?"

I explained to him that all the dressing rooms were full and that I did not feel like making any demands.

3. "He doesn't give a damn about us."

"But you are our guest choreographer, and you are director of a company." I grinned: "So what?"

He gave me a somber look, as though all the life had ebbed out of him.

"What's the matter, are there difficulties?" A foolish question, because in a ballet company, and certainly one on tour, there are always difficulties.

He sagged onto a chest with a deep sigh and wiped his sweating brow. "Ah, the company is impossible, nothing is good enough for them. They wanted the best hotels, three stars, and they got it. But now they all want more money, overtime and compensation, otherwise they refuse to work."

He thumped the chest with his hand and blew his nose into a towel. "Instead of being happy to perform in New York they complain. Idiots." His voice was husky and barely audible; I had seldom seen him so emotional.

"Come, I'll arrange dressing room for you," but by the time we arrived at the dressing rooms there was a delegation of dancers waiting for him and he was conducted into an office. Once inside, he turned toward me again, I saw his lean head, miming more than it spoke, but his voice was inaudible, stifled by the dancers talking at him in raised voices.

"I have somebody I want you to meet. I promised her you would do a work for her." Promised?

In the large, dark room in the Dakota, a thin, somber-eyed girl was sitting by the open window, some kind of elder sister to Lolita, I imagined.

"This is Nastassia Kinski. We did a film together but, at the moment, she has no work, no director is interested in her." I knew he had been working on a film again, but had no idea whether it had already been made, or whether it still had to be shot. I had never seen Kinski's acting, so there was little I could tell her.

"She will do anything," Rudolf went on. "She needs to keep working." It was touching to see how he persisted, full of good intentions, but I felt it must be painful for her to be praised as though she were a superfluous white elephant.

I looked at her blank face, "But are you also a dancer?" I asked, and added by way of explanation, "because I am a choreographer."

"Yes, but you can make something special for her." Into the ensuing silence Rudolf immediately leapt, "Kerdoing!" "Nastassia is very dramatic and full of surprises, exactly your cup of tea!"

It was an awkward situation. In desperation I said I had seen her father—"He is your father, no?"—in *Nosferatu*, and that the film had been shot in Holland. She looked at me blankly at that announcement. What did she expect of me, and what did Rudolf expect?

"You have to get together and talk, exchange ideas." Rudolf suddenly seemed like a marriage broker, "and if something interesting comes out of it, maybe there is a part for me in it, too."

It was one of the most silent dinners I ever experienced at Rudolf's.

Back in Paris, on the day following our return, there was an orchestra rehearsal on the Opéra stage—an irresponsible assignment for the dancers, immediately after the heavy season at the Met.

The soprano, Michèle Lagrange, was nervous. She had sung a few rehearsals of the first and fourth songs to piano accompaniment, before the dancers had departed for New York.

"But," she warned me, "the orchestra tempi are quite different from those on the Gundula Janowitz recording you use in rehearsals."

She looked at me with concern, a pleasant woman with vivacious eyes. "I have spoken to the conductor, but he wouldn't listen."

The few times I had heard her sing in the studio had really made me appreciate her; she sang Strauss's composition lovingly and interpreted the songs beautifully; the sound, intensity, and changing hues of her voice moved me deeply.

She was open to every suggestion and each request from the dancers, and tried to accommodate everyone as far as she could where the tempi were concerned.

I told her that Janowitz, as well, who had sung the ballet in Vienna, had admitted that she did not sing nearly as well as on the recording. "On a recording you can take a break between songs and redo passages endlessly, until it can't be done any better. Singing this piece live is a different story altogether."

The Paris weather was gray and drizzly for the time of the year, a cold shower after the saunalike climate in New York, and that morning the dancers stood shivering and utterly exhausted in the wings; drowsy, wan faces and a listless mood—no surprise.

The stage did not provide a much cheerier setting: the backdrop was still hanging in sad creases and folds and the bare working light gave the dancers an even more fatigued and colorless appearance. No one uttered a word, gloominess all around.

"Listen, you have only one rehearsal with the orchestra following this one, so at least try to learn the tempi, because they may be quite different from what you're used to. Force yourself to respond in time *to* the music, not behind it. Once your dancing starts lagging behind the music, it'll be hopeless."

But I wondered whether the dancers even heard me; they were like zombies, sleepwalkers.

Just before I entered the auditorium, Elisabeth Platel approached me with cautious steps: "Rudi, we only arrived late yesterday and we couldn't make classes this morning, they started too early. If we dance full out this rehearsal there'll be a risk of accidents, no one's warmed up. Please don't hold it against us."

"The management should thank its lucky stars we came at all," someone added, "and we can't agree yet whether we want to rehearse tomorrow, the day of the premiere. What we need to be able to dance well is rest."

"But how do you expect to dance a reasonable performance if you do nothing more tomorrow and only mark it out today?"

The orchestra started up and there *were*, indeed, differences, some quite considerable, but not insurmountable as long as the dancers pricked up their ears. I knew the music through and through, of course, and could see minutely where the dancers would fall behind. They did not come to grips with the music, allowing it to take them unawares.

After what I saw as the initial run-through, I first went over to the orchestra to put in a plea for a few musical adaptations by the conductor and singer. Lagrange was prepared to go to any lengths, but the conductor reacted grumpily and said in reply to all my questions, "*Non. Impossible.*"

He was acutely aware of the mood among the dancers and armed himself in advance; I had the impression he would not surrender an inch of his territory.

When I returned to the dancers on stage, it appeared that a number of them had already left for the dressing rooms; French courtesy knew no bounds that day. I had no inclination to charge around the immense building—the staff apparently had the day off as well—to retrieve the deserted *étoiles* myself.

"Merci," I said to the others. "*Dormez-bien, et à demain.*"[4]

The orchestra pit was already deserted, only Lagrange was standing somewhat forlornly with the score in her hand. I waved to her, too depressed to talk.

Oh Amsterdam, Oh National Ballet . . .

Rudolf was ill from the trip, something to which I was not accustomed from him. I sat on the edge of his bed awhile; we drank tea, I related my disastrous day, and, before he could complain about the dancers, I cut him short: "But Rudolf, you're exhausted yourself!"

Toer had arrived and we wove in and out of the labyrinth of tiny streets behind Rudolf's home, leaned over a Seine bridge, and stood staring into the falling dusk.

When we arrived home again, Rudolf was seated at the table shrouded in sweaters and shawls and his face gave the impression he had been drinking heavily.

"I have a fever," he whispered, "feel my forehead." Burning hot. Slurping his tea, he walked through to the room at the front of the house. "I hope I can make the performance tomorrow."

When we left him alone, he was reclining on the large settee, almost hidden among the cushions, watching a random television program with great concentration.

"Goodnight, Rudolf."

There were, indeed, problems at the dress rehearsal, as Toer and I had foreseen. Usually, on such an occasion, the mood is one of excitement and anticipation, but now it was as if everything were taking place in a weird vacuum, as though all involved were gazing at one another through a steamy window.

A number of passages in the ballet were not quite right yet but, as a whole, the first fully-danced rehearsal was not bad; the points requiring improvement seemed easily adjustable at a second rehearsal. However, when the cur-

---

4. "Thank you. Sleep well, and see you tomorrow."

tain had fallen and rose again, the dancers from the second and third song walked up to the footlights and called into the theater—in the direction of Rudolf, who had come after all—that they refused to dance *Letzte Lieder* with the singers and the orchestra; they would do the performance only if it took place to a tape accompaniment.

Poor Lagrange was inundated with comments that were quite offensive and very embarrassing.

I made my way to the stage, followed by Rudolf and a large part of the staff, where the group or, rather, several groups, stood dotted about the stage: the negatives, the more positive ones, and those who carefully opted first for this side, then for the other.

"We're not dancing like this," Guillem was crying. "Can't you hear that she [withering look at Lagrange] can't keep time? You're the choreographer. You surely can't be shown up tonight? It's awful like this."

"I saw that you were awful, yes, and I think you'll be shown up if you dance the way you have done now," I snapped at her. "I already told you, all of you, in New York, that you should particularly concentrate on the musical phrasing."

"But the singer is hopeless; she doesn't follow us for a moment."

Lagrange stood beside me with a distressed smile and tried politely to be accommodating: "Where? Where were the difficulties?"

"There just happens to be a conductor in this, too, and it is he who dictates the singer's tempo." I had to keep a check on myself so that I did not shout.

"Then he must adapt and listen carefully to the tape. We'll only dance to the tape."

How awful that there had been no time to rehearse a double cast for the two protesting ladies; then everything would have been solved, quite simply.

"Can't we go through it all once more?" suggested Platel and, relieved, the singer turned to go back to the orchestra. But the orchestra pit was empty, conductor and orchestra had opted to call it a day in a very demonstrative way.

"I'm sorry for you, but I'm still on the singer's side. Either the ballet is done live, or not at all."

"Then I won't dance."

"Fortunately, that's not my business, but your director's." But when I turned around, Rudolf appeared to have beaten a hasty retreat as well.

I was baffled. Was *I* supposed to find a solution to this dreadful chaos among the dancers?

Anna Faussurier, pale, stationed in the wings, had to go and search for Rudolf and put the problem to him.

Kader Belarbi, the only non-*étoile* in the cast, tried to reassure me: "Tonight everything will be fine, *tu verras*,[5] the people are just heavily overworked." But for me there was no way it could work out fine any more; that much was clear to me.

I thought of Charlotte Margiono from Holland, who was to sing the second half of the series of performances. She would need to be a virago to survive this.

It was a bad, or maybe only an average performance, but the one who had danced worst and with the least inspiration had the most success with the audience. She had left out whole chunks of the choreography, dancing with a face like stone and not looking at her partner for a moment. But the audience cheered her and shouted, "Bravo."

Du, holde Kunst . . .[6]

I saw no reason at all to go on stage and receive the applause, to Rudolf's annoyance, nor could I face going to the dancers' dressing rooms. What could I say to them?

I asked Kader to greet a few people on my behalf and, for Lagrange, I left some flowers and a note.

Whether or not I saw Rudolf after the performance I do not recall; I must have, as we were staying with him, but it is erased from my memory.

It was the last work I did for the Opéra and Rudolf would not work there for long afterward, either. And that I regretted. For him.

5. "You'll see."
6. Oh, precious art . . .

I had told Rudolf I wanted to relinquish my appointment as artistic director of the Dutch National Ballet, within the not too distant future, in 1991.

"But why?" asked Rudolf.

"Because I did that job since 1965, Rudolf, twenty-four years. Don't you think that's enough?"

"Don't be foolish," he responded, "don't give it all away. Be clever, put somebody next to you, who does the heavy work but keep your finger in the pie." But that was not what I had in mind.

"There comes a time for younger people to take over. And I know we do have capable candidates within the company, people I trust."

"When I stop," Rudolf said suddenly, "then I'm going to do all the things I could never do before."

"Are there still such things then?" He seemed to have done everything in his gargantuan life.

"Oh yes! I've made plans with John Taras (one of Balanchine's ballet masters) that, toward the time I stop, we'll hire a bus together and travel around, visiting all the good restaurants in the world. We're going to eat, drink, laze around, just simply enjoy life. Fat, dirty old men we will be." He squawked with laughter at that unlikely prospect.

"And when *you* stop work," suddenly he seemed enthusiastic at the idea, "You'll have more time for me, we can do things together. We'll go to my homes and stay there as long as you want. My ranch near Washington is ideal for you to write a book. I'd love you to use it."

I must have disappointed him, for in that first year of "freedom" I was busier than ever and traveling all the time. Whenever he asked if I at least had time to come and view his latest acquisition, there was something that hindered me, sometimes merely the fact that I was happy to be at home in peace for a short while.

In March 1988 he turned fifty. His actual birth day I had, as usual, forgotten, but I received an invitation for an official celebration to be held later in the year in New York, during a guest appearance by the Paris Opéra Ballet: all his friends were asked to be present for a special performance dedicated to him, with a celebratory tribute as grand finale.

Right up until nearly the last moment, it was uncertain whether I should be able to leave Amsterdam; a great deal had happened in and around the Dutch National Ballet and, to be perfectly honest, I was not really looking forward to such an undoubtedly pompous birthday party. But my airplane ticket had already arrived and, just in case, I hired a tuxedo at the last moment, although at the back of my mind there was still an idea that I might not leave. I *did* go, however: Rudolf only turned fifty once, a milestone for a dancer.

On the morning of the trip I threw a few clothes into a bag, stuffed a hundred guilder note into my pocket—all I had in the house—and asked the financial department at the ballet in the morning whether they could rustle up a hundred dollars for me in a hurry. I tore off to Schiphol Airport only to discover there that I had left the one credit card I possessed at home. But that would not be a problem because those invited would be bound to receive some sort of retainer, I thought.

At Kennedy Airport there was, indeed, a car waiting to take me into town—perfect organization!—and the hotel turned out to be a very aristocratic affair: a tip for the chauffeur, one for the boy who carried my weekend bag and minute tuxedo case into the hotel, and the man who brought it all from the entrance to reception.

At the front desk, eyebrows were raised when I had to admit to not possessing a credit card.

"In that case we must ask for a deposit of one hundred dollars," the lady said, but the hundred were already rather depleted by the tips. "Is seventy dollars okay too?"

I just managed and, to the girl who ushered me to the lift and on to my room and the man who carried my things upstairs, I mumbled words to the effect of "Only Dutch guilders, change some money first."

My two tiny pieces of luggage drowned in the sumptuous suite but it amazed and pleased me to notice again how the contents of such a small bag can cause a fair amount of chaos in a large room!

The speedily converted guilders produced a little under forty-five dollars but, fortunately, the hotel was lavish in providing and replenishing baskets of fruit. And there were also ingredients for making coffee and tea on hand as well.

I purchased some food for breakfast in a small shop and thought I would thus be able to survive my five days in a grand hotel.

When, after some hesitation—was he allowed to know we were in New York?—I called Rudolf, I heard the voice of Wallace, who was indeed intercepting as many calls as possible. "Rudolf is very tired and far too busy. I am worried about him." The tone in which he said that last bit made me wonder; surely Wallace had not seen Rudolf anything other than tired and overworked?

Only later did it become clear to me that Wallace was one of the very few who knew that Rudolf was seriously ill.

"Shall I come over to you, this evening?" But Rudolf had rehearsals in the evening and a long interview following that; he would only be free around eleven o'clock. However, it was indeed the intention that he should be unaware how many people, and who, would be present for the anniversary performance, a rather naive thought on the part of the organizers, for there were posters hanging at the theater announcing the event, with the words "special guests" followed by some fifty names from the entire theater world, from Liza Minnelli and Margot Fonteyn to Miss Piggy.

In the hotel, I had received a regular scenario for the coming four days, complete with predress rehearsals and dress rehearsals for the parade, box- and table-seating arrangements; nothing was left to chance. The first day was blank, a welcome surprise, but also somewhat awkward for me, with barely any money in my pocket. I considered asking Wallace, or Maude, who was staying with Rudolf, for some assistance but on second thought I found the situation too ludicrous; I should have to make do on my own.

New York was sunny and relaxed. There was a massive AIDS demonstration that day, with thousands of people making their way along the wide avenues. The remainder of the time I spent loitering on street corners and seated on benches, absorbed in my favorite pastime: gazing at passersby, always a fascinating kaleidoscope show that, in all its random array of intricate scenes and gestures and expressions, could never be so convincingly and compellingly recreated on stage.

The following day there was a gathering at the Metropolitan Opera House; I saw the Opéra dancers again, pale, jaded, and overworked, and, from the wings, Rudolf, rehearsing Maurice Béjart's *Songs of a Wayfarer*, with one of his favorite Opéra dancers, Charles Jude.

There hung an aura of mystery around this fiftieth birthday and the festival linked to it, with people guessing and whispering that this particular performance might well be Rudolf's last, that from then on he would work only as choreographer and artistic director. Was that why I watched the rehearsing birthday boy through different eyes?

He looked appalling: gray, unshaven, and hauntingly thin, his practice clothes were in tatters and rags as ever and the eternal woolen hat sagging to one side over his perspiring brow.

Jessye Norman, concealed in the orchestra, sang the Mahler songs; the sound of her voice, consoling, plaintive and brimming with joy all at once and Rudolf's silhouette, hovering over the half-dark expanse of the stage, melted into an image that sank its teeth in me.

Weary, breathless, clinging in vain to the final bars of the ebbing music, his figure assumed the proportions of a monument: danced to exhaustion, the battle done, he passed me by, led by the still young and powerful Charles Jude, one last time he turned toward the auditorium—that vast and gaping void without an audience—thrusting out a surprised and plaintive childlike arm. "Is it all over? But I'm not ready yet."

A little later, he came up to me in the wings and saw that I was overcome; he was scornful, but I saw he was happy and flattered, as well. "What's the matter, why are you emoting like that?"

"Because I realize that maybe I'll never see you like that again."

"Not again?" I was obviously not the first person to confront him with that remark. "What do you mean, do you want me to retire?" He looked at me derisively. "I'll have to disappoint you, my dear. I'll still dance for a long time." And then he was gone.

Later that day, there was a rehearsal of the parade: all the guests were requested to report to the rear entrance of the theater, where further instructions would be given; everything was still shrouded in great secrecy.

I arrived shortly after Margot Fonteyn, who was hovering uncertainly at the porter's reception desk.

"What's your name again?" I heard one of the porters asking her. "I can't find your card."

"But this is . . ." I walked over to her to help her, but Fonteyn giggled. "It's all right, he doesn't know. I am forgotten."

She fumbled around in the box herself, found her nametag, pinned it onto her lapel, and was then allowed into the theater where, only a few years earlier, she had received ovations that often lasted for more than half an hour.

In the wings, Rudolf's friends and colleagues were placed in a long line and, one by one, on cue, we rehearsed our walk across the center stage, a strange and almost amateurish experience. But then, we *were* "amateurs," lovers and practitioners of that one art, dance, and friends and admirers of the man who professed that art so fanatically and with every fiber in his body.

During the performance, I was less moved by Rudolf than in the rehearsal the previous day; the mood in the audience was inflated and Rudolf did everything to be as perfect as possible.

Oh, if only he had messed up once, shown his fatigue and inner conflict, his faults and frustrations . . . But he was perfection itself: a perfectly fitting costume, immaculate makeup, not a gesture that was over the edge. Even if the tempi were not how he wanted them, he did not protest or complain, or clap in irritation and annoyance, or push his hat away from his eyes with the gesture of a weary Greek peasant.

He gave us the unapproachable Nureyev and I so yearned for the unadorned, flesh-and-blood Rudolf.

After the performance, at dinner, he told me ("Give me advice." But he rarely took advice,) that he was considering an offer to appear in America for a whole year, in a musical, *The King and I*.

"It's a challenge, every night on stage. And I have to sing, too."

"Yes, but it is definitely not Bach you will have to sing. Do you really want to listen to that kind of music for a whole year? Why?"

He said that *The King and I* guaranteed he could appear on stage evening after evening, "something the Paris Opéra doesn't allow me," and that he needed the dollars badly.

"I'm going broke, you know. Everything I earn goes to the taxes in France." Taxes were a real obsession for him.

"And the Opéra, does the management agree to your being away for so long? And what happens to your dancers? What will they think?"

He said he had stipulated that he should be able to return to Paris from time to time for a few days and all the rest he would be able to arrange from America.

"So you signed already! Why do you ask me then?"

"No, I still have to have talks in Paris. Of course the Opéra will refuse, but in the end they will agree."

It was inconceivable that he should want to commit himself to a trivial and dated musical, thus risking everything he had built up in Paris. Paris was a city that suited Rudolf like no other, the grand choreography of boulevards, parks, and monuments, palatial buildings, panoramas and expansive squares, the breathtaking river with its wealth of bridges, the spirit of the past on every street corner: Delacroix, Gautier, Voltaire, Berlioz, Chopin, Georges Sand, Flaubert, Géricault.

Paris was the city where Marius Petipa, the choreographer on whose ballets Rudolf's fame was founded, had been trained as a dancer, to blossom in St. Petersburg, and Rudolf had traveled that road in reverse. From 1859 until 1907, Petipa had been the first French ballet leader in Russia; Rudolf, after Serge Lifar, the second Russian ballet director of the Opéra.

But the artistic decision, as well, to do things that were not at all in his line for so long upset me; he, who was such a refiner, and had such exquisite vision where music and theater were concerned.

With the salary he earned from *The King and I*, he confided in me, he could make a fantastic purchase: "At last I shall have my house by the water. You'll be astonished when you see what I want to buy."

I had no notion of what he meant and it scarcely interested me, I was tired of his never-ending house-buying mania. I looked at his thin, worn-out face, the probing, feverish look in his eye, and the laugh that sometimes no longer seemed a laugh but a self-defence mechanism.

"Stay in Paris. Don't do it, Rudolf."

"Okay, enough. Basta!" He broke off the conversation abruptly, irritated by my lack of support in this uncertain question.

To my astonishment, at the end of the party that was held in the foyer of the theater beneath the enormous paintings by Chagall, he asked me to stay a day longer. "I'll make sure they change your ticket."

I stayed, but the following day Rudolf was so tired and had so much going on, that I hardly saw or spoke to him. In the evening, before dinner, reclining on his carved four-poster bed, he said, "Let's talk here," but he hardly uttered a word. Was he asleep?

After what seemed like an age, I heard the sound of his rasping, disappointed voice: "No one in the theater said a word about yesterday, no one told me how I danced; they all behaved as if nothing had happened."

Later that evening, at the door, just before my departure, he suddenly took me by the arm and drew me back into the hall.

"I have been back to Russia. I saw my mother. Do you still have that film?"

Of course I had it. At my question as to what it had been like to see her again—he had received permission to go back to Ufa because his mother was dying—he reacted defensively.

"She didn't recognize me. She looked at me and said, 'Who is he? Who is that man?'"

He laughed abruptly, a joyless laugh.

The car I had been promised to take me to the airport did not turn up at the hotel the following day. It was pouring rain in New York and the porter was doubtful whether it would be so simple to find a taxi on such short notice. Was I going to miss my flight now, as well?

My heart pounding, I eventually leapt into a taxi that was speeding past, and wondered whether the seventy-dollar deposit the hotel returned when I checked out would be enough to pay for the return trip to Kennedy Airport. What should I do, get out earlier or tell the chauffeur about my financial predicament the moment I saw the meter approaching the fatal sum? As we left the city behind us, I told him of my dilemma; after all, he had a friendly and confidence-inspiring face.

"What do you think, that I'd let you get out here, in the middle of the road? Of course I'd take you. You could pay me back on a next visit, but," he added rapidly, "for seventy dollars you could even go part of the way back with me."

Delightful city, New York, and such pleasant people!

Rudolf called me from London: "I'm fired at the Paris Opéra; they threw me out." I was speechless.

Understandably, his decision to do *The King and I*, with all the consequences for his enormous French company, had not been accepted by the Opéra management.

What had he brought upon himself? He would become "homeless" once again; his roving life would begin again from square one, now that he no longer had a home base. The directorate in Paris had given him daily activity, requiring plenty of time and energy, but it had also meant he had a base, a place where he *had* to be for a great deal of his time, whether he wanted to or not. With no permanent company, he would again go from hotel to hotel, from theater to theater, from country to country, with the exception that, whereas he formerly appeared in metropoles and large theaters, he would now have to be satisfied with—and was—far smaller towns and more provincial theaters.

"They're glad to be rid of me," he complained. "They had intended to do so for a long time." But even if that were true, then he had given them reason enough.

The young Patrick Dupond ("Too modern, no style") took over as artistic director.

Homeless or not, he had meantime acquired another new home, or, rather, a whole island.

"Isola dei Galli," an island off the Neapolitan coast of Italy, had belonged to Léonide Massine, who had made it his own as early as 1920, while still a member of Diaghilev's company. In later years, he had attempted to organize— not particularly popular—summer courses for young dancers there and, on his death, he left the island to his son, Lorca, another choreographer.

"It is like Ithaca, a miracle. Nobody there, I can be absolutely alone, nobody can invade me there. The wind, the sea, the sun, nothing else. Paradise!" And recalling our collaboration in Vienna, where Odysseus returned to the Ithaca for which he had so yearned, only to find it crammed full of apartment blocks, thoroughfares, and telegraph poles, the population clinging on to the raft *Medusa*. "It has nothing to do with our Viennese 'Ulysses.' Thank God, I escaped that, just in time. This Ithaca is quite private."

It later became apparent that Rudolf had once again thrown himself into a colossal venture at an astronomical cost. An inconceivable number of repairs were required and, despite Massine's summer courses, there were few facilities. To ensure electricity and water, generators were flown over and all building materials and the workmen had to be ferried across daily. And all that, organized Italian-style. Poor Douce was responsible for the supervision.

Despite all the problems, Rudolf insisted he was looking forward to being in America for a long time. "The audiences there love me, they make me feel welcome and I'm always sold out." Always? I thought of Chicago, eleven years ago.

"Well, Ruditchka, good luck and enjoy the work there." What else could I say? I had protested with enough arguments about the accursed "*King and him*."

Billy Forsythe was making—and how proud of it Rudolf had been, how he had waited for it—a brand new choreography for the Paris Opéra, on Nureyev's initiative.

With Rudolf in mind, Forsythe called the ballet *Impressing the Tsar*. As he began the new work in the Paris studios, however, the tsar was preparing to leave for a lesser realm.

In April 1989 I had to call Rudolf; Henny Jurriëns, the dancer of whom he was so fond, had died in an automobile accident in Canada with his wife.

The line was silent for a long time; then he coughed.

"Yes, I've heard already. It's too depressing. Everything is depressing."

Long silence.

"I can't talk about it, Rudi, not now. Do you mind? It's too awful."

Silence, and a small cough.

"But I'm very sorry for you."

23 ⟶ Red Angel

When I next saw him, a year or so later, he made a feverish and excited impression, as though he were about to embark on a new life.

"I think I am going to take up conducting again," he said, "I am getting tired of dancing, and maybe it is tired of me, too. But, anyway, it is too much effort, my body refuses."

"I don't understand. Why conducting? What can you achieve in that now? Music is just like dancing, you have to start young." But Rudolf denied this and retorted that there were other examples of people who only developed as orchestral conductors later on in life.

"But then they surely came from the music world; they were orchestra members, of course, waiting their chance."

"I will start with the music I know best, *Serenade, Apollo*; it's music I know by heart, I can dream it."

But being thoroughly familiar with compositions as a ballet accompaniment did not seem to me a guarantee for being able to conduct an orchestra satisfactorily.

"You wait and see," he said abruptly and with pride.

I was traveling through France together with the sculptor Gertjan Evenhuis, photos and catalogues of whose work I had previously sent Rudolf and, on the return journey, we paid him a visit.

He was alone in the house and seemed really happy to receive a couple of visitors. He strode off to the kitchen and returned with a bottle of wine, plates, and glasses.

"Where is Manuel?" It was unusual to see Rudolf doing the honors himself.

"Fired. I didn't need him anymore," he sniffed, pushing the plates toward us. "I'm almost never here, anyway, these days."

We sat together in silence for a while; the atmosphere was strained.

"Don't you have anything to ask me?" he asked, "lost interest in what I do?" And without waiting for a question he informed us: "I'm conducting a lot and I love it. I have a young orchestra from Vienna and we have lots of offers, all over the world. Athens, Italy, maybe even Russia."

He and Gertjan became acquainted uncertainly, a cautious reconnaissance of territory, but the latter responded guilelessly to Rudolf's sometimes prickly questions, so that the tension soon eased.

"You have to go to the Opéra tonight. I have had Bob Wilson make a new piece for us, *Saint Sebastian* by Debussy. I'm curious what you'll think of it, opinions are very divided. That's all I'm going to tell you."

Seeing Wilson was always an adventure and, weary though we were from our exhausting automobile journey, that evening we were seated in Rudolf's box. The theatrical piece, however, contrary to my hopes and expectations, was rather disappointing. The score was clearly not Debussy's most inspired composition and I was puzzled as to why Wilson had not scrapped the inconceivably pompous declamations, so hypocritical in tone, or used them to give the spectacle an ironic twist.

The performance dragged on, scene after overloaded scene, complete with dancers disguised as polar bears, walruses and penguins. It seemed as if the evening would never end, although rumor had it that all of Paris was talking about Sylvie Guillem as the fiery red angel who appears in the snow-white kingdom at the end of the piece.

On our arrival home, Rudolf grinned when he heard our disappointed reaction. "I thought so. But it is a matter of taste. It has cost us a fortune, anyway."

We dined with him once again. Douce was there and a theater manager from New York and, this time, Douce's housekeeper Madeleine emerged from Rudolf's kitchen.

"I've borrowed her from Douce," Rudolf grinned. "It's easier so."

"And cheaper," Douce added with a hint of cynicism.

Through the half-drawn curtains, Paris was visible, bare and wintry still, blurred silhouettes in bluish gray and sepia; Rudolf's abode was lit by a profusion of candles. "Well, I have to make it look good when I finally am home," he said, but Douce whispered that he was really celebrating a belated birthday party. Dozens of oysters were served, that no one but Rudolf would touch.

"Well, it's for my own birthday." We saw the entire mound of shellfish disappear into Rudolf's eager mouth one by one. "The wine is the best of the best. Drink!"

Douce disappeared almost at once after dinner; the atmosphere between Rudolf and her left a lot to be desired once again. Poor Douce; it seemed as though Rudolf treated her like a ball at will, knowing that if he threw her away she would always bounce back in his direction.

I saw Gertjan casting stolen glances at the dozens of paintings hanging all around the room, barely discernible by candlelight.

"You like?" Rudolf sounded wary.

"I don't know, I have to take a closer look."

"Well, don't worry, they are excellent pieces, that I can tell you." He walked about the house with Gertjan, showing him his objets d'art and enquiring after the work upon which Gertjan was engaged.

"Could you make me a painting which is roughly a copy of, or complement to, this work? He pointed to a classic portrayal of a man seated on a blood-red cloth against a dark landscape.

It was the same question I had heard him ask Toer many a time.

I could not fathom Rudolf's desire for a counterpart to a particular painting; one above each entrance to the dining room perhaps? Besides that, it was a strange question to put to a modern artist; if he had examined Gertjan's work closely, it must be clear to him that he had no affinity at all with such an intrinsically classical nude in a romantic landscape.

"Nobody wants to do this, it seems. Is it so complicated?" Rudolf did not seem to grasp that it is less usual in contemporary painting to copy an existing piece than in the art of dance, where audiences are bombarded with old masterpieces in all sorts and sizes and interpretations.

Despite Gertjan's resolute refusal, Rudolf was very taken with him, pinching and feeling him all around—something which might easily have been offensive and was only appreciated in the nick of time by the bepinched, who was reddening in confusion—and said to him: "You would be an excellent partner, like iron."

Later on in the evening, or rather, night, I went to see Madeleine in the kitchen. She was one of the most placid people I have come across, the type of woman who puts herself completely at the service of others, and seems to have the well-being of the people for whom she works as her only goal.

"*C'est trop petite*," she complained. "*Trop fatiguant.*"[1] And, indeed, the kitchen was relatively small and awkwardly situated, with a single door opening directly onto the room where the dinners were held. During the sittings, which often lasted for hours, the housekeeping help was obliged to camp out in the space, which was filled to overflowing with ovens, refrigerators, dishwashers, and pantry cupboards. There was no room for even a comfortable place to sit.

At half-past one in the morning, she left, white as a sheet from fatigue.

"I'm sorry, but my time is up, Monsieur Nureyev."

I wondered how she went home; Parc Monceau was some way from the Quai Voltaire. If she took a taxi, would Rudolf pay for it?

"Was he really such a good dancer?" Gertjan asked when we were alone. "Seeing him now, it's hard to imagine anymore."

I was used to it, but for someone seeing Rudolf for the first time, his sometimes so awkward manner of moving around must be conspicuous.

"Was?" I said. "Is. He still dances."

---

1. "It's too small," she complained. "Too tiring."

24 ⟶ Make Believe

In February 1991 Margot Fonteyn died, the ballerina with whom his name had become established in the western hemisphere. Fonteyn's death—not unexpected for Rudolf, he had known about her illness for a long time—not only seemed to make him sad, but bitter, as well; he sounded as though he felt betrayed or abandoned.

"I have nobody left, I feel deserted. You know how Margot died? So lonely, so forgotten. That's the way it will be for all of us: done away with."

He had recently lost Gorlinsky, his financial manager, as well, leaving Rudolf behind in sudden great anxiety concerning his possessions.

"I don't know where everything is, what I own. I need help, but these days you can't trust anyone anymore. They're simply out to rob you of your money" —the very same words I had so often heard him utter about Gorlinsky.

Increasingly, I had the impression that a circle had formed around Rudolf that was closing in on him more and more. In his frequent nocturnal telephone conversations—heavy and laborious, as though his weariness were imposing itself on me through the connecting wires—he often made me feel he had abandoned all hope of finding a way out; there was a tone of resignation or disillusionment in his remarks that I had never noticed like that before. And it was not a façade, that was clear.

In the four working periods I had spent at the Opéra in Paris, and during the many preparatory visits there in between, I had seen Rudolf dancing frequently and in a widely varied repertoire.

Even though he had no longer danced premieres in the company he led until 1989, he had often appeared on stage nonetheless, as second cast. I do not think he grasped the awkward position in which he thus placed the choreographers, albeit unintentionally, when, as the great star he still was and company director to boot, he attended rehearsals as second cast.

Rudolf was such a soloist in heart and soul that by his manner of working or the remarks he made, he managed to play first fiddle even as second cast, and was always dominant. If *he* were in the studio it was impossible to ignore him, even if the idea was to concentrate on the first cast.

In Paris, besides his own, enormous repertoire, Rudolf danced an extensive number of ballets by a variety of choreographers. Naturally, he was way past his prime at that time—he was around forty-six when he became artistic director of the Opéra—but, for every role, each production, he clearly fought like a lion and threw himself into it with every fiber of his body and with an absolute, occasionally even naïve, eagerness.

Is that why so much of what he did seemed rather strained? Rudolf often gave me the impression that he never quite spoke the language of choreographers other than the old masters impeccably or without effort. And it was not because, in a perpetual rush, he did not allow himself time to become familiar with a particular style; the private sessions he had desired, and organized himself, for *The Ropes of Time* and *Ulysses* spoke volumes about that.

In actual fact, Rudolf's body was not an ideal one for dance, lacking the elongated muscles and really pliant joints that made for long, lyrical lines. In relation to his torso, his legs were fairly short and all his mobility seemed to stem from power and effort. There were seldom moments when he *let* himself be borne along, as it were, on a gentle breeze: if he moved, he did it *himself* and whoever saw that was two hundred percent aware of it. And the audience admired this show of energy, as well.

No matter how high he leapt, he never gave the impression of grace or buoyancy: he pushed off with power and effort and sailed or circled through the air with that same power, a tense mass of energy, never losing contact with the earth.

Modern dance requires a motion impulse coming from within, an internal mainspring spurring the back and limbs on to movement, often asymmetric.

Classical dance—and Rudolf was first and foremost an exponent of academic ballet—appears to consist of externally proscribed forms, achieved via rigorous patterns and requirements. The inner being and the dancer's imagination seem to receive little scope and attention, certainly in the early but so formative years of study.

It was hard to allow Rudolf to be an individual, no matter how much of an individualist he was. Sometimes I said to him, "Find your own expression here, let your arms respond naturally, don't pose. Move as you feel." But he always seemed to end up in polished crystallized positions, rehearsed and "classical."

Sometimes—maybe in desperation—he would indulge in making faces or grotesque, somewhat froglike movements: legs wide, knees bent low. Frog jumps.

"This what you want?" he asked, partly in rage, partly in the hope that he was on the right track.

He even suffered from the same problem in his own contemporary chore-ographies, like *Manfred, The Storm* or *Washington Square*, where he sought after a more modern idiom but remained unable to become one with it.

Strangely enough, he never quite assumed the role he was interpreting on stage either. At the most intense of moments, when partnering the ballerina in work that had to be carried out to the millimeter, or in the middle of a series of daredevil pirouettes and leaps, he might suddenly direct a down-to-earth glance at the wings, as if to register who was watching him and how people were responding to his efforts.

He was rarely dissatisfied after a performance; he would curse now and then, but that was usually about a tempo that the conductor had set in wrongly, a light that had hindered him, or the corps de ballet who had been mess-ing about. I seldom heard him speak negatively of his own achievements; "I wasn't *that* great," every now and then, but never so dejected and disheart-ened as other dancers when they feel they have worked below par.

Rudolf often worked below par, and anything else would have been im-possible, in the light of the amount of work he wished to do. I think he took that into account in a realistic way and did not consider it any further.

The world of academic dance, filled by Marius Petipa with an impressive number of evening-length ballets, is a world of transparent make-believe; in among painted forests and palaces fabricated from planks and cloth and with painted wood for marble, dancers and ballerinas portray fantastic tableaux by means of daredevil technique, to the sound of compositions that, all except those by Tchaikovsky, are reminiscent of an operetta group in their hollow banality.

In the second half of the nineteenth century, the choreographer and his ballet ensemble served as a travel agent for trips to unknown, exotic regions, rather like Jules Verne and his books did in literature. In the theater, the audience was transported to legendary lands like Bessarabia, Egypt, Greece, or Africa, with vivid but stereotyped portrayals of ethnic groups: Indians, Arabs, pirates, Moors, or odalisques, all represented along Western and often caricature lines.

In the midst of this "barbary," the dream world of the hero or heroine in the story unfolded itself through pure classical ballet, providing a means of escape from the horrors of reality into a realm of nymphs, the souls of dead princesses and wood spirits, floating away in translucent mists.

Rudolf believed passionately in the formulas and discussed them with enthusiasm, recalling performances in Leningrad. The patterns of style and the axioms of such ballets he defended with passion, as though they were the Ten Commandments. With great authority, he would declaim upon how such works should be staged and what was absolutely essential from a dance- and theatrical-technical point of view.

He amazed me, then, this man who admired avant-garde theater. He was all eyes and ears for whatever was new and yet still worked with a fanatical belief to get dancers onto imitation horses, fighting with wooden swords, and to have princes step out of picture frames and come to life in a world peopled with ravishingly beautiful maidens, caricatured old men, and brave but uninspiring heroes.

"Isn't this magnificent?" How often I heard him sigh at the sight of one of Petipa's choreographies, arranged by him. "It's absolute perfection."

Life itself, however, was not to be a perfectly wrought choreography, even for Rudolf, and its performance began to show increasing worn-out patches as well. Where it was once an ensemble piece with a large cast, the dance of his existence became ever more sober; from a choreography with an excessive decor by Petipa, it changed into a solemn, penetrating solo sketch à la Balanchine.

But Maude was still there for Rudolf; he rang her almost daily, invited her to his performances and on holiday. He adored her.

"If Maude is gone I will change my life; Maude will be the last woman I want around me. After her I don't want any other. Fini. Basta."

25   ⌒   *Tidal Kiss*

Gerhard Brunner had asked me to make a choreography for Nureyev for the dance festival in Vienna, to Peter Maxwell Davies' *Vesalii Icones*.

"Rudolf's definitely going to end his dancing career now and I want to have that ballet created as a tribute to him." Probably for taxation reasons, Rudolf had had himself naturalized as an Austrian and begun working with an orchestra put together in Vienna, and he was thus still in touch with Brunner.

I promised to speak to Rudolf to find out whether he still *really* wanted to dance, or whether he would be content with a far more expressionist piece. "If he wants pirouettes and leaps, if he wants a classical piece from me, then I won't do it."

But Rudolf appeared to be amenable to anything. I had shown him photos of an image created by Gertjan Evenhuis, *Tidal Kiss*, a work with a strongly theatrical slant: the figure of a man striding forward in a glass cage placed on four columns, in which rising and falling water washes over the figure or leaves it high and dry, as in ebb and flow.

"That would be the only piece of scenery," I told him, "and, besides that, there are three dancers, a boy, a younger man, and a bearded elderly man."

"And I am the old man?"

"Yes."

He was silent for a while. "Can't I be the man in the water?"

Not so long ago, he would have demanded the role of one of the two younger men; now he was angling for the role of the mythical figure of indeterminate age.

"But the ballet lasts a half hour. Do you really want to be in a cage, naked, for such a long time?"

I told him I had thought of asking Gertjan himself to be the "waterman"; he had given performances in his aquarium before.

"Everybody will only look at him, a beautiful naked man in a bathtub. I may as well stay home."

I went back to Vienna, selected two dancers, Christian Musil and Krystian Rovny, and promised Gerhard Brunner I would try to arrange a meeting with Rudolf, something that would not be easy to realize, as we were all fully occupied.

Rudolf insisted we meet him on his Italian island, but for Brunner and me that was far too roundabout. He had already tried several times to talk me into spending a vacation on Isola dei Galli with him, but I was busy and wished to spend my scarce free time in my own way.

Besides that, Maude had told me how difficult the situation on the island was.

"There's nothing wrong with the house itself, but there is no electricity or running water; we had to import hundreds of bottles of mineral water to fill our bath. And there's no beach. If you want to swim you have to clamber down below, because the house is high up on a rock. I am too old for that, I just go there to please Rudolf."

He himself was occasionally picked up off the island for dinner by friends with a helicopter, but otherwise everything went by motorboat, and an experienced captain was needed for that. None of it seemed particularly attractive, especially as a location for a meeting.

The new piece was intended for September 1991, a date not feasible for me. Rudolf then proposed first rehearsing alone with him in the summer vacation and then with the other two dancers on the island, where a studio had been built back in Massine's day.

"But why the hurry? Surely it would be better to postpone it until next season? Everything can be far better prepared then."

"Maybe next year my body doesn't want to move anymore. I want to do it as soon as possible."

When I told him I wanted to go to Chios on vacation instead of to his island he growled, "Chios? I hope you get massacred on Chios," and hung up.

Things never went any farther than telephone calls, making appointments and subsequently postponing them. His voice sounded weary and dull and I could hear from the way he spoke of the project that he no longer believed in it himself, despite his frequent, "When do we start?"

For as long as I had known him he had worked unceasingly. I do not believe there has ever been anyone in the entire history of the art who has danced such a superhuman number of performances as he did, and such physically demanding roles to boot. How he found the time and energy to work as a choreographer parallel to his dancer's existence was beyond me. The number of productions of evening-length ballets he made was enormous, his eight "full-length" ballets were danced by more than thirty companies throughout the world.

That work, too, always had to be staged in a limited time. He went about his work in a businesslike and efficient way, as though he were assembling a machine, piece by piece.

His own productions had gradually begun to form a path of stepping stones in a swiftly flowing river. The more of his works there were spread around the world, the easier it was for him to appear, time after time, as guest in those ballets: two birds with one stone.

"I've laid my eggs everywhere," he said with glinting cuckoo's eyes. "They'll never be able to forget me, nowhere!"

Sometimes, he gave me the feeling his unquenchable zest for work came from uncertainty, from fear of being forgotten as soon as he stopped tearing around the world at a less breathtaking tempo.

He had asked Wallace to register all his productions and guest appearances on film. He asked Robert Tracy, who had developed into a writer, and me, too, to write about him, urging us to publicize his ideas, his working methods, to commit his ballets to paper. One of his final wishes was that a book of memories should be made about him, with contributions from well-known painters, photographers, and writers.

As proof that he was there, that he existed or had existed? How could he imagine he would ever be forgotten!

Later on, when I understood he had known for years that he was HIV-positive and so almost certain (but how many escape clauses does each human being build in for himself?) that being alive would be over for him within the foreseeable future—later on, I saw his urge to work as an attempt to leave a minimum of time and energy in which to be confronted with the impending doom.

"I am a human being and I fight," he said to me, as if to teach me a lesson, when he thought I resigned myself too easily to certain things. "You mustn't just let it happen, you must grasp it, mould it, see that you do with it what *you* want."

"But I'm not at all sure that what I want will be an improvement."

"You have to believe in yourself, right or wrong. Take that from me."

He had barely spoken to anyone about being HIV-positive; Maude he had told in the initial stage and later Wallace. But even to Douce, in his immediate vicinity for years, he had never said it in so many words: "I understood it from the doctor's visits and from the hospital I brought him to from time to time for tests. That was known to be the place where AIDS-patients were treated. But I had to respect his silence and so I never asked him a thing."

He appeared in Amsterdam one more time, the RAI once again: *Giselle*, with a pickup company. I was out of the country at the time, but Toer went along.

The performance was not sold out and Toer felt that the level of the entire production was rather depressing. He organized a supper afterward at his home for Rudolf, and the latter brought along his doctor, who often accompanied him on his trips in later years.

"It was a strange, uncanny evening," Toer told me. "Something was clearly and badly wrong, as though we were both thinking of bygone days, but could not bear to broach the matter."

Gerhard Brunner made one more attempt to get us together. It transpired that there was one day on which Rudolf would just be returning to Paris as I was passing through. "Let's meet on that day at two o'clock at Rudolf's."

When I arrived in Paris, at exactly the agreed time, there seemed to be no one home. To be quite sure, I rang the bell of the studio apartment as well, and the door was opened by an unfamiliar boy of around twenty, with long blond hair.

"I'm trying to find Mister Nureyev."

"*Ah entrez,*" said the boy, speaking with a heavy accent, "*Moi, je suis le neveu de Rudolf.*"[1]

The apartment had altered a great deal, there was a penetrating odor of

---

1. "I'm Rudolf's nephew."

cigarette smoke, things seemed neglected (no Manuel anymore) and on the walls, many works of art from Rudolf's collection had been replaced by half-naked pinups, torn from magazines.

Other voices, other rooms . . .

The boy spoke nervously, with downcast eyes.

"Do you know when Rudolf will be home? I have an appointment with him." But Rudolf apparently did not keep his nephew informed when he took off on his travels or would be returning home again.

"Hasn't anyone rung from Vienna, either?" But the boy knew nothing. I went back outside, where Gertjan, who had come along to discuss the set, was waiting in the car; I had said to Brunner that we had very little time.

"What shall we do? There's no one there yet."

We decided to wait for an hour, if we could park the car inside the court-yard on the Quai Voltaire. But the concierge was already scurrying out: "*Non, ces places sont seulement pour les habitants, pas d'autres,*"[2] polite, but unrelenting.

I foresaw that Rudolf would arrive home late, that we should first have to dine at length and that, at the last minute, the *Tidal Kiss* project would be discussed, with the net result that Rudolf would keep it at bay again.

"Let's go; if anthing concrete is agreed upon, we'll hear about it."

A week later Brunner rang me, Rudolf had arrived in Paris far later than expected. He had waited for hours for him at the airport. "I'm afraid we'll have to forget the whole idea," he added. "Rudolf doesn't look as though he'll ever dance again."

When I left for New York in spring 1992 to work with Evenhuis, I hoped to see Rudolf there. In the weeks leading up to my departure, I had spoken to him briefly, and his failing voice—absent almost—had worried me even more.

"I will conduct *Romeo and Juliet* at the Met," he whispered. "Quite excit-ing. Can you try to be there?" And, as if he felt that the weakness of his voice interested me more at that moment than the conducting, "Yes, I had opera-tion. In Vienna. Terrible operation, I think they messed me up there. Rather awful."

2. "No, these places are for residents only, no one else."

I knew I would not arrive on time for the performance of *Romeo and Juliet*, but thought he would be staying in New York for another few days.

When I met her on that first morning in New York, Jane Hermann, director of American Ballet Theatre, informed me that the conducting session had been a success for Rudolf: "I was happy I organized it for him, all his friends were there. I think he was grateful, but I was scared to death because his condition was so appalling."

There really was something seriously wrong, it was apparent from the veiled and roundabout way she spoke of his condition.

"But how on earth could he conduct such a heavy score?"

I called Rudolf's house, hoping to find him still there, but heard the voice of Robert Tracy, who lived in the apartment in Rudolf's absence—so more or less permanently.

"Rudolf left yesterday for his house in St. Barthélemy, you must have crossed each other at the airport. But why don't you come over for a coffee?"

We decided to go immediately. I wanted to know what was wrong with Rudolf.

"What? Didn't you know?" asked Robert. "Rudolf has AIDS. He never told you? And you hadn't guessed it, either? Heard no rumors?"

Of course I had heard the stories, more than once, for years, but I had refused to believe them; Rudolf's behavior had given absolutely no reason to do so. Of course I had thought about it, with his way of life—"He tosses them like pancakes"—but, miracle of miracles, he seemed to have had a lucky escape. That he was often exhausted and worn out was hardly surprising with a hectic existence like his. If he had known he was so close to death, then surely he would have spared himself?

Robert's announcement came like a deafening thunderclap. I simply could not believe that something like that was happening to the man who lived as though he would never die—while his way of life—his constant yearning for physical contact, the adventures he sought and found all over the world, his eternal pursuit of the ideal partner in his existence—put him near the top of the list of possible AIDS victims.

It lay like a stone in my skull.

In the apartment, there were two settees that had once belonged to Maria Callas.

"Rudolf said that he would like to be buried in these couches, as though he were resting awhile." I thought of the fire on the beach, Byron and Shelley.

"He doesn't want anyone to talk about his condition with him. The best is to pretend everything is normal. But he looks awful," Robert warned me on our departure.

"The last time, in Paris, I did indeed think he looked sick," said Gertjan, walking back to the hotel. "He had such a strange look in his eyes."

I had the feeling I had been blind, all that time.

Back in Amsterdam I called Rudolf's house in Paris.

"No, Rudolf is on the road, he has work to do. And he is busy with *La Bayadère* for the Opéra. It was Douce on the line and she sounded fairly matter-of-fact.

Was everything less serious than Robert had suggested to us in New York, after all, then?

The house, that was what struck me first. It made a neglected impression. Whereas everything once seemed positioned and handled with care, now piles of newspapers, letters, open and unopened, had accumulated on the tables; garments were strewn here and there on chairs and couches, and used glasses, cups, and stray pieces of cutlery lay among the collections of bronze statues and antique ornaments. In one room, boxes and bottles of medicine and capsules were standing and lying around in casual disarray.

The objects in the rooms had lost their warmth and luster; clearly no one had given them a thought for a long time. All attention was focused on one room, Rudolf's bedroom.

Douce met us in the hallway and gave us directions in a whisper: "Don't tell him you've come specially for him, that makes him suspicious. And don't mention his illness, he doesn't want that at all. The best thing is simply to talk of the future, as though there were nothing wrong."

A black dog shot through the room, recoiling in fear when he saw us and skidded and fell over while swerving, his ears flat to his neck.

"Prepare yourself for a great change in him but don't let him see you're shocked, no matter what."

"Rudolf has premiere of *Bayadère* on October eighth. Please come to Paris. Everybody will be there. It will be a great event."

I had received Douce's cable in Austria, where I was working on an opera production; Rudolf's first night fell on the very day I was planning to return to Amsterdam.

After living out of suitcases for three months, the idea of a stopover in Paris for a first night hardly appealed to me; I was longing for home. Besides, I had never really had a particular liking for premieres.

I opted to go to the second performance; after all, I was not really there for *La Bayadère* but because I wanted to see Rudolf.

Once again, my reaction on reading the telegram had been: if he can cope with the enormous production of a full-length ballet, then he cannot be seriously ill.

Together with Toer, I traveled to Paris, tense, but still in the expectation that Rudolf would overwhelm us with his willpower and energy as ever.

We wandered around the city for far longer than necessary, as though to postpone the moment of confrontation, to let soothing ignorance last slightly longer.

As we drew near to the Quai Voltaire, we grew silent, both overcome by gloom. Cars were racing by, people loitering outside galleries, walking their pets in the late afternoon sun, or disappearing into restaurants. The gateway to the courtyard suddenly loomed ahead of us.

It was tranquil inside, geraniums in a corner by the caretaker's lodge, vague aromas of food wafted out, and pale sunlight high on a wall. I glanced up at Rudolf's bedroom windows, the curtains were drawn.

"Maybe he's not at home," I suggested, hopefully. "He's bound to be terribly busy."

He is lying there in the darkened room, a lamp burning at his bedside. His eyes and mouth seem more pronounced now, burning and bulging as though all his senses reach out to the world through his face. Keen, eager, afraid to lose even a fragment of his surroundings.

"Toersky," a feeble gesture toward Toer, his voice hoarse and weak and, to me, motioning toward his bed, "sit down."

Don't show emotion. "Whatever happens, don't let him see you're shocked." I sit down on the edge of the bed, struggling to find my voice, and face that searching gaze, almost the way he looked at me on that dark beach in Greece, reproachful: "In a situation like this, your own emotions are of no importance."

The body of which he had always been so proud, that he had always tried to keep in superb shape by training, is thin, the leg protruding from under the blanket limp. I lay my hand on it, knowing how much store he sets by contact, touch.

He tells us about last night's première of *Bayadère*, the success he has had, but there is a haunted look in his eye and his words are punctuated by a soundless cough.

"Marvelous, they danced so well. You *have* to see." Short phrases, words flutter out on his breath, as though the slightest effort is too much.

"Solor." Wearily, he tries to turn his head toward the black dog that has entered the room and immediately cowers back again. "Come here," but the dog disappears in fear, its nails clicking over the wooden floor.

"I want him to sleep on my bed, but he refuses. I like him to be close to me."

Rudolf with a pet animal, the last thing that would ever have occurred to me. When the telephone rings in another room I see the agitation in his eyes, suspicion almost. "If it is for me, put it through," he tries to call out, but the telephone by his bed is already buzzing and he hastily grabs the receiver. He talks a little, utters a feeble laugh, and makes appointments: "Carla," I hear him saying, "what good idea, when are you free? What can we dance together? Something new?"

While he talks, my eye wanders around the room at the Byzantine abundance of colors and shapes, a room fit for a tsar, glowing darkly like an icon.

The television is on, with the sound turned down, and now and then two women enter the room or put their head around the door, only to vanish again: Marika Bezobrazova from Monte Carlo and Jeanette Bali from San Francisco. They have moved in with Rudolf and, together with Douce, taken it upon themselves to care for him, toiling day and night, looking after him, watching, listening, washing, feeding.

"My women," he will say later, still somewhat mockingly. "See? Always my women." What a blessing they are there for him, those women.

He puts down the receiver and announces that he has a great deal of work in store for the future, conducting, performances. "But"—even *that* crops up again—"there are still some gaps in my diary, I still have some free time left." Is it disbelief, is it confirmation he is searching for in our eyes?

It is absurd to talk about the future with him; I feel a hypocrite, a comedian. But what if it gives him hope, if he believes in it?

He tells us he wants to go to a performance that evening, Roland Petit's company is dancing in Paris, would we join him? Douce, standing behind his bed, gestures to us and says, comfortingly, that if he feels better in a few days, they'll go around antique stores together, lovely things have been put aside for him. Like a child being mollified.

He peers at Toer and me penetratingly, as if to unmask us. "Do *they* believe what is being said here?" and his remarks to Douce are as cutting and bitter as ever.

Later she will valiantly say she is grateful he gibes at her, that at least, then, he is his old, familiar self again. "Everything better than to see him silent and suffering."

We move to another room, leaving Rudolf behind with Solor, and speak to "the women" in hushed voices.

About a year earlier Maude had told me on the telephone that she was very worried about Rudolf: "He doesn't take care of himself; he should stop working and rest, you know. But he has a new secretary, an Australian boy he likes and trusts very much. Somehow that is a relief."

"Where is Rudolf's new assistant?" I ask Douce. "Rudolf seemed to have great confidence in him. Surely he can help you."

"We fired him yesterday. *C'était un peu un scandale mais il voulait trop de salaire.*"[1]

I was dumbfounded that at such fundamental moments in Rudolf's life a sort of Ping-Pong game was still being played with people.

"Was Rudolf in agreement?"

"*Oui, il le voulait. Absolument.*"[2]

At a sudden sound, Douce darts back into Rudolf's room; outside, beyond the heavy curtains the Seine and the Louvre are sinking into a hazy twilight.

Solor appears in the room, looking strangely spotted; he cringes and vanishes again.

"He can't cope with the situation, strangers around him all the time. He relieves himself all over the house, because we don't have the time to take him out. It smells."

There is an enormous bouquet of lilies, wrapped in cellophane, lying on the table—"*Il déteste les lys,*"[3] says Douce—sent by Madonna and, in the kitchen, in a plastic bottle with the top cut off, a mass of dark red roses from Jacqueline Kennedy.

When we take our leave, Rudolf is standing shakily beside the bed. "I threw

1. It's a bit of a scandal, but he wanted a higher salary.
2. Yes, that was what he wanted. Definitely.
3. He hates lilies.

up, all over poor Solor. He got it frontal," he says faintly while the women put things in order. "Make sure you see *Bayadère*, tell me what you think."

The following day we lunch with Douce before going to Rudolf. We had risen early and wandered around Paris, each engrossed in our own thoughts, sitting in Parc Monceau for a long time, watching the French go jogging by, a black bride and her groom being photographed among the flower beds, lush even now in the fall, and the unmistakable characters from the neighborhood shuffling past.

At Douce's, a great deal has changed as well; the quiet, caring Madeleine has died and Douce now has to cope with day-to-day matters alone as well. Her bedroom is more reminiscent of an efficient executive office than the well-groomed boudoir it used to be: a fax machine is spitting out messages almost constantly, two answering machines announce unceasingly, "*Maintenant je ne suis pas chez moi. Veuillez s'il vous plait . . .*"[4]

And piles of papers lie strewn around on chairs and across the floor. All of it concerns Rudolf.

Ninel Kurgapkina, the ballet mistress from St. Petersburg who has assisted Rudolf in the staging of *La Bayadère* is staying with Douce. She lets us in on all the colorful details, and yet with a very "cool" air, of her experiences at the Opéra, the lack of time—owing to which the fourth act has never been finished—and her battles with the scenery department. "They refused to make an elephant and," she looked at Toer and me fierily, as though seeking support, "what is *Bayadère* without an elephant? They had run out of money, they said at the Opéra, but I fought for it and finally rang Rudolf (who was resting in St. Barthélemy): "Rudolf, there's not going to be an elephant." But when Rudolf had rung Paris the elephant was there instantly. Did you see it, yesterday?"

Yes, indeed, we had seen it in the performance, an almost lifelike animal that was trundled on from the left and, when the hero had dismounted, vanished off to the right again shortly after.

Rudolf, at the end of his life, having to worry about a fake elephant.

Later, on the way to Rudolf, Douce stops off at a kiosk and buys a huge pile of that day's newspapers, for reviews of the premiere.

"Rudolf is anxious, he wants to know what the press writes." But in the

4. "I'm not home right now. Would you please . . . "

car, Douce's niece, a young, birdlike girl, who tells us she attends the nuns' school, reads the reviews aloud to check that nothing has been written about Rudolf's illness.

"*Nureyev, qui souffre de la maladie de notre temps*,"[5] I hear her girlish, child-like voice spelling out the review.

"No! Away, get rid of that one. He mustn't read that one."

"*Malade de SIDA*,"[6] I hear next, as though she were reading aloud from a school book.

"No good, either." Out of the whole pile, two, maybe three newspapers remain that pass the censorship and end up on Rudolf's bed.

"Is that all?" he asks, confused, when he sees a few papers land on his blanket.

A few visitors have already gathered. Here and there in the apartment small knots of people are conferring softly together, in an aura as though death has already come. Under the open lid of Rudolf's beloved old harp-sichord are some discarded newspapers and a full and heavy ashtray is lying on the strings. The only ones with constant access to Rudolf's bedroom are the three women and Charles Jude, a great support to them and to Rudolf; he helps when Rudolf has to be moved about, assisted in and out of the bath, and whenever technical household skills are needed.

Douce says how hard it is to refuse people entry to the house. "They come from all over the world and it's *his* house and maybe he wants to see them." But she would dearly have liked to have kept everyone out. "It's too much, we need all our energy for him."

John Taras comes in, white as chalk and overcome with emotion, he can hardly keep his tears in check. I recall Rudolf's busplan: to revel his way around the world with Taras, "to do everything that is forbidden."

I have known Taras since 1954; he was the first foreign choreographer I witnessed at work in Holland (in *Dessins pour les Six*) and I greatly admired him.

The doorbell rings once more. "Rosa has come up from La Turbie. She is staying upstairs, with Gouzel. But *they're* definitely not coming in. It would only upset Rudolf. But sometimes it's quite a struggle."

What a strange situation, letting in friends and acquaintances and keeping Rudolf's family at bay.

5. "Nureyev, who is suffering from the illness of our time."
6. Ill with AIDS.

When we're sitting with Rudolf again he seems exhausted, he moves his hand weakly, pushes his woolen cap way down over his brow, but a moment later he has a sneezing fit that takes so much out of him that I see the numbing fear of death in his eye.

"How was *Bayadère*?" he pants, "Did you like?" but when we confirm it he seems to have forgotten it already.

"Niarchos just called, after years. Invitation for dinner." He studies our reactions, "that means I'm famous again." It's hard to tell whether that last remark is sarcastic, or whether he means it.

"Tomorrow I want to go back to Saint Barth," he says with a determined glance in Douce's direction. "Charles is coming with me; the sun will do me good."

Douce panics:"It's a dreadful journey, first to America, then changing planes in Haiti. And then on by small plane to Saint Barthélemy. Sixteen hours' traveling. And the nourishing food he needs so badly cannot be found there, there's no hospital, no good doctors, nothing. If something happens to him there he's completely trapped." When I look at Rudolf I'm convinced he'll never be able to go, it's a dream, a chimera.

"The doctor says he can't stop him. If he wants to go he should," she says with a wan smile, as though parting with a child.

When we are leaving, Rudolf glances up for a moment and says, "Thank you for thinking of me." A remark that cuts right through the soul.

"We shall never see him again," I say, when we're outside.

Under the archway we see Rudolf's nephew tugging on a lead in vain. Solor is crouching pressed to the ground in fear, ears flat against his head, and refuses to move. The boy smiles shyly at us and drags the struggling dog a little farther over the cobbles.

Outside, the Paris traffic is roaring by.

Over the next few days, Douce tells me that Rudolf has gone to Saint Barth after all, and, from what she hears from Charles, he's a little better, he's more cheerful, goes outside and has an appetite. Hope?

When he returns to France, I go to Paris again. I tell him I have to be there for work—and that is true—but in fact I have come for him; the work is less important.

Apparently, Rudolf had a deep relapse on his return home; hardly any wonder, and the mood in the house is one of resignation, as though all hope has been abandoned.

I see his penetrating stare, burning and suspicious, as though he no longer believes what his eyes perceive.

"I can't eat," he pants, "I can't do anything anymore. Do you know how that feels?"

I massage the frail hand drooping over the blanket in my direction. "I can't feel anything there, it's dying."

Part of his hand is a waxen yellow, as though the fingers have already died. Suddenly I no longer remember how his hands were before, when he was healthy. Those hands with which he grasped his partners firmly, or at times dealt out well-aimed slaps.

Besides his three women, he has a new caregiver, a gentle black boy with the appearance of a giant, the picture of health and energy. I can see from the look in Rudolf's eye that he is pleased with this new presence in the house.

Nothing is said for a long time; I am uncertain whether he is tired or does not feel like talking; to fill the silence I stand up and stare at the paintings covering the walls up to the ceiling. "Is that a new one?" I try.

He tries to look up and then makes a hoarse, almost contemptuous sound. "Sardanopolis. It will all be destroyed," he gazes past me for a long time. "Destroyed, yes." As though afraid I have not understood him.

"How is your school?" he asks me then, in confusion, as though awakening out of a deep sleep. "Is Casenave still teaching there?"

I do not have a school and Roland Casenave, one time ballet-master with the Dutch National Ballet, died some twenty years ago.

"I stopped all that a year and a half ago, remember?" I say. "No more director. It's better like this. Do you remember? You called me an 'amateur director'?"

He suddenly looks at me fiercely and then says decisively: "No, you called *yourself* that, don't accuse me. It was on tour in Italy." He still remembers *that*, from the very earliest days of our collaboration and, I realize, he is right.

He sips some white wine and then Bezobrazova feeds him a mashed substance, "*des fruits de Monte Carlo*"; and he raises a faint, sad smile at the memory of that now unattainable paradise.

His mouth and throat are infected and he eats with great difficulty, wincing every time he swallows, but he does not complain; not a word, not a glance that begs for pity. He seems to accept his being ill like an animal, resigned, without protest.

"Is that ballet?" he asks as if in a feverish dream, "are they dancers?" I switch the channel away from some disputing gentlemen in a television discussion, and a boy with a rasping and desperate voice appears on the screen, seeming to sing a way out to Rudolf: "A million love songs later here I am"; the sound and the words and Rudolf's childlike concentration at that moment tear me apart so that I can barely control my emotions.

Rudolf's head falls to one side—is he asleep?—but he is staring at the wall. I hope he is listening, that the heartfelt cry of the boy singing so passionately will console him.

"There's a newspaper man at the gate," Douce warns me. "Don't talk to him. Hyenas." And she shows me a note by a man who writes that "it is in the interest of the world to know how Mister Nureyev is," and therefore urgently requests a final interview. I can just imagine the gist of his little article.

I spend the following morning at the Opéra, where young male dancers are preparing for the annual exams.

"No, not like that," the *répétiteur* calls out after a neck-breaking combination of steps from Rudolf's *Sleeping Beauty*, "Monsieur Nureyev wanted it like this and not otherwise," and the boys labor on, panting, tumbling, and cursing, and finally falling against the barre in exhaustion.

I think of the man lying at home a few miles away in a darkened room, who once conceived of all this.

Charles Jude, coming in after class, tells me about the time he spent with Rudolf on St. Barth, how difficult and frightening it sometimes was, being with a man fatally ill, so far away from his familiar world.

"It was worst when I noticed his memory sometimes no longer worked. He had lapses and no longer knew where he was and who I was." Platel stands in a corner, listening. "What a terrible time," she sighs, "as though it will never end."

I have arranged to meet Douce at her home and to go to see Rudolf together, before I return to Amsterdam. As I stand in the hall, ringing in vain several times, the concierge appears: "Madame François asked me to tell you she has been called away. Monsieur Nureyev has collapsed and been admitted to hospital. This is the number of the hospital where you can call her."

But I do not call. It is all quite clear.

27 ✐ *Argos*

In the first month of 1993, with Sonja Marchiolli assisting me, I am working in Athens with the Lyriki Skini Ballet Company. Greece in winter; during the day I sometimes walk around in my shirtsleeves, in the evenings we shiver with cold in the barely heated Attalos Hotel.

On the evening of 6 January, Sonja and I are on our way to the opera house to attend a performance. As we wend our way through the labyrinth of narrow, winding, shopping streets linking the main boulevards, we notice a large, smooth-haired mongrel, at whom we must have glanced overencouragingly as we passed; he follows us, trotting along with us faithfully, occasionally pausing to sniff at garbage on the pavement but always waiting for us innocently on the next street corner.

He has an aura of natural friendliness, as though we have known him for years: when I pat him on his black, smooth-haired coat, he sits down patiently, head to one side.

Steering through the traffic that is racing along at a terrifying speed, I tell Sonja about Solor, the timid dog, seemingly shy of humans, that Rudolf has gotten himself, and that reminds me of this Athenian dog, despite the difference in character.

Rudolf has not been out of my mind since my last visits to Paris, and here in Athens, as well, he crops up repeatedly in my conversations with Sonja, memories, fear, premonitions. Hope, even.

"Oh," says Sonja, "didn't we have a fantastic time with him, then? We were so lucky to have known him."

When we stand still at a traffic light, I give the dog a nudge against his thin ribcage and advise him to go back: "No, no farther. Just stay here." But he still risks his life in among the traffic and stands quietly waiting for us on the other side.

I tell Sonja how Rudolf had hoped that Solor (he sometimes called him Soloria, so maybe even the dog was one of Rudolf's "women") would sleep on his bed at night, his yearning to feel the warm, faithful animal's body close to him. That seemed to me to reveal so much of his loneliness, the unspeakable fear he could only, would only, share with an animal.

When we arrive on the Akademikos, near to the theater, the dog is still beside us among the operagoers. Sometimes I feel his muzzle brush against my hand. When we stand still he looks at me with argus eyes.

"Here we are, boy," I say, "we're going in here." And to Sonja, "You'll see, he'll still be sitting here when the performance is over."

As we walk into the hall to pick up our tickets, Petros Stassinos, one of the members of the theater management, comes over to me.

"I have terrible news for you," he says. "Nureyev died today."

I had expected it, daily, I had prepared myself for it, I waited for it; but now, now it is irrefutable, I feel numb and empty, emotionless, I am at a loss for words.

Only when the theater director appears in front of the curtain and we hear a cry of horror go through the auditorium as he announces Rudolf's death to the audience, does the reality hit me. Rudolf is no longer among us.

We leave the theater at the intermission. I am feeling dreadful. Outside, we stand there, Sonja silent, somber. I gaze around: the dog has not waited for us.

Always keep Ithaca in your mind.
To arrive there is your ultimate goal.
C. P. CAVAFY[1]

1. Constantine P. Cavafy is Greek poet Konstantinos Kaváfis (1863– 1933). The quotation is from "Ithaca," written in 1911.

When Toer and I arrive in Paris in the evening, one of the first things we see is a huge poster with a portrait of Rudolf, pasted on the wall in a métro station: "*Une étoile s'éteint*"—a star is extinguished.

He shot through the firmament like a comet, leaving a brilliant trail of light behind him; you can almost hear the rush of power he generated on his way. I knew him for almost twenty-five years, a major part of any human life.

Now, those years seem to have shot past, light years, no more than a fiery flare across the heavens, vanished as swiftly as he came.

We move into the Hotel Voltaire, some ten doors away from Rudolf's apartment.

In reception, we see Marika Bezobrazova almost immediately, but Maude, Wallace, and Jeanette appear to be staying there, as well. Later in the evening, we meet up with more and more familiar faces from the world of ballet, even dancers from Japan have come over. We flee the hotel, no conversation now.

It is late, the gateway to Rudolf's house, contrary to custom, is still wide open, we see that police cars and security are posted beside the entrance.

"Where do you think he is now?" I ask Toer.

Later, Maude and Wallace will tell us that Rudolf has been brought home from the hospital that evening.

"Rosa and his other sister were there, and Gouzel and his nephew." Had peace finally been made with his family then?

"No, Gouzel refused to let Jeanette and Marika in the house, she wouldn't let them near Rudolf."

So Gouzel had gotten her revenge and to be honest, after all that had happened, I could quite imagine that.

Tessa Kennedy, a friend of Rudolf's for years, and Jeanette join us. We recall memories as though it will bring Rudolf back to life.

"Around the time he was making *Washington Square* (in 1984), he called me up to say he had to be admitted to hospital, it was something serious, and could I come immediately," Maude tells us.

"When I found him there I was upset by his condition; he looked as though he wouldn't live for another two days. I knew instantly which disease he had. When he came round, he looked at me and said, "Maude, you know what I have in my blood?"

"Yes, Rudolf, I understand what it is."

"It's strange, he never once used the word AIDS to me. 'You know,' he said, 'I can't complain, I have brought it on myself.' And he has never complained. Later he had operations in Vienna and a very drastic one in Paris, but I never heard a complaint. He must have suffered immensely, mentally as well. But I do not think he ever confided in anyone."

A lonely struggle.

The next morning, we go to Rudolf's apartment. The coffin, Wallace had already informed me in horror, has been placed on the low table where he usually took his breakfast—tea, toast and honey—while going through his mail.

That intolerable and inconceivable muteness, motionlessness that will become unbearable; but, above all, the excruciating absence of the one who is still present. Or seems to be.

I leave the room, away from this confrontation, this bleak, rectangular silhouette.

"In a situation like this, your own emotions are of no importance." I *hear* the rebuke in his voice.

Shelley; a small ceremony on the beach was what he had wanted, the surf, the sound of rolling waves.

I see Rudolf's sisters and for a moment I am uncertain which of the two is Rosa. Both are dressed with extreme sobriety, like peasants even, a black scarf wound around the head, in the fashion of pilgrims in an orthodox monastery.

Rosa comes and sits down next to me. "Rudi," she says in amazement, "Ay, Rudi. Amsterdam."

It is twenty-two years since we met in Leningrad, for one short afternoon; the robust woman who made such a carefree impression has become a small, imposing figure of Tolstoyan sobriety. Her face is one of supreme goodness, a being full of intense power.

The other sister has the bearing of an intellectual, angular features and an independent, spiritual air about her. She might be a French writer of the Yourcenar type, or Simone Weil.

Within the room, a few people are clustered around Rudolf and, to my joy, I see that Rudolf's black caregiver, his "buddy," is there, as well. Tessa is on her knees beside the coffin, Larquié is examining Rudolf's medals of honor, laid out on the coffin, in a businesslike way, as though studying the insignia of a car.

Being there in Rudolf's silent presence, in that room full of memories, oppresses me and seems to go on forever.

Douce, her face tense, ambles aimlessly from room to room, clearing up and rearranging something, anything, I think, to keep her mind from that one thing. Never again will she need to urge Rudolf to hurry.

Eventually, the small procession, five cars in all, gets under way, Rudolf's final journey through the gates of the Quai Voltaire. The roads along the route to the Opéra have been cordoned off, it will be the first time that Rudolf has reached the theater from his house in only a few minutes.

In the square outside the theater and on the steps in front, there is a large crowd, the most impressive tribute.

The Opéra foyer is quite full; people are standing all the way up to the balconies encircling the entrance and, row upon row, the Opéra dancers line the steps curving away to either side of the main staircase.

While a small ensemble plays music by Bach, Rudolf is borne into the hall by the male soloists of the company, his hope and expectation they were, Jean Guizerix, Charles Jude, Manuel Legris, Wilfrid Romoli, and the pallid Kader Belarbi, the companions he searched for so desperately all his life, so yearned for. Angels of death they are now.

Poems by Pushkin, Byron, Michelangelo, Goethe, and Rimbaud are recited, all in their own language. The coffin is borne outside to the strains of Mahler's *Songs of a Wayfarer*:

> *Auf der Strasse stand ein Lindenbaum,*
> *Da hab' ich zum ersten Mal im Schlafe geruht!*
> *Alles! Alles! Lieb' und Leid, und Welt und Traum!*[2]

---

2. "On the road, there stands a linden tree. There I first found rest in its shade. All was gone, All! Love and grief, the world and dreams." (From the fourth of the *Songs of the Wayfarer* by Gustav Mahler.)

The journey to the cemetery is long, Sainte Geneviève des Bois is more than twenty kilometers outside Paris. During the journey, Rudolf's "buddy" tells Toer and me how he traveled with Rudolf to the Quai Voltaire yesterday evening and of his shock when, suddenly, and though no one had warned him, everyone went and he was left alone with Rudolf in the deserted house.

"It was my first confrontation with death and I was scared."

But he also tells us how Rudolf's final days had been, that he had still had some pleasure with Rudolf.

"I would tickle him and occasionally pinch him in the chest, he liked that. And if he felt a little better he would sit up straight, in my arms, and then he would laugh a little. I think he sometimes enjoyed it."

A poignant image and, knowing Rudolf, a characteristic one, as well.

On arrival at the churchyard—it turns out to be a Russian cemetery, in passing we see the domes of the church through the leafless trees—our procession lingers until most of the buses and cars have arrived with the other mourners.

Rudolf's family and close friends follow the bier down the broad churchyard pathway, and in the crowd, among friends and acquaintances from all over the world, I see Zizi Jeanmaire, Joan Thring, Luigi Pignotti, Noëlla Pontois, John Taras, Anna Faussurier, Monique van Vooren, as well, an entire past comes to life. Franck Duval, Rudolf's little "KGB agent" from bygone days, emerges from the crowd and grabs my arm; gladness, despite everything.

Among the many graves, we pass a stone so colossal that you cannot miss it, SERGE LIFAR, DE KIEV the inscription says, concise, but majestic. A few people from the procession linger by the stone, kneeling or making the sign of the cross in the orthodox fashion. Rudolf's obsession comes to my mind; it no longer matters now.

Suddenly the motion stops short, we have arrived; the gaping pit in the earth.

Millions of love songs he had, each day anew: dance, painting, music, dancers, friends, opera, oriental tapestries, films, meals, his harpsichord, the theater, books, travel, his mansions, antique furniture, his companions; they filled his life to the brim.

The people whom he brought together during his lifetime, many hundreds of them, there they stand, without him.

"A million love songs later, here I am . . ."
The grave is appallingly deep, a gloomy, dark shaft.

In Paris once again, I wonder about Rudolf's timid, cowering dog and ask Marika Bezobrazova what happened to Solor in the end.

"Ah, I've found him a good home," she smiles, "with relatives in the countryside on the Riviera. There's another dog there he gets on well with and they have an enormous garden. He'll be very happy there."

An Ithaca, after all.

Amsterdam–Athens,
February–June 1993

28 ∼ *Epilogue*

I wrote these memories of Rudolf Nureyev in gratitude. His association with the Dutch National Ballet, which began in 1968, meant a life-giving injection for the company, which was in a precarious state at that time. Nureyev's arrival at our studios heralded a decided change for the better.

Nureyev meant a great deal to me as a professional, even though I by no means admired all he did, or shared his ideas anything like all of the time; working with him almost always meant learning something new and facing the facts of dance and theater life, and the fickleness of that world.

But it was my personal life upon which his influence was greatest. His friendship was extremely warm and generous; thanks to him I met many interesting and worthwhile people, and experienced many exciting, acerbic, and euphoric situations, which I would not have missed for the world.

Nureyev worked like a giant, lived like a giant, and made gigantic mistakes as well. He knew I did not always admire him unconditionally and, for that reason, it amazed me that our friendship endured for nearly twenty-five years, despite our vehement clashes and disagreements.

The fact that Nureyev worked in Holland a great deal, with Dutch dancers, musicians, and choreographers will not, I am afraid, receive the attention outside Holland I believe it deserves. Holland is a small country and, even in the world of art, that often means it plays a small—insignificant—role.

I felt that, if I did not record our collaboration and my Dutch and maybe rather unorthodox view of the phenomenon Nureyev, then many facts and events might be lost.

These memories were too precious, and they mean too much to me to allow that to happen. They have helped me a little to keep Nureyev alive.

Rudi van Dantzig

1993

29 ✧ *Afterword*

Nearly fifteen years have gone by since he died, Rudolf Hametovitch Nure-yev. Rudolf, son of Hamet and Farida. Fifteen years, hard to believe.

In one way or another he is always present in my life. Even if I do not think of him daily, I am reminded of him by photographs and books, scattered throughout the house, by the sight of an icon he gave me after a premiere, a many-armed candelabra—a Christmas present—or by Toer van Schayk's designs hanging on my walls.

But more trivial objects are forever conjuring up memories of him too; prosaic things even, evoke situations or events from the past, if *only* a for a fleeting moment: a colorful pullover, one of the many woolen caps he sported, towels, a pair of boots. They were things he gave or lent me, mostly from times when I stayed with him in Paris, or New York. "It's too cold, put that on; is much warmer." And when I returned one of those caps or pullovers after use: "You can keep. I don't need anymore," adding with a little smile: "I have better one."

During the early years of our friendship, Rudolf showed surprise at Toer's and my interest in Russian and Greek icons. When I asked him if he had not been raised in the Russian Orthodox tradition, his rather curt answer was: "No, I am Muslim." Not: "I was brought up a Muslim," but: "I am ...," which seemed to change the context.

Today I find it hard to imagine, but in those days—around 1975—I had rarely given the Muslim faith any thought, and we, the "West," had hardly been confronted with it. What would his position be nowadays? Would he be annoyed by the current tendency to judge all Muslims alike, by the appalling situation in the Middle East—Iraq, Gaza, Palestine—and the growing variance and distrust between "their" world and "ours"? I would have wished to discuss this with him, to know where he stood, to hear him explain his views and convictions.

Rudolf did not practice his beliefs, or not openly at any rate; I never saw him at prayer. But he had a striking fascination for oriental head-gear, and with an almost sensuous pleasure he would drape colourful shawls around his head, and preferably wore voluminous burnouses to match. "This reminds me of home," he would sniff the air in oriental markets, strolling among the stalls, "Delicious!"

"Why did you continue working with him if there were such difficult situations and if his behaviour was so impossible?" It was a question I often had to answer, and one I sometimes even asked myself. Of course I had been filled with incredulity when our collaboration began with *Monument for Dead Boy*, but at the same time I had felt extremely flattered, for did such things really happen, a world famous dancer who created a sensation wherever he appeared showing a sudden interest in the work of a practically unknown choreographer from a small country without any ballet tradition?

Rudolf and I were polar opposites: while in difficult situations I turned silent and morose, Rudolf would throw out all his rage and frustration at once, loudly, but therefore impotently too. After such tantrums he would sit in a corner of his dressing-room or in the studio, a confused, slightly embarrassed child. The beauty of it was that his rages were always short-lived, and I was frankly puzzled whether these rapid changes of mood were innate, or arose from tactical consideration.

Having endured quite a number of these squalls I decided it must be the former. I became more and more convinced that he loved, or *wanted* to love, life far too much to be hampered by even a single moody and therefore wasted evening. For him, dinner after an emotional working day equalled the smoking of a calumet of peace.

I had hardly counted on a follow-up to our first collaboration, expecting Rudolf to see this work with our company as a stop-gap, a minor experiment. When things eventually turned out otherwise, I was pleased, for his decision would doubtless have an enormous influence on our company's existence. Personally, I felt overwhelmed: Rudolf's performing with us would be challenging, but I was certain that on the whole it would make us grow. We would be exposed to many new experiences and we would be judged critically, compared, but the name "Nureyev" would act as a safe-conduct too. A dancer of his reputation would not associate with mediocrity.

Being together with Rudolf, working and getting to know him outside the studio as a human being was fascinating and full of unexpected, occasionally unwelcome situations. Along with our association came events I would never have experienced otherwise, and might never have been able to deal with. But Rudolf's trust and expectations helped me to make decisions: I just *had* to. "Don't just sit there like sleeping beauty, I need decision now, I will not wait forever," and a door was shut forcefully.

I would not have been surprised if, after I had choreographed for him once or twice, he had cried off from that part of the arrangement; after all, the results were not all that exceptional. The fact that he continued to believe in my work came as an invigorating and perhaps addictive injection. At his explicit request, I created four ballets for him, with him in the principal role of course, but then there was that last commission—*Sans armes, Citoyens!*—for the Paris Opera Ballet, in which I had not cast him. Although he was very disappointed, he accepted it quietly. . . . He never stopped surprising me.

Even though our collaboration ended after *Sans Armes*, our friendship continued, and this counted most for me. Evidently there was more between us than "just" work: we thought of each other and he valued the friendship between him and me—and Toer.

Along with Anna Pavlova, Nureyev was and is the most famous name in ballet-history. Mention these two names together, and the link to ballet will be made. Legendary though Nijinsky may be to ballet lovers, even *his* name is diminishing now and will hardly be mentioned, I fear. History no longer counts anymore, it seems. These days it is here, and now, the thrill of the moment.

Nureyev's career in the West, with all the attendant publicity, good and bad, but always front page material, has done more for male dancing, and male dancers, than anything or anyone before. One may wonder whether Baryshnikov would have taken that same position, had he escaped from the Soviet Union before Rudolf. In many ways, Baryshnikov was a better dancer, more stunning than Rudolf and his technical feats were more spectacular. He also performed with greater ease and possessed uncanny and dazzling natural gifts, as though presented to him—and us—on a golden platter.

But it was Nureyev's theatrical escape, his theatrical behavior and his stage personality, like one possessed even, that attracted all the attention; his urge to be recognized, to be the first, to show us in the West what dancing should really *be*. While dancing, he was also lecturing to his audiences, his colleagues, the young ballet students, and the critics alike: "Look, I'm showing you the truth!" At times, Rudolf seemed like a preacher, a fanatical visionary—right or wrong—the sacrificed "chosen one," but the one who symbolized victory as well.

To my knowledge, Nureyev was the most active dancer in ballet history, giving more performances and dancing more roles in classical *and* modern choreographies than seems humanly possible. At one stage, the Coliseum Theater in London launched a three month ballet season during which three companies came and went, but one dancer stayed in place like the sun: Rudolf guested with all three, one after the other, "never off"—or "Sun King" indeed.

In the West, before Nureyev made his appearance, ballet companies were mainly known for the names of their top ballerinas: Fonteyn, Ulanova, Plisetskaya, Hayden, Le Clerq, Alonso, Haydé, Fracci, Chauviré, but during and after Rudolf's time, male dancers became as renowned and admired as the females worshipped before them. Nureyev emancipated dance enormously, and with a generous gesture. Unmistakably; loud, and clear.

Nureyev has already gone down in history, dance history; of that I became aware when he made his last appearance on stage at the Paris Opéra, and during the following days, as I saw the deep awe of those beholding him. Even then, there was an unbridgeable distance: we staying, he poised for departure. Wonderment and awe.

The same feeling came over me as I was watching class in the studios of New York City Ballet. Stanley Williams was teaching a group of very young dancers from the company, children almost. The class had been going on for quite a while and the barre- exercises were over, when all at once, Balanchine entered the studio. Williams halted the class. I saw the young dancers looking at their illustrious choreographer and artistic director, their uneasy reaction—and to my surprise, some girls even giggling nervously.

Balanchine himself did not seem to notice, moving laboriously, occasionally supporting himself at the barre. He did not take the shortest route across the studio to the central position next to Williams; instead he shuffled along the walls, around the young dancers. The two men spoke together for a moment, then Balanchine watched the class for a short while, leaning on the barre, afterwards retracing his laboured way back. Suddenly the atmosphere in the studio became uneasy, embarrassed even. Only when Balanchine had reached the door did one of the boys in the class open it for the visibly ailing choreographer. When he had disappeared, I saw two girls in a corner crying.

At that moment, I could clearly sense how age and fame can cause immense inaccessibility and solitude as well. Toward the end, solitude surrounded Rudolf as well; he already seemed to be drifting away, like one who had fallen by the wayside, a wanderer now.

I like to think of Rudolf during his last days in hospital in the arms of the friendly black nurse, arms folded around him like a mother would do, protecting him, rocking him gently into a soothing sleep. That friendly, quiet young man who knew nothing about Rudolf's fame, or about his career; he simply cared for Rudolf as a man who needed protection and love in his final moments. Sometimes, when Toer and I hear the music from *La Bayadère*, the opening of *The Kingdom of the Shades*, we almost always respond as one: "Did you see him too? How he ran, how he moved, how he utterly absorbed the music and seemed to radiate?"

And there is the voice of Gary Barlow, the singer from the group Take That: "A million love songs later, here I am," he sings and Rudolf's face, in painful concentration, listens as if he wants to obey the singer. A voice that beckons him, wants him to wake up, to enjoy, to drink life in to the fullest one more time.

No, Rudolf will not be forgotten; Rudolf the fighter, the realist, the star that left a radiant trail in the memory of thousands of people.

The star has gone; its light is still visible.

INDEX OF NAMES

Rudi van Dantzig was a pupil of Sonia Gaskell, a Russian dancer who had studied ballet in Paris with the St. Petersburg ballerina Lubov Egorova. After moving to Amsterdam, Gaskell became artistic director of the Dutch National Ballet in 1961. During van Dantzig's first years as Gaskell's student, she encouraged him in choreography; in 1955 he created his first ballet, *Night Island*, strongly influenced by the works of Martha Graham.

When in 1971 Gaskell left the company—for which she had gathered a large George Balanchine repertoire—van Dantzig became director of the Dutch National Ballet, a position he held for 20 years. He created about seventy ballets for his company, among which *Monument for a Dead Boy* and *Four Last Songs* are his best known, together with his versions of *Romeo and Juliet* and *Swan Lake*. Most of his works were created in close cooperation with designer/ choreographer/dancer Toer van Schayk.

Van Dantzig worked in the United States with companies such as the Harkness Ballet, American Ballet Theater, Boston Ballet, Washington Ballet, and Houston Ballet. His ballets have been performed by companies in London, Paris, Toronto, Marseille, Florence, Winnipeg, Athens, Berlin, Munich, Copenhagen, Oslo, Helsinki, Beijing, Tokyo, Hong Kong, and Cape Town, and he is a permanent teacher with the National Ballet School in Toronto.

In the Netherlands he received two Royal decorations and in Germany the Cross of Merit. He was granted the Silver Medal of Honor from the City of Amsterdam, and in Moscow he received the Benois de la Danse.

He has written five books, among which his first novel, *For a Lost Soldier*, was translated into English and German and later made into a movie.